Young People's Views on Sex Education

Why does Britain have the highest rates of teenage pregnancy in Western Europe? What can sex education programmes do to improve the poor sexual health record? *Young People's Views on Sex Education* asks both these questions and puts forward suggestions for policies to improve the situation.

Based on observation of sex education programmes and in-depth interviews with young people, the authors aim to understand more about adolescent attitudes to sexuality and their sexual behaviour in order to develop policies which will meet their needs more appropriately and effectively.

Issues covered in this interesting and accessible book include the ways adolescent informal culture affects sex education programmes and practice; the impact of gender inequality on sex education and safer sex behaviours; legislation and policy frameworks which affect sex education policies; the way young people see legislation and evaluate sex education programmes; and the impact health professionals can have in school sex education.

The authors contend that the insights into the values and views that young people bring to bear on the sex education they receive should have an important role to play in the development of policy and practice of those involved in sex education work.

Lynda Measor is a Senior Lecturer in the School of Applied Social Science at the University of Brighton. **Coralie Tiffin** and **Katrina Miller** are Senior Lecturers in the School of Education at the University of Brighton.

Young People's Views on Sex Education
Education, Attitudes and Behaviour

Lynda Measor with Coralie Tiffin
and Katrina Miller

London and New York

First published 2000
by RoutledgeFalmer
11 New Fetter Lane, London EC4P 4EE

Simultaneously published in the USA and Canada
by RoutledgeFalmer
29 West 35th Street, New York, NY 10001

RoutledgeFalmer is an imprint of the Taylor & Francis Group

Typeset in Goudy by Taylor & Francis Books Ltd
Printed and bound in Great Britain by
Biddles Ltd, Guildford and King's Lynn

British Library Cataloguing in Publication Data
A catalogue record for this book is available from the British Library

Library of Congress Cataloging in Publication Data
A catologue record has been requested for this title

0–750–70895–6 (hbk)
0–750–70894–8 (pbk)

This book is dedicated to the memory of Peter Edward Stafford,
23 August 1936–28 February 1999

Contents

1 The Issues Outlined

Introduction

This book is based on research into adolescent sexuality and sex education in England. At the heart of the work is an interest in the provision of appropriate and effective sex education for adolescents. We had a commitment to the idea that effective and appropriate sex education can be developed only if we know more about adolescent sexuality and the viewpoints which young people bring to sex education. We need more understanding of pupil perspectives and adolescent informal cultures and the attitudes of young people to sexuality in the modern world. The research therefore aimed to take an adolescent-centred approach to sex education, working with pupils to advance our awareness of their views.

Any work on sex education in Britain in the 1990s must take account of the considerable controversy which encircles the subject. In the last decade-and-a-half significant legislation relating to sex education has been introduced. In those years successive governments have been lobbied by moral groupings which have taken polarised stances based on ideological positions.

Sex education is currently one of the most controversial and politicised aspects of the school curriculum. It engages adults with distinct cultural, political and economic agendas in heated and acrimonious debates in which student voices are largely unheard (Trudell 1993: 2). Any research into this field runs a risk of finding itself part of the controversy. We argue that a focus on what young people themselves think about the controversy and the issues is essential and aim to develop our understanding of the perspectives that adolescent 'users' bring to the sex education they are offered. This knowledge might enable us to move beyond the claims and counter-claims that are put forward by adults in the debate. In this research we look at the policies on sex education which have developed in the last decade-and-a-half in Britain and seek to evaluate the response of young people to the sex education programmes which have grown within the policy framework.

The research considered sex education provided in secondary schools in the south-east of England. We were interested in young adolescents and focused on sex education programmes offered to pupils aged 13–15. The schools in which we collected data were mixed comprehensives. We focused exclusively on the secondary school level, and there is no attempt to deal with the issues which arise in relation to sex education in the primary school context.

The other point we need to make concerns homosexuality: we do not seek to exclude homosexuality, nor the concerns which face young people in early adolescence who feel they may have a same-sex sexual orientation. Our problem is that the young people we studied made little mention of it. In the schools we studied we did not find young people who were prepared to talk to us about their feelings and reactions in respect of homosexuality. Although unsurprising in itself, this reluctance also may reflect some inadequacies in our research style or in the approach we made to young people. But, this is a study based on the views which young people were prepared to share with us, and we aim to reflect those views. We include some material on homosexuality, but it originates by and large in other people's research.

We take the view that the delivery of effective and appropriate sex education requires a grasp of theory relating both to adolescent sexuality and to its connections with gender and identity. We were concerned that much of the research that is done into sex education is untheorized (Allen 1987; Ingham 1994). There has been a burgeoning of theoretical work in the social sciences on the issue of sexuality in recent years (Weeks 1985; BSA 1994). Work on sex education which employs these insights is beginning to appear (see for example Jones and Mahony 1989; Holland, Ramazanoglu and Thomson 1992; Lees 1993), but there is little evidence of its take-up by the more practitioner-oriented literature on sex education. Because a grasp of theoretical work is essential to a fuller understanding of the issues, and specifically for the formulation of effective policy, our aim was to marry the theorising with data collected from contemporary sex education work.

The project is a small one: the research covered five schools in one region, south-east England; we can make limited claims on the basis of our findings; our funding was small-scale; and there are several issues, uncovered in the course of the research, which are in clear need of further investigation. Throughout the book we draw attention to these issues. The study is exploratory: we researched innovative sex education programmes and aimed to draw attention to issues which are not fully covered in other research into sex education. We were interested in forming hypotheses capable of leading sex educators into areas of investigation and understanding which we consider significant to the development of more effective policies and programmes. The size of the study limits the generalisability of the findings; other sex education programmes in other areas of the country, or indeed in other countries, will require their own research.

Patterns of Adolescent Sexuality

Research has established a partial picture of the characteristics of young people's sexual behaviour and their attitudes to sexuality and to sex education, although there is still a good deal that we do not know. In the late 1980s there was an increase in research into sexual behaviour in general because of concern about HIV/AIDS. This led to a number of surveys about young people (reviewed in detail by Wight 1990 and Breakwell and Fife-Shaw 1992). On the basis of this research there are some things of which we can feel reasonably sure. The most significant finding is that in Britain a high proportion of young people – defined as those under the age of 19 – are sexually active: 65 per cent of the teenagers interviewed in the Health Education Authority's survey of 4,436, 16–19 year-olds reported that they were sexually active. Of these, 79 per cent had had sexual intercourse, 64 per cent had engaged in mutual masturbation and 49 per cent had engaged in oral sex (Health Education Authority 1992). Research consistently indicates that in western countries premarital sex has become the norm. Fewer than 1 per cent of women, and no men at all, in the age-group 16–24, had their first sexual experience within marriage (Welling 1994).

There is evidence from surveys to suggest that young people are becoming sexually active at a younger age. In the past four decades the median age of first intercourse has fallen – for women by four years from 21 to 17 and for men by three years from 20 to 17 (Wellings *et al*.1994). It is important to note that this fall in the age of first intercourse began in the 1950s and not the so-called "permissive" 1960s.

There has also been an increase in the number of young people who have sexual intercourse before the age of 16. Welling's work suggests that nearly 1 in 5 women and more than 1 in 4 men under the age of 20 had had intercourse before the age of 16 (Wellings *et al*. 1994). From various surveys around the country the figures suggest that 20–25 per cent of all young people are sexually active before the age of 16 (see e.g. Clift and Stears 1989). It is important to note that these changes in sexual culture are the same across all modern western nations. In their 1989 survey in the United States Brooks, Gunn and Furstenberg (1989) suggested that in 1950, 7 per cent of white American girls were sexually active by the time they were 16; by 1982 this had risen to 44 per cent. Current figures estimate that about 60 per cent of unmarried 18-year-old girls are sexually active, a figure which is consistent across Western nations (Hayes 1987).

Research has begun to provide us with some information about adolescents who have a same-sex orientation (Epstein 1994). We have significantly more research on male than on female homosexuality. It suggests that young gay adults begin to realise that their sexual feelings are different from those of the majority at about 9 or 10 years of age. From Sigma's survey of the sexual lifestyles of gay and bisexual men in the UK in 1991, 22 per cent recognised their feelings before they were 10, and 97 per cent by the age of 20 (Weatherburn *et al*. 1992). Other recent research with gay men has found that the average age of first sexual experience is 15.7 years (Weatherburn *et al*. 1992). It is clear that we need more research in this field in order to develop effective policy.

The Problem – the Sexual Health Record of the UK

From the research that we have mentioned it is clear that a high proportion of young people are sexually active, a significant percentage beginning to be sexually active at an age younger than the law allows. This is true for both heterosexual and same-sex-oriented adolescents. The situation is that pre-marital sexual experience has become the norm for young people. It is clear that adults have diverse responses to this picture of adolescent sexuality. Their views, based on pre-existing morality and political attitudes toward young people and perhaps toward sexuality, make this a difficult topic to discuss. In this research our approach aimed to focus on the extent to which this youthful sexual activity has negative consequences for young people. It is clear that Britain has a poor sexual health record, with rates of teenage pregnancy and sexually transmitted diseases (STDs) which are significantly higher than those of other European countries.

Teenage Pregnancy

The figures on teenage pregnancies dealing with 1996 were released in December 1998. They show that 63 in every 1,000 women under 20 years of age and 9.4 in every 1,000 girls under 16 became pregnant (Office for National Statistics 1998). The Office for National Statistics confirmed that numbers had risen for the second year running: there was an 11 per cent rise in teenage pregnancies in 1995–96 from 8.5 to 9.4 per 1,000. More than 75 per cent of the girls who became pregnant were 15-year-olds, about 50 per cent of whom had abortions (*Guardian* 12 December 1998). This reverses the downward trend for the previous four years for England and Wales. In 1970, before contraception was available free to young people, the conception rate among 15–19-year-olds was 8.24 per 1,000 (OPCS *Population Trends* (England and Wales) 1993). In 1996, in England and Wales, 94,000 teenagers became pregnant, 8,800 of them when they were under 16 (ONS 1996).

These are the national rates, but they vary regionally. The highest rates of under-16 pregnancy are associated with areas of social and economic deprivation (Pearson *et al.* 1995: 386). We considered it important to present the figures that apply to the specific area of south-east England studied in the research. The figures are age-specific per 1,000 of the population:

- The conception rate for 11–19-year-olds was 18.1. In 1992 in the 11–19 age group there were altogether 737 conceptions. There were 10 live births in the 11–15 age-group and 361 live births in the 16–19 age-group.
- The abortion rates in the area were 1.6 for 11–15-year-olds and 16.2 for 16–19-year-olds. In 1992 in the local area there were 37 abortions in the 11–15 age-group and 328 abortions in the 16–19 age-group.

Sexually Transmitted Diseases

STD is another sexual-health problem in Britain, and HIV/AIDS has of course added a new and urgent dimension to the issue. We need to bear in mind when considering these figures that there are other routes of transmission for the virus than sexual contact. The heterosexual spread of HIV has been less rapid than was feared in the mid-1980s (Tappin *et al.* 1991). Nevertheless, one-third of the 17,000 people in Britain known to have the HIV infection are under 24 (Communicable Diseases Surveillance Centre 1992). If we assume an 8–10-year incubation period for HIV/AIDS, most of these young people would have contracted HIV in their teens (Health Education Authority 1997). We know from research that, in terms of HIV infection, the majority of young people do not perceive themselves to be at risk, and this has consequences for their sexual behaviour. Research also shows alarmingly low rates of awareness of common STDs like chlamydia and little perception of risk of infection (Health Monitor 1997).

'Teenage fertility rates for England and Wales, closely followed by the rates for Scotland and Northern Ireland, are higher than [in] any other economically developed country with the notable exception of the United States' (Corlyon 1999: 6). British rates are significantly higher than those in Germany, France, Sweden and Holland. The birthrate in England and Wales for the 15–19 age-group was 33.3 in 1990 compared with The Netherlands at 6.4 and Switzerland at 4.6. Other countries, notably Scandinavia and also Holland managed to make significant improvements in this area during the 1980s. In Denmark the conception rate for 15–19 year olds was reduced from 47.6 to 25.4 per 1,000 between 1977 and 1985 (Corlyon 1999: 6). Rates of STDs were also lower. There is no evidence that sexual activity among young people is any lower in those nations, but the consequences appear to be different. There is evidence that these varying rates are, at least in part, based on policy differences. In all of the Scandinavian countries young people have better sexual knowledge than their UK counterparts; moreover, these countries have a network of specialist clinics for young people. Similarly, the negative consequences of sexual interactions vary in different nations and the reasons for these variations need to be explored. The attempt to understand the implications of adolescent sexual activity, it seems, requires a complex formula.

The Policy Response

If the research we have outlined offers an accurate view of the behaviour of young people, then policy makers and practitioners need to decide on a response to it. The major changes in attitudes and in behaviour which have taken place over the last forty years have implications for the provision of sex education which need consideration. For our purposes, what is really significant is what these figures indicate about the attitudes of adolescents towards their patterns of sexual behaviour. Most adolescents express a liberal attitude to premarital sex, favouring the view that premarital sex is acceptable in the context of a long term relationship (Moore and Rosenthal 1993).[1] Young people assert that given the proportion of young people in the UK who are sexually active, there is a need for effective sex education in Britain.

It is important for parents, teachers and all those who work with young people to be aware of what is happening in the present adolescent generation with respect to sexual values and behaviour. 'Education about sexual health is likely to be most effective if educators take into account the current beliefs and practices of their target audience' (Moore and Rosenthal 1993: x). We are aware that this statement is likely to appear controversial to many adults, but we emphasise again that our purpose in this work is straightforward: we seek to offer the viewpoint of young people on these issues and to allow their views to be heard.

Successive UK governments have declared, in *The Health of the Nation* (DoH 1992) and *Our Healthier Nation* (DoH 1998) programmes, their aim of improving the sexual health of the British people. Health education interventions are widely seen as the most appropriate strategy for meeting health of the nation targets, and for the more general objective of improving young people's sexual health. The widely quoted claim that 'education is the only vaccine we have against HIV/AIDS' reflects this view. Despite this commitment to offering sex education, there are profound difficulties and controversies surrounding existing provision. Sex education seems to be an inherently problematical area of social policy.

Adults involved in sex education in Britain have real doubts about the sex education programmes which currently run. The Sex Education Forum, the umbrella organisation for thirty-nine agencies involved with sex education, expressed its concern in 1992: 'School sex education is a patchwork of concern, doubt, confusion and mis-management in which good practice and intentions often founder' (Scott and Thomson 1992: 10).

British adolescents too seem to be very dissatisfied with the sex education they are offered, according to research on this issue. There has been sustained criticism of sex education programmes by adolescents, who claim to have been offered a surfeit of moral exhortation and a deficit of explicit relevant information (Farrell 1978; Allen 1987; Ingham 1994). Theoretical research backs up their criticisms (Jones 1985; Fine 1988; Frankham 1993; Trippe 1994) and reaches a number of gloomy conclusions about the relevance and effectiveness of the work.

Controversies in Sex Education

We have suggested that a range of tensions have combined to thwart the development of a co-ordinated national programme of sex education in schools in Britain. What we have is sex education which, in the view of young people, fails to meet their needs and which manifestly fails to improve the sexual health of the nation in ways achieved by other countries. It is important to understand more about the reasons for this failure, and the chapters which follow look in detail at the data collected in this research and aim, through an exploration of the data, to develop and elaborate our understanding of the problems.

Defining Sex Education

Part of the problem may relate to the confusion or, more accurately, controversy over what sex education should be. 'Sex education' is a label with a wide use. Individuals and agencies use 'sex education' to describe what they do, but in practice offer rather different things. A number of disciplines and bodies of knowledge compete for space within the field of sex education. Traditionally sex education in Britain has been framed in the context of physiological and biological knowledge; such sex education draws much of its content from biology and the sciences, and has strong affinities with theories of physical development, growth and physical change. It therefore commands a strong knowledge base in the powerful and high-status scientific disciplines considered essential in this approach.

In more recent years, sex education has come to be used as a shorthand term for the much broader subject of personal relationships, sexual health and education about sexuality (Sex Education Forum 1997). This approach is much more related to the social science disciplines of psychology and sociology. These disciplines are considered as important to this approach as are the scientific disciplines to the more traditional approach to sex education. It is important to remember that religious thinking can also have significant influence on debates relating to what sex education should be.

Postmodernist theorising has been applied to sex education, resulting in a shift in perspective on the issue. Sex education is considered to have an important role in the regulation of society: it is a technique of 'governance' (Foucault 1979). Sex education thus has importance in socialising a new generation, not only into prevailing attitudes about sexuality but also into critically important ways of thinking about and being in society. It claims to be about producing sexually responsible individuals, but acts in addition at a more fundamental level to constitute our notions of 'intimate citizenship' (Plummer 1996: 7). Sex education is a site for modern forms of monitoring, regulating and the 'disciplining' of society (Thorogood 1992).

Reiss (1990: 125) points out that what is defined as sex education has changed over time: 'The history of sex education in schools is one of a widening of the notion of sex education.' If postmodernist insights are taken into account here, this is precisely what we might expect. Foucault argued that sexuality is an important area for modern forms of social control. It plays a critical role in the individual's self regulation and touches some deeply felt emotions about identity and self in the world. Sex education cannot therefore be left to chance;

postmodernist theories would suggest that we should expect increasing statutory regulation of sex education.

Such theories are valuable in making us look again at the kind of regulatory discourses which operate in our world. They allow us to scrutinise what may be taken-for-granted notions about institutions in our society. There is however, little space in postmodernist theories for any notions of resistance to the over-whelming power of discourse. We also need to remain aware of the plurality of the discourses which carry power to define what happens in modern society. We have mentioned the way in which scientific knowledge, social science-related approaches and religious views may compete over sex education. Sex education has shifted significantly over the last century as values have varied. The messages about appropriate sexual behaviour sent out by adults to adolescents are now much less clear than in the 1950s. There is no monolithic scaffold of values: a number of discourses about sexuality prevail in the modern western world, and we should expect to see them represented in a variety of forms in sex education. Competing definitions of sexuality make fissures in any blueprint which might be communicated.

Young people learn about sexuality in a whirl of contradictory forms – and we should expect to be able to discern the paradoxes which as a consequence feature in sex education. We should be able to see also the confusions this produces for young people in our society. Trudell (1993) made an important point when inquiring into what counts as successful sex education. The problem she identified is that in this controversial area viewpoints vary, so that there is no single accepted outcome which would be valued equally by all concerned. Sex education, as we have said, has become a political issue in recent years (Chapter 2 considers these issues in more detail and examines current legisla-tion and policy). Sex-education work is controversial, and it is important to outline the different areas of disputation.

Generation and Sex Education

Sex education brings into focus tensions around generation and issues about the way we acknowledge or refuse to acknowledge the fact of adolescent sexuality (Moore and Rosenthal 1993: 40). There are important issues in our society about adolescents' *right* to sexuality. The issue has produced heated and bitter controversy in Britain in recent years. A conservative view takes the line that it is important to protect the 'innocence' of children. A liberal or more radical view starts from the acknowledgement that we live in a sexualised culture. The last thirty years have seen complicated shifts in many family and household structures, shifts that are likely to have affected concepts of marriage and sexual standards and to have made for significant changes in sexual practices – all of which will affect young people, too. It is the case that children receive much of their sex education in informal ways, such as from television programmes and their peers (Balding 1997). Even if we wished to regulate the information that children receive, it would be impossible. In a highly sexualised world, the liberal view argues, sex educators should be working to offer young people protection, and to ensure that accurate information is available to them from sex education programmes run by well-trained and reflective individuals.

Gender and Sex Education

It is important to keep gender to the forefront of any examination of sex education programmes, for much of the controversy around sex education is gendered. Feminist critics have a number of arguments against British sex-education provision. One such argument is that sex education incorporates and offers to young people an image of the 'normal' woman. This is a specifically heterosexual image and one which stresses marriage and motherhood as the 'proper' routes for women to take through life. Feminists suggest that the ways we teach sex education are influential in constructing female sexuality and femininity in docile and non-powerful forms. Fine's work which alleges that there is a 'silence' on the subject of female desire and a missing discourse of female sexuality is relevant here as this is an essential element in the construction of a passive femininity (see e.g. Fine 1988).

Issues of gender need to be kept on the agenda of school sex education, both politically and at the level of practice (Trudell 1993: 56). Feminism has drawn our attention to issues of power which characterise relationships between the sexes, and these raise important political questions about the extent to which sex education should challenge taken-for-granted power networks.

Definitions of Sexuality – a Compulsory Heterosexuality

Heterosexuality is defined in our society as the central form of sexual expression and all same-sex sexuality is marginalised. School sex education has an exclusive focus on heterosexuality: one view of how sexuality is expressed and acted upon is prioritised and privileged, and any other form of expression is made marginal or 'other'. Weeks for example suggests that we are:

> Enslaved within the circle of meanings attributed to sexualities, and public lives are dominated by the institutionalisation of heterosexuality. Heterosexuality has long been the dominant category of sexuality and one which affirms masculinity and the dominance of heterosexual man.
>
> (Weeks 1985: 164)

The same processes are at work in the construction of feminine identity and sexuality. 'Heterosexuality is uninterrogated' and it is 'pivotal to conventional feminine identities' (Adkins and Merchant 1996: 26). Legislation of course has a powerful role in deciding what material should be included in school sex education and Section 28 has had real implications here.

Sex Education and Discourses of Desire and Danger

What is presented as sexuality in the sex education programmes we have has been criticized. Jackson (1982: 22) argues: 'What passes for sex education is in fact education about reproduction rather than sex education and is rarely about sexuality in its broader sense.' Other critics point to the fact that sex education has created a discourse which associates sexuality with danger rather than pleasure, with an emphasis given to the dangers for women especially of sexual expression. It is important to note that these messages stand in marked contrast to the other discourses relating to sexuality which we find in modern industrialised society, including the world of advertising and the mass media generally. We live in a sexualised society in which desire, albeit mostly male desire, and the expression of that desire are seen as of paramount importance.

Distribution of Themes

The remainder of this book is devoted to an exploration of these issues. In Chapter 2 we focus on the policy framework for sex education which exists in Britain and the development of legislation in the last decade-and-a-half that has represented a significant shift in approach.

Chapter 3 looks at the impact which the controversy over generational rights has had on sex education programmes in Britain. The main area of interest is the views young people themselves express about the policies and legislation that have been made for them and in their name. We consider their reactions to the aim of 'protecting' their innocence. It is important to state at this point that young people expressed nothing but resentment and bitterness about the legislation, which they considered restricted their entitlement to knowledge and experience.

The central empirical finding of this research is that girls and boys respond differently to sex education programmes, and that boys react more negatively than girls. Our data indicate the importance of informal gendered cultures for understanding patterns of sexual attitudes and behaviour among adolescents. Chapters 4–7 deal with different aspects of gender, and their significance for our understanding of what takes place in sex-education lessons. Chapter 4 outlines the theoretical approach taken in the study, beginning with an account of theories of sexual and gender socialisation. Social learning and feminist psychoanalytic theories are assessed and the work of Chodorow and Horney is combed for relevance. Chapters 5–7 examine different aspects of the data. We suggest that without a grasp of some of the issues involved in the development of gender identity we will not develop our understanding of either the processes of sexual socialisation or of adolescents' responses to the sexual socialisation received in the sex education programmes.

In Chapter 8 we explore the discourse of sexuality which is presented in the sex education programmes we studied, and consider the claim that the discourse emphasises danger and neglects desire. The focus is on how young people view the notion of sexuality presented to them. We were interested to document the paradoxical situation in which young people find themselves: health campaigns which have been developed in Britain in response to HIV/AIDS have opened up a debate about sexuality and have led to open discussion of a range of sexual behaviours; yet this openness in public discourse stands in contrast to formal school sex education programmes in which the legislation and a prurient media interest have over the years constrained what can be discussed

In Chapter 9 we consider the implications for policy and practice in sex education of understanding more about the perceptions and cultures of adolescents. One of the main concerns of this book is the effectiveness of sex education, which recently has been under scrutiny. What is distinctive about this study is that we have sought to assess effectiveness and identify good practice from the viewpoint of the pupils. We were interested in what young people identified as important and what they specified they would like to see offered in their sex-education lessons. In this final chapter we consider what are the most effective and appropriate strategies for teaching sex education to adolescents from *their* perspectives.

Background to the Research

The Sex Education Forum and other concerned agencies and individuals responsible for sex education have been alert to young people's criticisms of their provision. These agencies have launched new initiatives in an attempt to improve the situation by providing sex education which responds to these criticisms and to the changing pattern of adolescent sexual behaviour. Sex educators, of course, work in a political atmosphere which exhibits considerable hostility to liberal approaches. Sex educators work in a situation which is full of contradictions, pulled in different directions by the wish to respond to the changing needs of adolescents and the need to respond to the HIV/AIDS threat. They simultaneously have had to bear in mind the difficult political situation in which a right-wing lobby has pressed hard for conservative policies.

We have selected examples of sex education programmes launched in this complex and controversial policy context and which sought to negotiate the contradictory pressures. We aimed to identify innovative programmes established locally and to explore whether they satisfied the demands made over a number of years by adolescents or answered their criticisms. These sex education programmes were innovative and progressive in both content and pedagogy, while managing to avoid local or national controversy. We have endeavoured to develop an understanding of the reactions of young people to these programmes and to the policies underlying them.

We began by studying the sex education that was offered in a number of comprehensive schools in the south-east of England. We discovered a number of different service providers in this field. Although teachers and schools were an important source of sex education for the adolescents in our study, we found that health professionals are playing an increasingly important role both in the school setting and the youth-work context. In addition there is an increasing number of situations in which the sex educators are themselves young people in peer-education programmes. However, the main focus in the research was on the work done by teachers and health professionals in schools.

We looked at five school-based sex education programmes. To ensure the anonymity of the schools we called them Gainton, Tonford, Ferryfield, Streamham and Whitefarm. In Tonford and Gainton schools we researched sex-education provision that included health professionals contributing to the schools' programmes. The programmes, each funded by a different Health Authority, involved multi-agency teams of health professionals delivering a series of one-day programmes. Each team comprised of 6–8 health professionals, including family-planning doctors and nurses, doctors and nurses working in GUM clinics, school nurses, health education advisors, HIV/AIDS advisors and health workers. The schools involved suspended the year-9 curriculum for the day (14–15-year-old pupils). Each programme covered a variety of topics, but contraception and STDs were the most important. The third school, Streamham, was aiming to develop the use of health professionals in its sex education programmes and had invited local health professionals to talk to the pupils, but did not have the funding to develop a full programme of the kind that Gainton and Tonford had. We include material provided by teachers as well as by health professionals in Streamham school. The sex education programmes in the fourth and fifth schools, Whitefarm and Ferryfield, involved only the schools' teachers. The decision to choose schools which had different programmes was taken to assist evaluation of the pupils' views of diverse styles of innovation.

The sex education programmes we studied provided copious clear information about growth, conception, reproduction and the range of STDs, including HIV/AIDS. They dealt also with sexuality, acknowledging adolescent sexual activity. They produced explicit information about methods of contraception suitable for adolescents and explained where teenagers could access contraceptive supplies.

The sex education programmes suggested a 'democratised' model of sexual relationships, stressing collaborative and consensual interactions characterised by the open communication of feelings and responses. Boys and girls were urged to take responsibility for contraception, and also for emotional issues.

Methodology

It was with these ideas in mind and these concerns predominating that we designed a research process which focused on working with adolescents in the settings where they were offered sex education. Our research incorporated both qualitative and quantitative strategies. Originally our design contained only qualitative approaches, because we felt that these methods were suited to the sensitive areas of adolescent experience. There has been substantial quantitative research on sex education (see Allen 1987). While this work has given us an essential grasp of the outlines of young people's attitudes and perspectives on sex education, it has left a number of questions unanswered. We know very little about the details of the interactions between pupils or with their teachers in sex-education classrooms. As Trudell has pointed out: 'The everyday dynamics of students and teachers have been largely unexamined in the sex education literature and excluded from the debates among policy makers, academics, school personnel and health educators' (1993: 171).We need, in her view, to 'understand what counts as sex education in the daily life of schools' (ibid.: xiii).

This research used qualitative approaches to explore the adolescents' own understanding of their experiences, in the hope that the information thus yielded would offer us a solid basis on which to define priorities for sex education. The research was therefore based originally on participant observation of each sex-education programme, followed up by unstructured interviews with both pupils and health professionals in schools and youth-work settings.

During the field work we found that those running sex education programmes conducted their own evaluations, and these used more quantitative techniques. They were willing to make their data available to us, some of which we have included. Both health professionals and teachers evaluated their own work through questionnaires in Tonford, Gainton and Streamham schools. We decided to give a similar short questionnaire to pupils in Ferryfield and Whitefarm schools. This involved about 30–40 questionnaires for each class, depending on the number of pupils present.

All the questionnaires requested some basic information, and then asked five open-ended questions about pupils' responses to the sex education programmes. The questionnaires were administered either by the researchers, in the case of Ferryfield and Whitefarm, or by health professionals or teachers, in the other schools. They were completed by pupils in their classrooms immediately after sex education. The teachers and health professionals conducted their own analysis of their questionnaires, but then allowed us access to the raw data in the original questionnaires, and it is our analysis which is presented here. We analysed both our questionnaires and those of the health professionals and teachers within a few weeks of their completion: 685 questionnaires were completed. Pupils completed them with varying degrees of thoroughness, seriousness and care, as well as of literacy.

The questionnaires differed, asking different questions, and in different ways and with different formats. Some were more rigorously designed and administered than others by the health professionals involved. Because of the wide variation in the questionnaires, we have not attempted a statistical analysis of their content. What all the evaluations had in common was an emphasis on open-ended questions to gain insight into pupil reactions. In response to these methodological disparities we have quoted from the answers to the open-ended questions to illustrate themes.

The data presented is therefore taken from participant observation of the sex-education lessons, unstructured interviews and focus groups in the five schools, and from the questionnaires given to pupils. Qualitative and quantitative data, gathered by different methods from different sites by a team of three researchers offered opportunities for data, methods and investigator triangulation. Because we were working in five schools we were able to use a constant comparison model, employing both theoretical sampling and analytic induction for data analysis and validation. In our analysis we have tried to give a flavour of the spontaneous comments of pupils. Our principle has been to illustrate the themes that occurred most frequently and most eloquently in the pupils' comments. The aim is qualitative: to allow the 'voices' (including the spelling mistakes) of the individual young people to come through the analysis.

There is a final note to add. We feel that there are difficulties in researching sexuality and sex education with adolescents, problems which we do not consider have been adequately acknowledged by much research done in this field. We are far from convinced that the basic tools of qualitative research are sufficient to overcome the sensitivities of adolescents to this topic. We have aimed, therefore, to develop methodologies that would be helpful in this respect. It is important to state that we are not convinced that our research fully answers any of these criticisms. We used focus groups, based on friendship, because we suspected that we would get better data from groups of adolescents who knew each other well. We also employed a range of trigger materials in schools, presenting the pupils with material and exploring and discussing their reactions to it. We experimented with a strategy of peer researchers that sought to turn pupils who were key informants into data collectors, following Pollard's model (1985). However, it is important to state that this was unsuccessful, largely, we think, because within pupil informal cultures it is not acceptable to ask questions about sexuality of your peers.

Oakley *et al.*'s influential article (1995) on sex education programmes looks at the problems involved with evaluating interventions and is critical of the methodology involved in almost all of the studies. The research team calls for improved design of evaluations. However, a study like this will entirely fail the tests set in Oakley *et al.*'s article, as it is a small-scale study and offers no attempt to create control groups or deal with drop-outs. We hope, nonetheless, that a rather different set of methodological constructs will shed light on some issues about which we currently have little information.

Conclusion

Despite the commitment in Britain to offer sex education there are profound difficulties and controversies surrounding the provision. Sex education seems to be an inherently problematic area of social policy. This may relate to the fact that in sex education the question of sexuality, usually considered to be a 'private' matter, receives rare open scrutiny. We can see a good deal about a particular society's view of sexuality by considering its provision of sex education. The controversy which surrounds the development of policy in this area relates directly to the issue of the appropriate boundaries to state intervention: 'School sex education along with law on abortion and censorship mark the political front line between the personal and the public' (Thomson 1994: 10).

It appears that sex education today is often undertaken without an adequate understanding of the changes that have occurred over the last few decades in the social construction of sexuality and sexual practices. We need to bear in mind that such changes have impinged differently on distinct groups in our society. Religion and ethnicity each contribute significantly to the effect which cultural change in sexuality has upon individuals and the community. Nevertheless, as Connell and Dowsett (1992: 1) have pointed out: 'Conventional ideas about both sexuality and sex research have been under more or less continuous challenge for the last two decades.' The political tensions which have shaped the development of sex education are rooted in the way that governments have responded or refused to respond to changes in the structure of the family and sexual relations. There is a growing body of evidence, to which our research adds, that in Britain since 1979 the 'gulf between the public agenda of sex education as defined by the "gatekeepers" and policy makers and the needs and opinions of young people [has] widened' (Thomson 1994: 55).

Note

1 Religion does affect adolescent sexual behaviour and these liberal attitudes may not be as common amongst those who come from particular religious groups (Moore and Rosenthal 1993).

2 Legislation and the Policy Framework for Sex Education

Introduction

In this chapter we set out the legislation and the policy framework established for sex education in the last decade-and-a-half. It is important we have a grasp of the legislation because, 'Without acknowledgement of the context in which teachers work it can be easy to focus narrowly and critically on the individual practitioner as responsible for teaching content and strategies regarded as unacceptable' (Trudell 1993: 176). We look first at the controversies which have encircled the development of legislation in Britain since the early 1980s, tracking the contradictory currents by which policy has been constructed. There is evidence of an increasing level of state intervention over recent years, which goes against historical precedent in this country. We go on to look briefly at the history of sex education and the state's intervention in matters of policy relating to sexuality. This is followed by an outline of the legislation – of 1986, the amendments of 1987 and 1988, the Education Acts of 1993–94 and 1996 – and an attempt to evaluate its impact.

Sex Education – Definitions and Legislation

There is a government-backed commitment to provide sex education to young people educated in British schools. Circular 11/87 and the Welsh Office Circular 45/94 state: 'The Government believes that all pupils should be offered the opportunity of receiving a comprehensive, well planned programme of sex education during their school careers' (DES 1987b/WO 1994).

There is no consensus, however, about what sex education should consist of in Britain. 'The debates have taken place against a background of conflicting social, religious and cultural views' (Scott and Thomson 1992: 133). Sex education has become a highly political and controversial matter, and we need to trace the processes involved in that development. When we discuss controversies over sex education, what is really at issue is controversy over adolescent sexuality and the responses of government and other agencies to shifts in adolescent behaviour and attitudes.

A History of State Policy on Sex Education

Understanding the origins of the messages delivered in sex education and the history of their development is important. In *Dangerous Sexualities* (1987) Mort studied the early English sex education programmes and exposed the intense controversy which surrounded their development. The account which follows is heavily dependent on his historical research.

The issue of government intervention in sex education is an interesting one. Mort points out that the late nineteenth and early twentieth centuries saw almost no formal intervention by the state. Little sex education was provided in schools, though one early and highly controversial attempt to introduce a sex education programme occurred in 1913, in Dronfield in Derbyshire, where a local head teacher, Miss Outram, attempted to provide basic instruction in sexual matters. Her actions resulted in a storm of protest, stilled only by the outbreak of the First World War.

The work of the sexologists[1] contributed to the slow shift in thinking that began at this time, and public debate over sex education was initiated. Pressure for the provision of sex education came from voluntary groups rather than government agencies. There were two social initiatives which proved influential in the early decades of the twentieth century, usually referred to as the 'social purity' and the 'moral hygiene' movements. Comprised of influential activists, these two movements agitated for the provision of sex education, but failed to provoke an official government response.

In 1911 a pamphlet backing the importance of providing 'knowledge' and entitled 'The Manifesto of the National Council of Public Morals' campaigned for sex education, holding that the solution to national immorality lay in education. Young men and women should not only be offered physiological information but introduced to the lofty ideal of the sanctity and significance of marriage. The pamphlet argued that the contemporary approach, which combined repression, through fear, with resource work for the 'fallen', was no longer adequate. The manifesto called for positive education to channel the sexual instinct towards socially approved goals and considered this essential to counter the older and more negative moralities. *The Lancet* in 1913 discussed the need to offer *positive* images of sexuality for young people.

The National Birth Rate Commission issued a model syllabus for use in elementary schools in the early 1920s. The commission emphasised the importance of 'heterosexual monogamy', which it claimed should be cemented by a spiritualised love in order to transform the 'animal' like nature of sexual activity. The model syllabus consistently emphasised the polarisation of male and female sexuality, and included strong warnings about 'active and dangerous female sexuality' (Mort 1987: 190). The document perpetuated the double standard by insisting that male self-control was problematic and that girls had to help boys to act responsibly (ibid.: 19).

While continuing to believe that the best agency for sex education was the family, the hygienists considered the lives of the working classes to be inexcusably immoral. Such people could not be trusted to educate their children 'properly', and the hygienists justified the intervention by professionals, outsiders and even the state to provide the right kind of information for young people. The hygienists recognised that there was likely to be resistance to sex education programmes in working class areas, and fear of that resistance inhibited the development of such programmes. Throughout the First World War and the inter-war years, the Home Office, the Ministry of Health and the Board of Education remained cautious about the introduction of sex education into schools, despite the work being done by the sexologists and by reformers like Stopes.

The Second World War produced no major re-think by the state, although many medical people and the eugenicists strongly supported the introduction of sex education into the curriculum. The programmes backed by the voluntary pressure groups reflected the wider ideas of the time about sexual behaviour. In the late 1930s and 1940s, however, there was a new political concern with sexuality, underpinned by an intent to preserve and extend healthy marriage and parenthood (Clarke 1991: 23). The aim was to encourage the stabilisation of family life, and chastity in marriage was an essential, but one that was most likely to be assured by a fulfilling sexual relationship. Reformers considered that sex education had a real role to play. In a rather English style of compromise, voluntary organisations were given money to conduct sex-education work in schools. Surveys showed that many of the schools and training colleges supported by progressive local authorities took advantage of the Board of Education's – deliberately ambiguous – programme in order to introduce their own sexual-hygiene programmes, especially for girls (Mort 1987: 200).

Despite widespread public concern about the nation's sexual and moral health it was not until 1943 that the Board of Education officially dealt with the provision of sex education in British schools. This year saw the publication of the Board of Education document *Sex Education in Schools and Youth Organisations*, which made space for sex education in the secondary schools' curriculum (Mort 1987: 200). In the 1960s and 1970s state sex education was adopted in the majority of schools.

The British state has shown a marked reluctance to legislate in relation to sex education, and even less willingness to develop a national or co-ordinated response to questions of public sexual health and personal morality. When the state did act it was in response to pressure from popular political movements. This meant that sex education developed piecemeal – through the efforts of voluntary bodies, some innovative LEAs and higher educational institutions, and with significant local variations. The aims of sex education continued up to the late 1960s to be framed by the preventive imperatives of public health.

Throughout this period there was no nationally agreed curriculum framework within which sex education was taught (Farrell 1978; Allan, 1987). Local authorities had responsibility for providing curriculum guidance to schools in this and other areas. The provision of, and approach to, sex education was inconsistent throughout the country (Thomson 1994). Central government avoided public confrontation of questions concerning the aims of sex education by allowing this local control of – and hence variability in – provision. There were important implications of this pattern. While there was a growing consensus between educational, health and voluntary agencies, this was not reflected in Parliament, the media or public opinion. As a result 'the consensus was vulnerable to attack' (Thomson 1994: 45).

By the mid-1980s there were several contradictory pressures at work. There was a wave of panic, rooted in the sudden realisation that the whole hetero-sexual population was potentially at risk from HIV. The spiralling statistics on HIV/AIDS infections pushed government agencies into decisive action, and resulted in public health campaigns which were more explicit about the threat than those of a number of other countries.

At the same time, however, there were growing pressures in the opposite direction, arising from a range of moralist lobbies which had emerged in the years of Conservative government. Organisations like the Responsible Society, Family and Youth Concern and CARE – Christian Action for Research in Education – demanded a more restricted definition of sex education, one which would constrain what could be taught under this name in schools. Such groups took a traditionalist and repressive line on adolescent sexuality, arguing that sex education should emphasise continence and chastity. The public health campaign about HIV/AIDS did not therefore immediately translate into educa-tion policy. Schools were given a framework for sex education which embodied growing tensions between the public health interest and the moral right-wing (Thomson 1994: 50).

The Legislation

Legislation defined the broad parameters of the content of sex education. In the eighteen years of Conservative government a series of Education Acts and Circulars from the Department of Education and Science as well as related legislation in local government changed the approach to sex education quite considerably.

Education Reform Act 1986

The Education Reform Act (No. 2) of 1986 (DES 1987a: Section 1(2)) required schools to offer a curriculum which 'promotes the spiritual, moral, cultural, mental and physical development of pupils at the school ... and prepares such pupils for the opportunities, responsibilities and experiences of adult life'. Sex education clearly had a role to play in that, but backbench Tory MPs, supported by the small but vociferous moralist lobbies we have identified, wanted legislation to go further. They introduced into the 1986 Education Act amendments to progress the aims of the moral right-wing. The government struck a balance between the imperatives of public health, the backbenchers' pressure and its own moral rhetoric. The result was a compromise: an amendment was passed which devolved control over whether sex education was taught at all to school governors, imposed the requirement to consult with parents, and gave governors the power to grant parents the discretionary right to withdraw their children from sex-education classes.

The amendment established in legislation the requirement that sex education be taught within a moral framework. Section 46 of the Education Act (No. 2) (DES 1987a) required that the LEA, governing body and headteacher 'shall take such steps as are reasonably practicable to secure that where sex education is given it is given in such a manner as to encourage those pupils to have due regard to moral considerations and the value of family life'. This emphasis on the 'moral tone' of sex education placated the moralist lobbies, but did not give them all they wanted; the pressures of the crisis over HIV/AIDS prevailed. It is important to note that the parental right of withdrawal, which could have compromised the public health interest, was not granted; nor was funding withdrawn from agencies like the FPA and the Brook Advisory Service, for which the moralist lobbies had campaigned.

In the following year the Department for Education issued guidance to school governors on their new responsibilities for sex education which went further than had the legislation and more forcefully pushed a prescriptive and moralistic framework within which sex education should be taught:

> Teaching about the physical aspects of sexual behaviour should be set within a clear moral framework in which pupils are encouraged to consider the importance of self restraint, dignity and respect for others and are helped to recognise the physical, emotional and moral risks of casual and promiscuous sexual behaviour. Schools should foster a recognition that both sexes should behave responsibly in sexual matters. Pupils should be helped to appreciate the benefits of stable married life and the responsibilities of parenthood.
>
> (DES 1987: 4)

The guidance went further than the requirement to encourage pupils to have 'due regard to moral considerations' laid out in the 1986 legislation.

The guidance also dealt with the controversial issues of contraceptive advice for under-16s and confidentiality, which had already captured public interest in the Gillick ruling of 1986.

> Good teachers have always taken an interest in the welfare and well being of pupils. But this function should never trespass on the proper exercise of parental rights and responsibilities. On the specific question of the provision of contraceptive advice to girls under 16, the general rule must be that giving an individual pupil advice on such matters without parental know-

ledge or consent would be an inappropriate exercise of a teacher's professional responsibilities and could, depending on the circumstances, amount
to a criminal offence.

(DES 1987b: Section 26)

The Circular also had specific advice about the way homosexuality should be
treated in schools:

> There is no place in any school in any circumstance for teaching which
> advocates homosexual behaviour, which presents it as the 'norm' or which
> encourages homosexual experimentation by pupils. It must also be recog-
> nised that for many people, including members of religious faiths,
> homosexual practice is not morally acceptable and deep offence may be
> caused to them if the subject is not handled with sensitivity by teachers.

(DES 1987b: Section 22)

Local government legislation, of course, also had an impact on the approach to
homosexuality that schools developed. Section 2 of the Local Government Act
1986, as amended by Section 28 of the Local Government Act 1988, forbade
any promotion of homosexual activities. The government clarified that Section
28 applied to the activities of local authorities, rather than to schools, and
Circular 12/88 from the DoE addressed the concerns raised by the Act. It states:
'Section 28 does not affect the activities of school governors nor of teachers. It
will not prevent the objective discussion of homosexuality in the classroom, nor
the counselling of pupils concerned about their sexuality.' It also pointed out
that the 'duty of confidentiality is the same for young lesbian women and gay
men as it is towards heterosexual young people'.

Implications of the Legislation and Circulars

The legislation has had implications for schools' governing bodies and for
teachers, and inevitably has affected the practices of both. The legislation
meant a transfer of control over sex education from local education authorities
to school governing bodies. This has had variable results, for school governors
had responsibility for school management, including financial management,
and it was easy for sex education to be overlooked. Gillian Lenderyou from the
Sex Education Forum has pointed out that sex education tends to be under-
prioritised.

The most crucial implications for practice in sex education work, however,
have arisen in relation to homosexuality and contraception. Section 28 and the
guidance in Circular 11/87, taken in the context of the Gillick ruling, had
'considerable impact on the way in which school sex education was and
continues to be perceived' (Thomson 1994: 49). There is significant evidence
that the majority of teachers found the law confusing and were anxious about

what was and was not allowed in sex and relationships' education (Biddulph 1988). In practice it meant the avoidance of teaching about homosexuality, and severe restrictions on work done on contraception. Section 28 and the guidance in Circular 11/87 had the effect of placating the moral right-wing and reinforcing the traditional model of sexual relations in sex education. The introduction of a moral framework for sex education in schools tended in the same direction.

The Education Act 1993–94

The controversial Sex Education Amendment (No. 62) to the Education Bill was passed without debate in the Commons on 19 July 1993. The amendment now forms Section 241 of the Education Act 1993 (DfE 1994a). The Department for Education wrote to all chief education officers and schools in September 1993 to inform them of the changes, effective from August 1994.

These changes were:

- Section 241 of the 1993 Education Act made the provision of sex education compulsory in maintained secondary schools in England and Wales. It required governors of maintained secondary schools to provide sex education (including education about HIV/AIDS and other STDs) to all registered pupils.
- It removed from National Curriculum Science reference to AIDS/HIV, STDs and aspects of human sexual behaviour *other* than biological aspects.
- It granted parents the right to withdraw pupils from all or part of sex education classes outside of the National Curriculum in both primary and secondary schools.

The implementation of policies for sex education in schools is monitored by OfSTED inspectors as part of school inspections. These inspections also consider the opportunities for spiritual, moral, social and cultural development in a school's curriculum.

Circular 5/94 and the Welsh Office Circular 45/94.

In response to the new legislation the Department for Education issued new guidance to schools on sex education in Circular 5/94 (DfE 1994b). This replaced Circular 11/87 (DES 1987b). It is important to emphasise that Circular 5/94, issued by Secretary of State for Education John Patten, offered guidance only, and did not constitute an authoritative legal interpretation. Nevertheless, there is evidence that it has significantly influenced both policy and practice.

Implications of the Act and the Circular

The Act and the Circular have significant implications for the work of those delivering school sex education. In this section we examine the respective aspects of the legislation.

Central Control

The situation for primary schools has remained unchanged, except that parents are able to withdraw their children from all or part of sex education provision. Governors of primary schools continue to decide whether to provide sex education and to develop a policy outlining where and how sex education would be provided. The situation in secondary schools, however, has changed significantly as a result of the 1993 Act. Since 1967 in England and Wales sex education in secondary schools had been under the collective consideration of LEAs, governing bodies and headteachers. The Education Reform Acts of 1986 and 1993 require that secondary-school pupils are provided with sex education, including education about HIV/AIDS and other STDs. School governors of secondary schools have lost the power to decide whether a school provides sex education. The 1993 Act has removed these powers from local agencies and governmental structures, and has created a national framework for sex education that is under the control of central government.

Observers of the workings of the amendment have pointed out that the legislation has the advantage of drawing attention to the importance of sex education in schools and that the national framework it created makes it more difficult to ignore sex education. There are nevertheless significant problems with this centralised structure. The legislation has increased central control at the expense of local flexibility and experiment. Under the old system of delegated control, developments in practice were pioneered by independent bodies like the FPA, as well as by specialists in LEAs and some institutions of higher education. The dismantling of the LEA's powers and the withdrawal of funding for specialist local advisors has meant the diminution of pioneering work.

Right of Withdrawal

Parents now have the right to withdraw pupils from the parts of the sex education programme that do not form part of the National Curriculum. But sex education which continues to form part of National Curriculum Science, or which arises during the study of other National Curriculum subjects, is outside of parental jurisdiction. Critics have pointed to drawbacks and difficulties attaching to these provisos. Questions were raised in Parliament about the implications of the legislation for cross-curricular teaching. The Department for Education has taken note of these concerns and has stated in guidance that if, in a given school, no pupils are withdrawn from sex education classes, a cross-curricular approach to sex-education provision is viable. If that school wishes to do so, it may continue to teach sex education in National Curriculum Science. In schools where pupils have been withdrawn, those aspects of sex education which are additional to the requirements of the National Curriculum are to be so structured in the curriculum so as to facilitate the withdrawal of pupils.

The guidance also stated that if discussion of sexual issues spontaneously develops in a curricular area outside of the sciences, that discussion is allowable even to pupils who *have been* withdrawn from sex education. 'Provided that such discussion is relatively limited and set within the context of other subjects concerned it will not necessarily constitute part of a programme of sex education' (DfE 1994b: Para 30). This has caused schools some difficulties in curricular construction, and teachers have expressed concern over answering questions and dealing with discussion without infringing the law.

Another criticism has been that the legislation opens sex education to politicisation in the form of local activism geared to encourage parents to withdraw children (Thomson 1994: 53). Critics have suggested that teachers and governing bodies face potential censorship of their work by local moral right-wing groups. In the face of this threat, it seems, teachers are themselves censoring the material they discuss in the classroom.

Perhaps the most searing criticism has come from those who consider that the legislation jeopardises the entitlements and rights of pupils. Incensed by the provision of the right of withdrawal, they argue that the legislation represents an attack on children's entitlement to sex education and an increase in the power of parents. These critics have suggested this parental veto is inconsistent with British and European legislation on children's rights.

Confidentiality

One of the most controversial provisions of Circular 5/94 concerns confidentiality and the provision of advice to pupils:

> Particular care must be exercised in relation to contraceptive advice to pupils under 16 for whom sexual intercourse is unlawful.

> A teacher approached by an individual pupil for specific advice on contraception or other aspects of sexual behaviour should whenever possible encourage the pupil to seek advice from his or her parents and relevant health professionals. Where the circumstances are such as to lead the teacher to believe the pupil is contemplating a course of conduct likely to place him or her at moral or physical risk or in breach of the law the teacher has a general responsibility to ensure that the pupil is aware of the implications. In such circumstances the teacher should inform the head teacher. The head teacher should arrange for the pupil to be counselled and

if the pupil is under age for the parents to be made aware.

(DfE 1994b: Sections 39 and 40)

The situation for health professionals working in schools is slightly different. School nurses are deemed capable of giving pupils information about where they can receive confidential contraceptive and sexual health advice and treatment, and of counselling individual pupils on health-related matters. There is an obligation to respect confidence, except in exceptional circumstances. As health professionals, school nurses are deemed competent to exercise professional judgement as to whether a young person has the maturity to consent to medical treatment, including contraceptive treatment, without parental involvement. The criteria for making such a decision are based on the Gillick ruling that 'any competent young person regardless of age can independently seek medical advice and give valid consent to treatment'.

Teachers working with teenagers appear to have found these guidelines confusing. The suggestion that teachers should report information disclosed about unlawful sexual activity by pupils to the headteacher, who in turn should inform the pupil's parents, has been seen to be particularly difficult and unjust. The Sex Education Forum (1994) has pointed to the great responsibility invested in the headteacher, who may instruct staff to follow the advice of Section 40 quoted above. Teachers could face disciplinary action if they failed to do so.

Most teachers seem to feel that their practice has been constrained by the guidance. As part of our research we attended training days organised for county-wide advice on the new legislation by one of the LEAs responsible for the programmes we studied. We heard voices there that urged a cautious line:

> Teachers don't know the answer to whether they can give contraceptive advice. There has not been a court case, so we don't know how the law would come down. The advice we give you is that under the new guidelines you cannot give advice.

A trainer at a conference on the new legislation organised by a local health trust summed up the position as she saw it:

> Schools are positive but frightened. The threat of being taken to court or even being thoroughly disapproved of is closing them down, they won't even talk about contraception for example. Teachers feel they are putting themselves at risk.

There is evidence from other sources that the effects of the new legislation are felt to be restrictive. The Brook Advisory Centre, which specialises in offering sexual health information and counselling to adolescents, is often asked to give talks to schools. Since the amendments to the Sex Education Act the trickle of requests has become a flood. Brooks Centre representatives have made it clear that teachers need more support to tackle this area. Teachers are concerned that the legislation has created conflict in their relationships with young people. The confusion and concern which have resulted from the guidelines on sex education have made it difficult for schools to plan and carry out coherent and relevant programmes (Roberts and Sachdev 1996).

According to the Sex Education Forum, 'young people now have no right to sex education nor to confidentiality concerning their sexual practice from their teachers' (Thomson 1994: 53). The process, initiated in the legislation of 1986, by which these rights have passed from the orbit of adolescence into the remit of adults, specifically parents, has been extended in that of 1994.

Moral Frameworks

The 1993 Act and Circular 5/94 employed a moral framework similar to that of the 1986 Act, and in fact continued to use some of the language of the earlier Act. They continue also to emphasise the importance of encouraging pupils to have regard to moral considerations and the value of family life. Sex education should 'provide knowledge about loving relationships, the nature of sexuality and the processes of human reproduction'. At the same time, however, 'it should lead to the acquisition of understanding and attitudes which prepare pupils to view their relationships in a responsible and healthy manner' (DfE 1994b: Section 8).

It is fair to say that our research shows teachers, head teachers, trainers and local authority personnel to have severe criticisms of the Act and the new restrictions that it has imposed. We found no support for the measures from individuals involved in sex education. The Avert Organisation conducted a survey of AIDS education in schools in 1990 and concluded: ' Many teachers do not share the "restraint and celibacy" approach emphasised by the DES' (Avert 1990: 10). Part of the issue here is that professional advice given by those who had spent many years working in the field of sex education was ignored by government when the legislation was drawn up. This has distanced sex-education practitioners from the framework within which they work. It has served also to reduce their confidence and sense of autonomy in their work. The emphasis on prescriptive morality and the insistence on a single framework of values within which pupils are supposed to live were opposed by senior teachers in the schools we investigated. A typical response came from one of the deputy-headteachers of Ferryfield, a committed Christian:

> I might be reading the text wrong, but I sense that the government wants to come from an Old Testament 'Thou shalt not ...' [position]. They're not real. It's just a different match up, and what bothers me as a teacher is that we have to work with what is – for the sake of the youngsters.

This is a clear statement of disagreement with the imposition of a moral framework which ignores the realities of life in a secondary school.

The deputy-head at Whitefarm took a similarly pragmatic stance in arguing against the ideological thrust of the legislation:

> Well, I think these things are part of life and school. You can't ignore any issue or push it under the carpet, which I think the government wants to some extent. But, basically, the whole back-to-basics moral-majority climate ... well, it is just one particular morality, and it's certainly not mine. I feel that it is so out of touch.

The headteacher at Gainton was in agreement, and made much the same point: 'No, I think the government is completely out of touch. I think it is very narrow.' Asked to say in what way the government is out of touch, she replied:

> Well, its draconian. I think they want a return to what they see as a golden age in terms of morals, which I don't feel ever existed – there were all those back-street abortions. I think sexuality is part of life, and the attitude to sex in this country is appalling.

Homosexuality

The approach of the 1993 Act and the Circulars to homosexuality was seen to presuppose a moral framework which is inappropriate and likely to have a negative impact on pupils. This aspect of policy met with considerable disapproval from sex-education teachers. Circular 5/94 and Welsh Office Circular 45/94 restated and confirmed that restrictions regarding teaching about lesbian and gay issues do not apply to schools. There is, however, considerable evidence that since 1986 discussion of and teaching on homosexuality has in effect been stifled in schools and that has been largely responsible for the stilling of voices. Gay rights' campaigners have repeatedly warned that the lives of homosexual teenagers were being put at risk because of this legislation.

Healthy Alliances

The other provision made in Circular 5/94 relates to the development of healthy alliances. In July 1992 the government published its strategy in *Health of the Nation* in which a number of targets in public health in general and sexual health in particular were set. Sex education, according to Circular 5/94, can make a substantial contribution to meeting those targets. The Circular also recommends the aligning of secondary schools' expertise and resources with those of health professionals:

> Teachers should take account of the range of expertise and other resources available to them including the contribution which health authorities, other health service bodies and health professionals – particularly doctors (including GPs) and school nurses – may be able to make.
>
> (DfE 1994b: para. 32)

The projects we researched had grown under the combined stimulus and constraint of the new legislation. The National Curriculum obliges all secondary schools to deliver a sex-education programme, and inevitably some were better placed than others to do so. *Health of the Nation* had set the targets, and 'healthy alliances' were means of addressing them. The NHS and Care in the Community Acts opened up space for new providers to enter new areas of work.

The Policy Context

It is important that we put these aspects of legislation into the wider policy context. In April 1994 the Health Education Authority announced that it was to withdraw ten of its sex and HIV-related educational publications after disputes with the government over the nature of its campaigning. Among those withdrawn was Nick Fisher's booklet 'The Best Sex Guide.' His earlier booklet 'Your Pocket Guide to Sex' was referred to by Health Minister Brian Macwhinney as 'smutty'. At that time the moralist lobbies were trying to get involved in curriculum matters: CARE for example produced a video on abstinence for use in sex education.

In 1996 Peter Luff, Conservative MP for mid-Worcestershire, having looked at a magazine his 10-year-old daughter was reading, attacked the 'squalid titillation, salaciousness and smut' featured in magazines aimed at teenage girls. He introduced a bill in the House of Commons to try to force such magazines to carry age warnings on sexually explicit material. He won backing from Home Office Minister Tom Sackville, who told the Commons that some magazines were using sex and exploiting the innocence of young people to make money. The publishers and retailers of the magazines agreed to set up a working party to draw up a code of conduct.

Initiatives in other areas indicate the development of increasingly restrictive policies, inimical to progressive approaches to sex education, at a time when the moralist lobbies appeared to be gaining ground. Throughout the late 1970s and 1980s equality of opportunity programmes were developed to address gender inequities, a vital element of which was a consensus about the importance of developing young women's critical abilities and communication skills – in all areas of the curriculum, including sex education (Weiner 1985; Burchell and Millman 1989). The influence of anti-sexist strategies in the education and youth sectors encouraged a more critical approach to sex education. The emphasis on gender difference in the sex education available was recognised and progressive local authority initiatives such as ILEA's Sexuality Unit developed strategies for teaching sex education which questioned sexual identity, gender roles and issues of control and consent in sexual relationships (Thomson 1994: 45). These initiatives were lost with the abolition of ILEA and with the increasing centralisation of those sex education programmes permissible under the legislation.

Education Act 1996

On 1 November 1996 the Education Act of 1993 was repealed, though there were no changes of substance to the law on sex education. Section 352 provides that sex education should cover both HIV/AIDS and STDs. School governors still decide each school's sex-education policy. The moral framework remains intact. All maintained schools are required to offer a curriculum which prepares pupils for the 'opportunities, responsibilities and experiences of adult life'. The insistence on the importance of 'due regard to the moral considerations and the value of family life' is maintained in the 1996 legislation.

Evaluation of the Policies

Our central purpose is to evaluate the response of adolescents to the policies set out in the legislation and other initiatives. The debate, as we have said, is full of heat and controversy, and there is little space for young people to voice their views. It seemed important to ask young people directly what they thought about policies on sex education framed for them, which did not consult them or discern their viewpoint. Observing their reactions to the sex education programmes they were offered was also important as was understanding more about their responses. Part of what is at issue is the contradictions of policy which young people find themselves operating in. On the one hand they encounter restrictive legislation, and on the other they are exposed to HIV/AIDS material which provides a more open discussion of sexuality than was previously seen in Britain.

Conclusions and Ways Forward

How then are we to take the debate forward about what the content and purposes of sex education should be in Britain in the 1990s? There has been bitter and polarised dispute about sex education in the last decade and a half in the UK and the subject has become a political one in a way that it was not in former years. Some elements of the mass media have unhelpfully sensationalised issues in the way they have focused on sex education in schools and youth work centres. The tabloid press has pilloried individual practitioners and shown no awareness of the difficulties of sex educators negotiating between the realities of adolescent sexuality and new legislation which reveals little knowledge of those realities. Linda Grant, writing in the *Guardian* (25 March 1997), has criticised the collusion of politicians and the tabloid press: 'Sex education has suffered the effects of sound-bite policies, of politicians knowing they can get on the front page if they talk about teenagers and sex.'

An atmosphere hostile to progressive sex education had come to prevail, creating problems for practitioners. During the Thatcher and Major governments those involved in innovative sex education clearly came to feel that they were at risk. The present Labour government has shown itself to be more open to innovative approaches, but the direction of future policy is not yet clear.

However it is essential to remember that the HIV/AIDS epidemic at the same time created strong pressures in the opposite direction. The research into sexuality which resulted from the threat of AIDS has facilitated the public discussion of sex and sexuality (Thomson 1994: 54). The campaigns launched in reaction to HIV/AIDS, and the current concern about teenage pregnancy rates, have sharpened the demand for effective sex education programmes.

Public health initiatives in relation to HIV/AIDS were progressive in approach, using more explicit language and attempting – if not entirely successfully – to get the specifically sexual issues involved in the HIV/AIDS threat discussed more openly. It is important to recognise that the government backed this campaign. Concessions were made to the moralist lobbies, as we have noted, but the lobbies failed to achieved all they had campaigned for. The promotion of 'healthy alliances' has had progressive outcomes, and we will present data which indicate that such outcomes are related to improved sex-education provision in UK schools.

Note

1   The name given to a group of – predominantly male – researchers concerned with sexuality, attempting to map and codify sexual behaviour and to study it 'scientifically'.

3 Generation and Sex Education

Introduction

In Chapter 1 we discussed the issue of generation, and pointed to its controversial status in the sex education field. Sex education brings into focus 'tensions around generation, and issues about the way we acknowledge or refuse to acknowledge the fact of adolescent sexuality' (Moore and Rosenthal 1993: 40). In this chapter we consider the reactions of young people to the arguments adults make about adolescent sexuality, and their reactions to the sex education programmes which result from the policy framework. We look first at the controversy between liberal and conservative views relating to the best way to inform and counsel young people about sexuality. We go on to look at the reactions of young people to the legislation passed in their interests by government. Finally we focus on the responses of pupils to the sex education programmes provided for them within the legislative and policy frameworks.

Political Controversy over Sex Education

The conservative view starts from the principle that it is important to protect the 'innocence' of children. Childhood, which is seen to persist until the age of 14 or 15, is defined as a time of innocence in this approach. In the United States the New Right sees sex education as something which can destroy the family and religious morality, and threatens God-given gender roles; it is therefore to be resisted (Hunter 1984: 63). Moral majority campaigners in Britain have taken a less heated approach to sex education, but nevertheless demand constraints on the education which is offered to young people.

Liberal and more radical views emphasise children's knowledge of and curiosity about sexuality. Research has consistently shown that young people's cultures are steeped in sexual awareness. The Goldmans' 1982 study, for example, focused on children aged 5–15 and indicates that we consistently underestimate their knowledge of and capacity to understand human sexuality.

The liberal and radical views start from an acknowledgement that western society is highly sexualised and abounds with overt and covert sexual messages. The media have a crucial role to play in the construction of western culture.

Young people are socialised into a world characterised by a vast array of media forms (Sachs *et al.* 1991). Much of their sex education comes from informal sources, such as from television programmes (Balding 1997). The widespread coverage in the media of AIDS and of sexual scandals involving the rich and famous means that even very young children are likely to be exposed to information about these matters. It is important to emphasise that sexuality is an element essential to consumer culture. The market asserts a 'right to wrap sex around any and every consumer item' and continues to do so because of the market success of the strategy (Sachs *et al.* 1991: 18). The media, which together constitute the main vehicle of consumer culture, provide powerful models of sexuality which are likely to be valued highly by young people. Nowhere in our society is there a clearer set of representations of and messages about desire than in the mass media, and the liberal–radical argument is that we 'cannot pretend these models do not exist or keep them hidden from our children' (Moore and Rosenthal 1990: 205).

It is fashionable – and easy – to blame the mass media for this highly sexualised culture, but what we as adults do counts for a great deal. The last thirty years have seen complicated shifts in family and household structures that are influenced by variations in sexual morality. Such changes affect young people's notions of marriage, relationships and sexual practices, perhaps more strongly than do media images.

Sex educators argue that there are policy implications arising from this context of the sexualised culture. They question whether protecting children's 'innocence' remains a reasonable aim: 'Adolescents are faced with sorting their way through this material' (Moore and Rosenthal 1993: 72), and the argument goes that sex educators should be working to offer young people the tools to do so effectively.

The majority of sex education agencies have been critical of the legislation passed in the last decade-and-a-half in Britain (Sex Education Forum 1994). In their view the legislation has shown little understanding of the cultural context in which young people operate. It makes little compromise with the reality of social change, failing to acknowledge that changes in the structure of the family and in sexual relationships cannot simply be reversed at the will of the politicians and morality lobbies. The legislation and policy framework have resulted in the isolation of young people from adult professional advice. Teenagers trying to make difficult decisions about their own path through these contradictory pressures are left alone, with little support from adults.

Recently some broadsheet journalists have engaged seriously with the issue. Yvonne Roberts, for example, commented:

> Of course I'd prefer that my 14-year old was into Little Women, Girl Guides and pony gymkhanas. But she isn't. Instead, she and thousands of other teenagers have to survive as robustly as they can living in the carnal zone which passes for daily life. It's time that we adults were grown-up

enough to accept that – in the seedy world we have created – our children deserve knowledge and genuine protection.

(*Guardian* 2 December 1998)

Liberal commentators have expressed their irritation with current sex education policies which fail to equip young people to negotiate a path through the 'carnal zone'. Jackson (1982: 137–8), for example, asserts that the 'chief aim' of sex education 'is apparently to dissuade [young people] from expressing their sexuality at all'. Wolpe also has been critical: she points out (1987) that British educators see sex education as preparing adolescents for the future rather than helping them to come to terms with their sexuality here and now. They argue that sex education needs to provide young people with a number of opportunities. In the first place it is important to ensure that accurate physiological information is available to young people from sex education programmes run by well-trained and well-informed individuals. Information is not, however, the only issue. Sex education should offer adolescents preparation for 'considered thinking' about sexual matters in our consumerised sexual culture. It is also important that sex education provides young people with a space in which they feel able to discuss their fears and to challenge the sexual norms of the adolescent informal culture they construct and are constructed by.

Some observers more pragmatically start from the statistics, which indicate a drop in the age at which young people are becoming sexually active. Given that this accurately describes the situation, it is the responsibility of adults to ensure that young people can protect themselves from the unwanted or negative consequences of their sexual activity. This is particularly important for young women: 'It is absolutely clear that many girls become pregnant through sheer ignorance. We need to create a climate where young people understand the consequences of their actions and their relationships' (Jowell 1998).

Adolescent Reactions to Sex Education Policy and Legislation

The legislation and policy framework outlined in Chapter 2 represents a shift towards the conservative approach to sex education. Thomson, writing for the Sex Education Forum claimed that the policy reforms of the 1980s were out of touch with what young people wanted or considered significant:

If schools did attempt to engage young people creatively in an exploration of values and morality they would find that young people hold strong opinions about what is fair and unfair and these opinions differ significantly from those envisaged by the politicians.

(Thomson 1994: 55)

We saw this to be an important claim, worth testing out in our research. We discussed the legislation with young people aged 15–16 in the schools we researched. They were surprised and angry at the government's actions and opposed the new legislation very strongly. We found no young people who considered that the legislation was fair or appropriate. We approached the issue by giving young people newspaper articles and headlines which discussed the 1993 legislation and asked for their reaction to it.

Right of withdrawal

Pupils were not in agreement with the government's view of the rights of parents over children. They challenged this view of the balance of power between the generations. A pupil at Ferryfield commented: 'It only gives parents the right. It should be up to the person.' Pupils at Tonford objected to this provision in the legislation because in their view it meant losing an opportunity to learn about such important aspects as HIV/AIDS:

> It could be that if a parent withdrew a child from sex education, it means they would have no education about HIV and AIDS.

> Well everyone should learn about it and its dangers, shouldn't they?

> It's just really important.

Pupils asserted their belief in the importance of sex education. There was an acknowledgement of their need for information and for help from adults. Any attempt to restrict their right of access to information was therefore resisted.

Confidentiality

A survey (HEA 1997) commissioned by the Health Education Authority asked young people aged 13–15 to give their reactions to the new legislation on contraception and confidentiality: 84 per cent said they would like to talk to their teachers about contraception, but 64 per cent would not do so if they thought their parents would be told. Our qualitative data offers a similar picture and elaborates some of the factors behind the figures, enabling us to see more of the young people's reasoning.

We explained government guidelines which put teachers under pressure to inform their headteacher and then parents if pupils discuss sexual activity or contraception with them. Pupils at Whitefarm reacted to this information by demanding: 'Why? Parents don't need to know that!'

· The same pattern of reaction is visible: adolescents are asserting their rights to an autonomous sexuality independent of their parents. They demand to be seen as grown up and mature enough to make their own decisions. Pupils at Ferryfield also suggest that the guidelines are counter-productive, as they make it more difficult to take sensible decisions about sexual activity:

If you went to a teacher and said, 'Look I'm sexually active, I want to know about getting some condoms', and they said, 'No, I can't tell you', then you'd probably go out and do it without, but if they give you advice you're less likely to get pregnant, aren't you?

There was no acknowledgement of any effective adult interventions to prevent adolescents engaging in sexual experimentation. At Gainton a pupil said: 'People will have sex anyway.'

Pupils accused the government of refusing to acknowledge the realities of the way teenagers live their lives. The assertion is clear: teenagers will engage in sexual relationships. They charged the policy makers with a kind of plurality of thinking:

The only way to go about reducing teenage pregnancy is through education. They say they want that, and then pass these laws – they are so contradicting. Let people know what they need to know.

There is also an assertion of entitlement by these pupils, who feel they have 'a right to know'. In the teenagers' view the approach has to include greater openness to have any hope of success:

If John Patten wants to decrease teenage pregnancy then we should be allowed to ask advice from anyone, in confidence, because otherwise we are not going to know about it.

If we aren't asking teachers and that, then more people are going to be ignorant and more pregnancies are going to occur.

There was a contrast drawn between the realities prevailing in the commercial world – where contraceptives are available to a teenager who can buy them – and the restrictions placed on teachers operating outside that consumer culture. At Streamham a pupil asked: 'How come you're not allowed to go to your teacher for advice, but you can walk into a shop and buy them?'

Pupils made another point in this context which we feel is important. They made it clear that they would not want to discuss personal sexual issues with the majority of their teachers, and we look at this issue in more depth in a later chapter. They stressed, however, that there were some teachers they felt they could trust and would want to be able to ask for help. Pupils at Whitefarm said:

If you have a teacher, like Miss Magges, that you can talk to, then that's great. You need a teacher that won't say what you tell them in confidence, you need to know that they won't tell.

> That is the problem now with a teacher. They'd have to tell – legally obliged to, etc. 'Cos it could get back to your parents, or whatever.

We consider it important to note that pupils do have good relationships with some adults and teachers in whom they feel able to confide. This is a significant issue in the lives of young people, particularly those who may have little support from home. They expressed resentment that government decree should disrupt the support which they had developed with some teachers, and so change and destroy a valued resource. It is also worrying that not all pupils display evidence of good relationships and honest communication with parents, and this issue is explored later in this research.

The moral framework

One newspaper article used for class discussion focused on the new moral framework that Conservative governments had established for sex education. The article described the government's insistence that 'lessons in right and wrong' be put on the timetable for secondary-school children. The journalists explained that teachers are expected to make it clear to teenagers that it is wrong to have heterosexual intercourse before the age of 16 and before 21 years of age in homosexual relationships. Teachers are charged with asserting the benefits of the female–male relationship for the bringing up of children. The article emphasised that government ministers wanted teachers to concentrate more on family values and morality than on the mechanics of sex.

A 15-year-old pupil at Ferryfield School expressed his disagreement with the thinking behind this policy:

> Right and wrong! There is no right and wrong. I don't think they should talk to you about family values because everyone's got a different family, parents and that.

We consider this reaction interesting as it starts from an awareness of the pluralist nature of society in modern Britain and acknowledges the diversity of family patterns that have developed in recent years. This pupil expressed his sense that there is no single set of consensus values about sexuality and family in his world. It is perhaps interesting to note that this comment came from a pupil in Ferryfield school which was the most working class of all the schools we researched.

Pupils at Whitefarm expressed irritation at the way in which the legislation ignored the realities of adolescent life and the values that prevail in it. One said:

> Well, it's the rights and wrongs to do with sex they are going on about, so they are saying, 'OK, you're not allowed to fall in love with that bloke until

you are 17, or whatever.' That's what they will say, but that doesn't happen, does it? If you have sex, you have sex. They can't really tell you what to do.

The data indicate that pupils are unlikely to be influenced by a policy which seeks to impose the view that sexual self-expression at their age is wrong. From pupils at Tonford we gain a picture of legislation that is entirely out of touch with the way they think, and the rights they are convinced they have:

> OK, if the teacher tries to say none of you are allowed to have sex until you are 16, everyone is just going to say, 'F—— that! I mean, like we'd really listen to you!' So, you are in a situation with some bloke, and you are really going to say, 'No, my teacher says it's wrong.' I'm sorry, but you know!

The pupils offer a picture of the values relating to their own sexuality here which is interesting. They accept that sexual relationships will develop between teenagers, and they suggest that they have the right to make those decisions independently of adults' views on the matter.

The Age for Sex Education

We discussed with pupils at Ferryfield School an article that looked at the controversy stirred when a health professional, operating in a youth work setting, gave contraceptives to a girl of 12. The pupils objected to the health professional's action. 'I do think 12 is a bit young', said one, and another agreed: 'Yes, that's not really right.' These pupils had clear views on the age at which sexual activity is acceptable, and considered 12 too early to begin sexual relationships.

Nevertheless the adolescents were pragmatic in their attitudes to this behaviour, as is indicated by the discussion the group had, which we reproduce here:

Pupil 1   Yes, but if that girl has made up her mind that she wants to have sex, then why not provide her with a condom?
Pupil 2   They should be available, shouldn't they?
Pupil 3   It's going to be expensive, giving out free condoms to 12-year-olds.
Pupil 1   What's cheaper, giving out condoms or having a baby, an unwanted pregnancy? If they want to stop people having babies, they are not going to do it by not giving out condoms, are they?
Pupil 4   Yes, but to 12-year-olds?
Pupil 1   If they've made up their minds to have sex, then you have got to give them a condom, haven't you?

It is important to note that these pupils were not libertarian in their attitudes. There is evidence in a number of studies that adolescent sexuality is rule-bound and full of moral judgements (Lees 1986; Measor 1989; Moore and Rosenthal 1993). The moral judgements may not be the same as those of adults, nor are they judgements that some adults would want adolescents to adopt; but they are real and strongly influence the behaviour and attitudes of their peers.

Content of Sex Education

One group of pupils at Streamham read a section from a newspaper article on the government withdrawing sex education, including the provision of information about HIV/AIDS from the National Curriculum. This particularly angered them, and a typical comment was:

> That's what we want to find out more about, HIV and AIDS. We want to find out more about it, so they're stupid saying that they want to withdraw it.

Pupils emphasised that they wanted more information because of their awareness of the dangers relating to HIV/AIDS. This is an issue we develop in a later chapter, but it is important to make the context of anxiety clear here:

> I worry that I'm going to catch it. How do you know if someone's got it or not? You can't tell.

Groups of adolescents we talked to at Whitefarm School criticised the exclusion from the Science Curriculum of information about HIV/AIDS:

> Would we not be allowed to learn about it in science, then? Because that would be better for us, because we could actually learn about bacteria picked up, and things like that, but we would know the actual facts of what happens.

Pupils are making the same demand that we have noted several times, already: they want full and accurate information; they feel they have an entitlement to it, and are intolerant of any attempt to deny them this right.

In summary, pupils were critical of the sex education they received because they felt the information given was not explicit enough. They were angered by any suggestion that there should be further restrictions on their rights of access. This is an issue we look at in more detail in subsequent chapters, although it is worth saying that it corresponds with what research tells us about the way pupils view sex education generally (see Allen 1987).

> The sex ed we have got now is just about non-existent. We need a lot more thoroughness. The legislation has just got to be totally rewritten. John Patten should be hung.

Such commentary is flavoured with the intolerance and fiery intemperate quality that often characterise the reactions of young people. However, that is not something to be condemned, but rather, in our view, welcomed. It is important that we take note of what adolescents are saying, and offer some respect to their viewpoints and judgements. Pupils resented the authoritarian nature of the new provision and expressed their anger against legislation that failed to take their viewpoint into consideration. A boy at Ferryfield expressed his outrage at government policies and indicated that, for him, the issues had a semi-political flavour :

> It [sex] is an open and natural thing in life – what has the government done? Taken away our books and banned information.

Young people did not approve of the new legislation and policy framework that had been established for them by government, resenting any attempt to restrict their access to information, knowledge and counselling.

We turn now to look at pupil reactions to the sex education schemes offered them in the context of this legislation.

Adolescents' Views of the Sex Education Programmes

'Too Little Too Late'

Our interest in this research is in understanding the pupils' views of the debates about 'childhood innocence', their entitlement to information and knowledge and, by extension, their right to access contraceptives and be sexually active. Research published over the last twenty years consistently suggests that the majority of adolescents have been disappointed by the sex education provided at school. They are resentful of any attempt to restrict their access to information and they reject attempts to protect their innocence. Farrell, writing in 1978 found that pupils objected to 'too little' information being given them 'too late' in their school career. Allen, in 1987, and Woodcock, Stenner and Ingham, in 1992, found teenagers making the same complaint; and in a Health Education survey published in 1994 nearly one-third of all the young people surveyed thought sex education was offered to them too late.[1]

The sex education programmes we studied reflected awareness of this criticism. They aimed to improve on what had been offered to young people, but found themselves having to work within the constraints of the 1988 and the 1993 Acts and Circulars of Advice. It is important to evaluate the extent to which they achieved a balance between the needs expressed by young people and the stipulations of the legislation. In this section, we consider pupil evaluations of the sex education provided in terms of whether it was what they wanted and needed. We look at a number of issues, including their evaluations of the depth, range and level of sophistication of the information provided. Pupils discussed the conservative and the liberal views on 'innocence' and the right to information. All of the pupils stated considerable opposition to Conservative government policy and the conservative approach, and expressed their resentment whenever they felt that adults were refusing to make information available to them.

The five schools we studied offered diverse programmes; and pupil evaluations of them varied between the schools. We begin by identifying the schemes and the approaches that gained a positive response from pupils, and attempt to pin down some of the factors that generated this response. We then look at the negative reactions, and attempt to develop an account of what it was that provoked adolescent resentment and disapproval. We can state with some confidence that pupils approved whenever they were offered detailed and explicit information, and objected to the provision when it failed to meet those criteria.

All five programmes were criticised for failing to deal explicitly enough with some of the information on sex that pupils wanted, though the extent of the criticism varied between programmes. Gainton and Tonford Schools, where there were funded and formally organised inputs from health professionals, faced far less criticism on this score than did the other schemes. Streamham School had *ad hoc* input from health professionals, and was in a middle position. Ferryfield and Whitefarm received the most criticism on this score, especially in relation to sex education provided by science teachers.

It is important to note that *within* schools there were wide disparities in individual views. Some young people felt that the level of information provided was accurately assessed and met their needs, while others were disappointed and, it is important to note, quite angry at the failings of the sex education schemes. We suggest that there were two factors which most influenced reactions. One is the variable *maturity* of pupils; the other is *gender*. It is clearly impossible to provide information matched to the developmental stage of each individual adolescent. The differentiation in maturity means that within the same year pupils will have widely varying experience, knowledge and appetite for information.

We have already indicated that there were significant gender differences in the response to the sex education work which held across all the schools, and that boys were more negative than girls. The questionnaires reflected the gender differences. The positive reactions came largely from girls, although a proportion of boys also approved of the schemes. In the next four chapters of the book we present qualitative data that demonstrate gender differences in the responses to sex education schemes, and describe the negative reactions that many boys displayed. The boys had a seriously disruptive impact on many of the sex education lessons we observed, which their actions tended to dominate. It is therefore useful to have their written evaluation as a way of indicating the reactions of those pupils who did consider the sex education schemes beneficial. It is easy to overlook their quieter reactions in a noisy classroom. The data offer interesting insights into the merits of using more than one method of evaluation.

Access to Information

Pupils made it clear that open access to information was important to them. Many girls in the Gainton and Tonford schemes specifically recorded their preference for: 'The chance to know everything.' They stated strong appreciation when 'the wraps came off', and they welcomed sex education 'where you could say anything'.

Some of the programmes offered a high degree of openness; others were less open in approach. Pupils were more approving of the former.

It is clear from the evaluations that many pupils were deeply interested in the material presented to them and valued the opportunity to learn about it. The numerous comments to this effect by pupils at Gainton and Tonford include the following:

I want to know this, it's useful.

You need to learn about it.

Adolescents welcomed the chance to learn about and discuss matters of significance in their lives, as the Streamham evaluations show:

It is important to know these things.

It helps to know. We need it.

If we seek to unpack these comments it is apparent that the sex education schemes were welcomed when they provided information that pupils viewed as useful and meaningful; that is to say, information perceived to have direct personal significance.

Levels of Information

Research suggests that pupils' main criticism of school sex education is that 'too little' information is given to them. At Gainton and Tonford, which had schemes provided by the health professionals, many pupils considered they had been given sufficient information. A large number saw the sex education as pitched at the right level and appropriate to their current needs: 'It's what we need to know.' 'You need to know about it; it is important to know these things.'

In the Gainton and Tonford evaluations many pupils stated their approval of the detailed information offered about sexual matters, for instance:

I think we were learnt everything that we needed to know.

It was quite good, because we got to know about everything.

41

A large number considered that the programmes had gone into the right amount of detail, as these comments indicate:

> I think it is quite good because they cover everything in detail.

> It was well detailed. We were told everything I want to know.

Negative reactions

Not all the schools adopted the same approach as used by Tonford and Gainton. The main complaint from pupils in the other three schools relates to the amount and the level of the information provided. At Ferryfield one pupil, voicing the complaint made by a good number, protested: 'I don't think we get taught enough, as we want more information.' The level of the information offered brought out the similar criticism: 'The sex education at school is just surface stuff. They never give us much deep into it. But I suppose we have been taught basic stuff.'

Pupils were particularly critical of the sex education delivered within the context of the Science Curriculum. At Whitefarm School a pupil protested: 'They cover all the biological parts but not the parts that we want to know about.' For some girls the school sex education had been rather oblique: 'Not detailed enough or open enough, because we were taught about plants and not humans.' This is a familiar reaction to science-based sex education, and the adolescents' negative response to provision that deals only with plants and animals is well documented. When Whitefarm pupils discussed the sex education offered by the Personal and Social Education (PSE) rather than the science department, a far more positive view emerged.

Selection of topics

Pupils had clear ideas on the topics about which they wanted information. When they were offered material they considered relevant and new they gave a positive reaction. We have to bear in mind that there were gender differences in reaction to the topics.

Contraception

Many pupils in the schools with health professionals' input made clear their appreciation of the direct and explicit information they were offered on contraception. Health professionals took contraceptive devices into school sessions to demonstrate their use and discuss them with the pupils, and these sessions were mentioned frequently in a positive light by female pupils. At Tonford School a girl commented: 'My favourite week was when we learned about contraception.' A girl at Gainton said: 'It was quite good, it tells you all about contraception.'

There was evidence that the breadth of information provided was welcomed:

I didn't know how many contraceptives there are.

I also found out that girls have condoms. I think they're called femy doms.

I was uncertain about the unconventional contraceptives.

By 'unconventional' this pupil meant that while she had a reasonable knowledge of contraceptives like condoms and, probably, the pill, other devices, the coil and the diaphragm for example, were far less familiar.[2]

Many of the teenagers considered information on contraception of direct significance. As one commented: 'I think that you should have most information on contraception as that is the most important.' It is important to note, however, that the welcome for work on contraceptives varied dramatically with gender, in ways we will demonstrate in subsequent chapters. When the programme offered specific information that 'shows you how to use contraceptives', 'shows you what to do with them' or ' shows you how to stop getting a girl pregnant', some of the boys also welcomed it. Young people appreciated sex education that offered them access to the information they wanted.

The health professionals demonstrated how to put on a condom, and this brought clear appreciation from the pupils. There were more comments on this topic than any other in the interviews and the questionnaires:

I liked the condom session best because it helped me to know what to do.

I know what to do now.

Pupils considered the demonstration appropriate to this stage in their lives: 'It was helpful to be shown exactly how to put the condom on.' In one class in Gainton, the health professionals were unable to demonstrate condom use, and pupils were swift to object: 'They didn't show us how to put a johnny on.' We must note, however, that the written comments in the evaluation stand in great contrast to the behaviour of many boys in classes where contraceptives were demonstrated.

Negative reactions

All of the negative reactions concerned the extent of the detail provided, which many pupils considered insufficient. The objections were graded according to what the schools provided. When schools did not present explicit information on contraception, pupils expressed their disapproval. At Whitefarm and Ferryfield, where there was no classroom input from health professionals, pupils complained that they had not been provided with enough information. Whitefarm pupils requested information that they considered or categorised as 'more adult'; this included information specific to contraception and pregnancy. They made specific requests, for example that there should be 'generally more leaflets given out and perhaps show us more literal and practical ideas, e.g. bring in a condom or the pill'.

The same view emerged at Ferryfield about the level of information, one pupil remarking: 'She should explain about the real nitty-gritty stuff, and the teachers shouldn't get all embarassed about it.' The issue of teacher embarrassment emerged as significant, and teachers were contrasted with health professionals in this respect. In fact, pupils at Whitefarm stated that they considered it a good idea to 'get somebody with experience in, e.g. nurse or family planning official, who knows what they are actually on about and who are not embarrassed to talk about it'. One girl discussed a programme she considered her school should adopt: 'Some schools have perfect sex education, I saw one school on TV which passed condoms round for the pupils to feel.' At the schools where teams of health professionals had delivered sessions there was less criticism of this kind, but it did not disappear.

The Streamham programme, with its *ad hoc* visits from health professionals, came in for more general criticism than did either Gainton or Tonford's. Streamham pupils felt that they had not been given enough information by the health professionals who had come into their classes. In interviews there, a typical opinion was:

> I don't think they teach enough about it. They tell you the basics, but never go into the detail, which they should to give us the information we need.

Even in the Gainton and Tonford evaluations there was considerable criticism from a minority of pupils, who objected to the sex education because they still felt information was being withheld from them. A significant minority of pupils was scathing about these sex education sessions, insisting that they 'knew it all before'. We can only speculate on the issues involved here. The first point to make is that the great majority of these comments came from boys. The charge was laid at all of the sex education schemes, including those delivered by the health professionals. Boys stated baldly:

> Very little was learnt.

> It was mostly stuff I already knew, so it was a bit pointless.

While there was less general criticism of this kind for the Gainton and Tonford programmes, there were nevertheless a number of pupils who felt they had not been given enough information. Both boys and girls agreed on this. Boys said:

They didn't tell us much.

Should put in more detail.

Not very thorough.

A significant minority of girls made the same complaint:

We do not get enough information.

I don't think we get taught enough, as we need more information.

It was useless, because they didn't explain in enough detail and they were worried, I think.

It was stupid (not enough info).

We need to have more information available.

The young people's objections seemed to be that they were being treated unreasonably, and like children rather than teenagers; there was not enough sophisticated information available early enough in their school careers:

I think we should be told more about what happens if we are pregnant and what to do.

Some pupils stated that what they really wanted was more direct information and perhaps advice on the advantages and disadvantages of each method of contraception:

I think we should be told more about the best forms of contraception.

In interviews we conducted with girls we were told about the pressure they perceived from family planning clinics to choose the pill as their contraceptive:

They really push you that way, once they know you are in a relationship especially.

Many girls spoke of their deep reluctance to take the pill. Stories about the unpleasant side-effects were legion, especially of girls putting on a considerable amount of weight when they took the pill. There was evidence of an anti-pill culture developing among these girls, and this is an issue on which we require more research. One of the reasons a minority of girls objected to the sex education is that they wanted more information and a range of opinion about the contraceptive pill.

A number of the boys had clearly experienced some sex education in a youth work setting where there had been an AIDS awareness week. They contrasted what the school had offered with what they had been given in the youth work setting:

> I didn't think much of it. I learnt more at youth club in AIDS week where we learnt to put a condom on and taeked about a lot of issues.

> I didn't learn anything that I didn't already know at school. They treated us as if we were nieve. I learned more at youth club in AIDS week, and real issues.

> Basically, I didn't learn anything, I learnt more at youth club at AIDS week. We talked about more real issues that we are likely to encounter in the next few years or so. I got the impression that they were treating us like infants.

These data indicate that the pupils preferred the approach taken by the youth workers. It is important in this context to note that the youth work sector is not constrained by the strict legislative controls under which schools have to operate. It may be that one consequence of applying ever stricter legislation to schools which the current sex education guidelines do, will be to weaken their ability not simply to tackle the difficult issues in a relevant and explicit way, but because unable to do so schools and teachers will lose their credibility as advisors on these issues in the minds of adolescent pupils.

Sexually Transmitted Diseases

Contraception was one of the topics that many pupils felt it was right to select for inclusion in sex education schemes. Pupils at Gainton and Tonford made it clear in their evaluations that they welcomed access to information about STDs as well as HIV/AIDS. There was less gender difference discernible in these reactions, as the boys, too, welcomed the information:

> The education I've received about sex is good because we've learned about all of the diseases you can get.

> I think it is important to find out as much about HIV/AIDS as you can.

As with contraception, the input on STDs was considered valuable by many of the young people. Boys and girls agreed: 'It is important to learn about HIV/AIDS.' The programme extended and broadened pupils' knowledge:

I'm glad I found out about how many diseases are linked with sexual activity. I only really thought about HIV/AIDS.

Pupils were aware of the 'need to know how many diseases there are'. Other pupils made such comments as 'I didn't realise that some STD's were that serious', and that they were glad the programme had 'told you the risks' and 'warned you'. Pupils emphasised the safety aspect of what they had learned, 'I liked finding out about STD's and how to prevent them, because it will keep me safe'. We wish to focus on this comment, and others with a closely linked tone, because they were so frequent in the evaluation:

It was good to know to be careful when we looked at the diseases.

It was helpful, because they want to make us aware of the dangers.

It was interesting, because I know to be prepared.

The input on STDs appeared to have had an impact on young people's values. They expressed an increased sense of responsibility:

It explained the infections that can be caused by sex, it made me understand how serious the sexual relationship can be.

You'll have to be careful now you know you can get lots of STDs.

Negative reactions

This appreciation did not extend to the Streamham project, which did not deal specifically with STDs. The health professionals at Streamham, who worked in family planning, had focused on contraception. There, pupils commented specifically that they wanted more information and objected to not being given it:

I think the nurse did her best, but I knew everything about what she talked about.

She didn't tell us any more about sexual transmitted diseases that we really should know about.

Similar comments arose from evaluations we ran at Whitefarm and Ferryfield schools:

Not enough info about STDs.

I feel I need to know a lot more about STDs.

It was boring because we knew everything anyway.

It is interesting to compare pupil approval for the schemes that offered detailed information with what the government has stipulated that pupils should be taught.

Timing of Programmes

The other major criticism that pupils have made of school sex education is that it offers them information 'too late' in their school careers. In the schools we researched the sex education programmes ran in Year 9, with the exception of Streamham where they ran in Year 10. Offering the schemes in Year 9 appeared to have overcome the problem of information delivered 'too late' for a large number of pupils.

Many pupils at Gainton, Tonford and Whitefarm reported learning things they perceived important and useful, and that were new to them as well. If pupils consider they are learning material that is new to them, then presumably sex education is not being offered too late. Pupils admitted in questionnaire responses: 'It was helpful. I learned things I didn't know.' Some pupils stated they felt a reduction in anxiety as a result of the information: 'I was confused but I understand now.'

The programmes were again welcomed because they offered pupils the opportunity to acquire *new* information about matters they considered important to them. It was the provision of material about contraception and STDs that was identified as particularly important. In Gainton and Tonford evaluations a typical comment was: 'I think I know a lot more about contraception than what I did know'. Pupils suggested that the information was targeted effectively to their needs: 'It answered a lot of questions I had about contraception and family planning'. It is also important to recognise in this context that pupils approved of the specific information about local facilities where they could access personal and confidential advice on contraception. In the Gainton and Tonford schemes pupils commented approvingly: 'They told us where the family planning centre is.' Again: 'It helped me know who I can talk to.' The health professionals stated that attendance figures at local clinics rise after they have visited a school and made local services known to pupils, some of whom clearly make use of the information.

In relation to STDs, the underlying principle was the same: the health professionals' sessions were endorsed because they offered new information to pupils:

It brought up problems I hadn't heard of before.

I liked watching the video on STDs. I thought it was educational, I did not know as much as I thought.

Some of the diseases I hadn't heard about.

Negative reactions

The majority of the Year 9 pupils studied did not consider that information had been provided too late in their school career. At Streamham, however, where programmes were delivered in Year 10, pupils felt differently: 'It was a bit late', said one; 'I think we should be taught more, earlier', opined another. One boy reflected on the context around him and commented that the sex education was 'a little late because most people already knew about sex'. There were specific criticisms about the timing of particular topics: 'I don't think we were taught all of it, contraception, AIDS, etc., early enough.'

We heard repeated reproaches from Streamham pupils that Year 10 was too late for proper sex education to happen; the request was that the serious work should be done in Year 9:

Diane   It's too late, it's too late in Year 10. You need the basics in Year 7, there was hardly anything in Year 9, that's when you need it, especially contraceptives and STDs.

Jane   Year 9, that's when you're getting older, when you really need to know, when you're getting involved with boys and starting relationships.

The different levels of maturity of the pupils had a real impact on the view that was taken here. Some pupils recognised that there had been limits to what they had been taught at school, but considered them appropriate for their age-range and their stage in life. At Ferryfield one girl commented that the sex education had been

fairly basic, but I don't believe that I need to know anything more. If I need to know more when I'm older I would go to a clinic.

They were taught in the same classes as pupils who appeared to be already sexually active and welcomed specific information on where they could obtain contraceptive advice and supplies for their current needs. A pupil at Tonford commented, for example:

It was good to get info about where to go and what's available to us and who to ask.

There is evidence in the evaluation at Tonford that pupils valued what was taught: the content was seen as having significance for their own lives. In the schools which had health professional input data from questionnaires indicated that many pupils welcomed the information they were offered and found it relevant; and even if they could not spell the medical terms, they wanted the specific information for themselves. Pupils welcomed sex education schemes that offered them direct and explicit information, about issues like growth and reproduction, and also accepted the fact of teenage sexual activity and gave information about the potentially negative consequences of that activity. Offering information on contraception and on the range of sexually transmitted diseases met with appreciation from pupils aged 14–15. They expressed a welcome for the programmes, and there were no signs that pupils considered themselves too young to hear about the material.

The amount of criticism the programmes generated seems to have been directly related to the amount of information offered and the extent to which the information was what the adolescents wanted. When the information was direct and detailed the programmes gained more positive reactions. Negative reactions were provoked by sessions that did not offer access to all of the information that pupils wanted, and which sought to protect their 'innocence'.

Adolescent Sexual Values

It is important in our view to note what teenagers across all five schools said about the information that was being offered to them. At the heart of this was the pupils' recognition, without disapproval, that many young people were sexually active by this stage in their lives: 'I think young people are sexually active. So we should do more sex education in school.' The young people across all the schools claimed the right to make personal decisions about their sexual activity: 'I think that more young people are becoming sexually active. I think that it's up to them to decide if they want to have sex.' They felt that policies or legislation perceived to be restrictive of their activities were unlikely to have any impact on behaviour:

> Well when you talk about all the dangers, it makes people more aware and they've got to be more careful, but when it comes to things like you've actually got to be 16 before you have sex, they just ignore that fact and do what they think is right.

The adolescents were prepared to rely on their own judgement where sexual behaviour was concerned. Efforts to control their sexuality were seen to have no chance of working:

In science we've done a lot on it. They know the message got through and we know everything about it, but they cannot make us change our minds if we decide to do something.

Pupils resented any adult refusal to recognise the realities of teenage life and to face the fact that many young people are sexually active. It is important, we feel, to register the amount of bitterness and disappointment that adolescents feel in this context. Pupils expressed their frustration that schools, parents and governments refused to recognise adolescent sexual values and face the fact that many young people are sexually active. Pupils considered that both teachers and parents displayed this attitude of denial. A girl from Tonford said: 'I don't think that the school thinks we should be doing anything with a boy (not just sex).' Other pupils made brisk assertions of individual sexual identity and demanded that schools should take appropriate action. One 15-year-old girl commented on the sex education she had received from Streamham school:

Not good. Too little, too late – by our age a lot of people have already done it.

A pupil from Ferryfield protested:

I think that teachers should wake up and stop being so naive and think that teenagers are not having under-age sex.

The problem as they saw it was that adults failed to recognise that adolescents needed not just basic information about reproduction and family life but sophisticated information about such issues as safer sex practices and about the whole range of contraceptive devices. Both genders expressed their dissatisfaction with the menu of sex education that was on offer. Pupils considered that the amount of information they were given was 'not good enough for the time we live in'.

It was clear that for many pupils the 'need to know' amounted to the 'right to know'. Pupils were critical if the nature and level of the information offered was 'not good enough for the times we live in'. There was in the minds of these teenagers very little justification on the part of adults to refuse them information.[3]

The other issue that arose in this context related to homosexuality. One pupil at Whitefarm commented:

I also think that homosexuality should be taught and not banned because of the legal age, which is 21, and then we will be able to understand more about homosexuals and their feelings, and not to treat them different.

There were also specific requests for the schools to deal more directly with homosexuality. At Streamham a desire was expressed for greater 'understanding that being homosexual is OK, and things in reality instead of always being so scientific'.

When individual teachers explained the government legislation, especially in this connection Section 28, young people expressed considerable resentment of the legislation and considered its prohibitions unreasonable. A number of very strong objections to the policy expressed by Section 28 were registered. We look again at these issues in Chapter 8, when we consider adolescent views of the failings of the sex education programmes.

It is interesting that the solutions suggested by pupils were radical ones. In the first place, they wanted more sex education that offered 'not just the basics, but real nitty-gritty'. They argued that easy access at school to contraceptive advice and supplies would be an effective strategy. At Streamham it was suggested: 'Maybe sex ed classes should give out some free condoms, then if they decide to have sex they have something to protect themselves.' A girl at Whitefarm said: 'They should give condoms out to everyone for safer sex and teach them more if they want to know more.' Another, from Ferryfield, said: 'I think they should have a condom machine in school.'

There is considerable controversy in this country and in the United States about whether sex education promotes or delays sexual experimentation. There is an increasing body of research evidence to suggest that sex education does not result in early sexual experimentation (Boethius 1984; Swedish National Board of Education 1986; DES 1987). Researchers are now in a position to be specific about the kinds of sex education that will be most effective. Kirby evaluated a range of different programmes, and established that those which gave instruction on HIV/AIDS together with assertiveness skills were significantly associated with a delay in the initiation of intercourse. Instruction about pregnancy and contraception was positively related to the use of contraceptives at first intercourse (Kirby *et al.*1992). Oakley's research suggests that providing sex education does not encourage sexual risk taking, but notes that sex education which promotes chastity alone may encourage experimentation (Oakley *et al.* 1995).

In a small study such as this, we do not hope to provide definitive conclusions to an international controversy, but we can draw attention to adolescent accounts. The view, expressed in many pupils' interviews, was that adolescent sexual relationships were in themselves 'not something to worry about', but pupils were acutely conscious that as adolescents they needed advice and information, and access to contraceptives, so that 'people are aware of what they are doing and can take the necessary precautions'. The right to make a decision about sexual activity implied for many young people the need to adopt responsible attitudes:

> I know that there are lots of people under the age of 16 having sex, but as long as you use contraception I think you should have sex whenever you feel ready for it.

There were other telling comments in this context. One pupil at Tonford School wrote: 'It helps knowing things, it helps to feel responsible.' In the Gainton evaluation the provision of information on 'grown-up' matters had a very positive impact: ' I felt interested and responsible when we were discussing the condom'. The input from the sex educators appears to have had an impact on the values that at least some young people bring to the issue, and again they stated an increased sense of responsibility:

> It explained the infections that can be caused by sex, and it made me understand how serious the sexual relationship can be.

> I found out how to be safe in sex. I want a long and happy sex life.

These adolescents did not think that sex education results in earlier sexual experimentation. Allen's 1987 survey of sex education painted a picture of responsibly aware teenagers who wanted help, like these pupils, to become fully informed. These adolescents were not claiming that information will delay or restrict adolescent sexual activity, but they do consider that increased knowledge makes sexual experimentation more informed and responsible.

These data have important implications for the timing of sex education programmes in secondary schools. There is of course a place for sex education schemes in primary education, and this was one of the points that pupils in our research made very strongly. Our research supports the opinion, expressed to us by many health professionals, that the watershed years seem to be the end of Year 9 and the whole of Year 10 of secondary school: young people are then on the threshold of initial sexual relationships. The data indicate that sex education programmes really need to be offered before this sexual activity begins, that is in Year 9 at the latest. This does mean that sex education schemes like Tonford and Gainton's, which offer comprehensive information on contraception and STDs, should be offered to pupils before they are 16. We suggest that Whitefarm, Ferryfield, Tonford and Gainton staff, and the health professionals who had input, had identified the right time to offer their sex education programmes. It is of course important to acknowledge also that whenever sex education is offered to young people the programmes should take account of what pupils have already been taught. There should be continuity throughout the secondary phase to build on information offered at the primary level.

Conclusion

This is a controversial account of the lives and views of teenagers, and we are aware that some individuals reading this material will have misgivings, even strong moral objections, to the provision to *children* of such detailed information on sexual matters, and of course access to contraception. Our starting-point in this controversy is the viewpoint of the adolescents themselves, and we have aimed to present it accurately. The question is, then: how should adults respond to the decisions that a significant percentage of adolescents seem to be making? Adolescents have a clear view about what they want from sex education, and made clear their objections to adult attempts to 'protect their innocence'. It is important to note that teachers and health professionals who work directly with young people are in agreement that adolescents make decisions about their sexuality and that it is the responsibility of adults to work within the framework set by the adolescents. The problem then becomes one of government legislation and policy, and these seem to work against the experiences of young people living in our highly sexualised culture.

Notes

1   This HEA survey found that of the young people sampled girls were significantly more likely than boys to think that sex education was offered to them too late: 37 per cent of girls as opposed to 24 per cent of boys made this criticism. Two-fifths of young people considered that too little sex education was available to them. Again, girls were more likely than boys to hold this opinion, and those in a higher socio-economic bracket were more likely to be critical than were those in lower income brackets. However, the young people in our survey did not always agree with those in the Health Education Survey. In this research the boys were in general much less positive than were the girls about the sex education they had been offered.

2   The Contraceptive Education Service commissioned research into knowledge of contraceptive methods. The sponsors were surprised by the lack of knowledge they discovered, and its uneven spread. There was a high level of general awareness regarding some contraceptive methods and services, but substantially lower awareness of others, and the research showed different levels of awareness among social groups. Only 30 per cent of those surveyed were aware that emergency contraceptive pills can be taken up to seventy-two hours after unprotected sex to prevent pregnancy. There is, it would seem, a real case for teaching this material in schools.

3   It is important to investigate the extent to which young people have been equipped by sex education with the information they need. Research suggests that adolescents in the UK are not knowledgeable about their bodies and contraception, and it is not surprising that young people said they wanted more information. Surveys of young people reveal considerable ignorance about physical development and sexuality (see e.g. Massey 1990; Moore and Rosenthal 1993). A similar picture emerges in relation to STDs: research suggests that while information about HIV/AIDS has in recent years been made available to pupils, they might still have little information about other STDs (Winn and Roker 1995; Turtle *et al.* 1997). Overall only 43 per cent of boys and 39 per cent of girls in the sample had received lessons on HIV/AIDS. The percentage rose from 14 in Year 7 to 77 in Year 11. Between one-third and one-quarter of all pupils had attended no lessons dealing with pregnancy or with STDs other than HIV/AIDS (Turtle *et al.* 1997). Other recent quantitative research suggests that we need to make a clear distinction between pupils' knowledge of HIV/AIDS and their levels of knowledge of other STDs. The figures show that they know considerably more about HIV/AIDS (Winn and Roker 1995).

4 Theories of Sexuality, Practices of Sex Education

Introduction

This chapter begins by exploring some of the theoretical positions that inform discussion of the development of sexual and gender identity in adolescence. It considers conceptual frameworks which focus on the nature of sexuality and its connections with gender. The analysis emphasises that an individual's sexuality is constructed in a particular culture and it aims to understand more about the role of gender and gender identity in the construction of sexuality. It then examines theoretical explanations of the development of gender difference in adolescence. Social learning and feminist psychoanalytic theories are assessed with reference to the work of Chodorow and Horney. Symbolic interactionist insights are employed to relate our qualitative findings to recent theoretical work on gender, including material on masculinities. Recent sociological work has explored the priority which is given to heterosexuality in our culture (Foucault 1981; Weeks 1981; Epstein 1998). In any attempt to understand the development of sexual and gender identity, consideration of the ways in which same-sex sexuality is marginalised is important.

We have said that one of the major empirical findings of the study was gender differences in response to the sex education programmes. The second part of the chapter introduces qualitative evidence taken from a set of sex education lessons which took place across all the schools we researched. It shows that boys responded much more negatively than girls. We know from quantitative research projects that gender is related to variation in response to sex education programmes, but little qualitative work has been done to offer insights on the issues which contribute to these reactions (see Woodcock, Stenner and Ingham 1992; Carter and Carter 1993). In Chapters 4–7 we apply theoretical material on sexual socialisation and the development of gender identity in an attempt to understand the different reactions displayed by boys and girls to their sex education. In this chapter we focus on the girls' reactions and the data we present are drawn primarily from a girls-only sex education lesson.

Theories of Sexuality

There is controversy over the nature of human sexual expression. Sexuality has been studied by a number of different disciplines and there is no real agreement among them.[1] At the heart of the controversy is the debate about the extent to which our sexuality is biologically determined, and is a 'natural', instinct, and the extent to which it is determined by social processes and context. Views about what constitutes 'natural' and 'normal' sexuality stem from, for example, religion, socio-biological traditions and psychoanalysis. These views influence both common-sense and institutional notions of sexuality, and consequently have implications for policy formulation.

Our theoretical starting-point in studying adolescent sexuality and sex education is that sexual behaviour and sexuality are at least in part made and shaped by social learning (Weeks 1985; Giddens 1992; Seidman 1992): whichever aspect of the sexual self is considered 'natural', learning is involved. Social construction theories claim that we learn 'scripts' for sexual behaviour, as we do for other forms of behaviour, from primary and secondary socialisation: 'Sexual behaviour is socially scripted behaviour and not the masked and rationalised expression of some primordial drive' (Gagnon and Simon 1973: 69). On this view the notion of 'the natural' is inevitably problematised: whatever attitudes or actions we may deem 'natural', they have been, on this account, deeply affected by social processes.

Sexuality and 'Nature'

The social construction approach is initially difficult and perhaps even disturbing. It contradicts well-established understandings, all of which assume that sexuality is fundamentally pre-social. 'It may be laid down by God, achieved by evolution, or settled by the hormones' (Connell and Dowsett 1992: 50). Social scientists challenge this idea on the basis of evidence for historical and cross-cultural variations in sexual behaviour and experience (Allan, in Connell and Dowsett 1992: 6).[2]

The social construction approach is perhaps difficult also because it seems to go against the 'common-sense' understanding of sexuality as a physical phenomenon. Social scientists, however, argue that we 'feel sexual experience in our physical bodies but it is not simply accessible to us as bodily sensations, it is actively worked over and made sense of' (Adkins and Merchant 1996: 25). How we make sense of it depends on the culture in which we live: the stories, scripts and attitudes circulating in our society, and what Foucault has called 'discourses'. We learn to interpret our bodily sensations through the scripts available to us, choosing some and rejecting others in a way that is active but that is also constrained by our society.

There are significant implications to this sociological approach. In the first place, it implies a need to ask 'questions about the historical, as well as sociological questions about the sexual' (Weeks 1996: 4). Second, social construction approaches 'imply that sexuality could be reinvented and remade' (ibid.). This is important for policy formulation within the sex education field, though it does not indicate that change will be easy to achieve or simple when effected. Both psychoanalytical and postmodernist work on sexuality is important here. Foucault has argued that we internalise 'normative control into the deepest recesses of subjectivity – the sexual' (cited in Evans 1993: 10). Change therefore is likely to be complex, involving interventions in some of the most individual aspects of the self.

Psychoanalytic Theory

Social construction theories are important, but may not tell the whole story. Psychoanalytic theory also has a contribution to make. Psychoanalysis does not dispute the importance of processes of socialisation for the construction of sexuality. Freud demonstrated that actual sexuality is not received biologically as a package: adult sexuality is arrived at by a 'highly variable and observable process of construction, not by an unfolding of the natural' (Connell and Dowsett 1992: 57). Psychoanalytic theory is useful because it acknowledges emotion and the intensity of desire. Connell and Dowsett draw our attention to the somewhat clinical view of sexuality implied by the social construction accounts. They point out that social construction theories of sexuality tend to lack an account of the 'source of the passion, compulsion, emotional depth and conflict that seems so much a part of our own experience of sexuality' (Connell and Dowsett 1992: 2).

Psychoanalytic work also draws attention to the fact that we may not be entirely aware of all of the emotional issues involved. It reminds us of the significance of 'experience hidden from awareness', and suggests that to understand sexuality we need to enter 'the world of the unconscious, repression, masks, denials' (Weeks 1991: 42). The psychoanalytic approach emphasises the importance of our early and intense emotional life to understanding the roots of some of our sexual reactions and processes.

Psychoanalytic theory takes seriously the severity of the difficulties for the individual which processes of socialisation produce. It points out that our sexuality and ultimately our identity are constructed in the context of conflict, repression and struggle. In Freud's view, the struggle is more difficult for women: 'Sexual identity is constructed in the context of male power' (quoted in Rose 1987: 173). Rose has pointed out that while sociological theories consider the internalisation of norms to be accomplished, via processes of socialisation, more or less effectively, a basic premiss of psychoanalysis is that it is not: 'Psychoanalysis recognises that women do not painlessly slip into their roles as women' (ibid.: 184). In Freud's later work, at least, there is an account which describes the process of becoming 'feminine' as 'an "injury or catastrophe" for the complexity of [a woman's] earlier psychic and sexual life' (ibid.: 185). More recent feminist work in psychoanalytic theory has begun to stress the 'injury' which is done to men in our society by the demands that current models of masculinity place upon them, and this will be dealt with in more detail later in this chapter.

Sexuality and Gender in Adolescence

This study focuses on young people at a crucial stage in life-cycle development in terms of both gender identity and sexual development. They are exposed to processes of gender socialisation and sexual socialisation at the same time. In this study we suggest that to understand what is going on in the processes of sexual socialisation necessitates an investigation of gender socialisation and the processes of gender identity construction. As Giddens (1992: 1) commented: 'I set out to write on sexuality, I found myself writing ... just as much about gender.'

Gender, clearly, is 'a pivotal category for [the] analysis of sexuality' (Seidman 1992: 132). Sexuality, like other aspects of life, work or culture, is gendered. We suggest that, at a fundamental level, learning about sexuality is integral to learning about gender: it forms a central plank in our notions of gender identity. Our gender identity will, in turn, affect the characteristics and practices of our sexuality. Giddens observed: 'Somehow, in a way that has to be investigated, sexuality functions as a malleable feature of self, a prime connection point between body, self-identity and social norms' (Giddens 1992: 15).

Another issue to be borne in mind is that sexuality 'is a social construct operating within the fields of power' (ibid.: 23). Patterns of gender inequality imply that inequality will operate in the area of sexuality. Feminist psychoanalytic work argues that the emotional and psychic costs of socialisation are different for men and women and, significantly, that they are higher for women than for men.

The young people in this study were simultaneously undergoing significant change in the simultaneous development of their sexuality and their gender identity. The dynamic relationship that obtains between the two processes can make it difficult to disentangle and make sense of adolescents' reactions. If Giddens is right – that sexuality is a prime connection point between body, identity and social world – then adolescents can be expected to react strongly to the messages they are offered during socialisation because they relate to core aspects of identity.

Gender Theory

There are theoretical issues here requiring exploration – in particular, the concept of gender – which are central to the interpretation of the data presented later. The starting-point is the feminist one which argues for the differentiation of *sex* and *gender* and asserts that gender is not simply biologically given and immutable. The argument is controversial, centring on the extent of biological determination of gender. Here the position taken is that gender is not solely or simply based on 'natural' differences between the sexes: biological differences are mediated in complex and powerful ways by influential social processes. Gender is socially constructed as 'two binary categories, hierarchically arranged in relation to each other' (Davies 1997: 11). Davies goes on to develop this idea further:

> The creation of this binary model is not the result of observation of natural pairs which exist in the world. Rather it is a way of seeing built round an unquestioned assumption of opposition and difference.
>
> (Davies 1997: 9)

Gender is socially constructed, but it is important to note that while the 'social patterns which construct gender relations do not express natural patterns, neither do they ignore them' (Connell 1987: 80). A structure of symbol and interpretation is woven around natural differences which can exaggerate or distort them and which counts as 'a social transformation of these differences', (Connell 1987: 81). Individuals select and employ symbol and interpretation to weave and construct gender.

Horney (1932), Chodorow (1971) and some of the more recent discourse analysis relating to this topic identify the social patterns involved. Chodorow's work on gender categories illuminates understanding of how individuals use symbolic resources to signal and express the 'binary divide' in daily life. Both Horney and Chodorow have suggested that societies place items, objects, styles, behaviours and values into categories; that these categories are gendered and are read as either masculine or feminine. The individual selects from these 'sets of culturally available, recognised and legitimated themes which are more or less identified' in a particular society with one gender or the other. These culturally legitimised ways of living and behaving, which signify gender, enable us to 'do' masculinity or femininity.

Work which deals with gender, language and discourse has extended our understanding of the processes by means of the various 'storylines' relating to gender, and by tracing 'discursive patterns which our culture makes available to us shape us as beings within the two-sex model' (Davies 1997: 11). The individual chooses and uses items, styles, storylines and language which signify masculinity or femininity and avoids those which signify the opposing gender.

This approach avoids the deterministic view which sees sex roles imposed upon passive individuals. This view instead emphasises the individual as active participant, selecting the components of a gender identity from the cultural elements to which she or he is exposed. Older work on socialisation has been heavily criticised for its failure to adequately acknowledge that the individual can resist the messages presented by formal socialisation and select from the full range of messages on offer.

We need to take account of issues raised by symbolic interactionists and by some postmodernist theorists who emphasise that identity need not be fixed once and for all. The suggestion is that there are 'in the late twentieth century a series of co-existing versions of both gender and sexuality' (Rose 1987: 170). Weeks (1989: 207) has pointed out that we are offered a range of scripts about both gender and sexuality which are presented in different languages – 'moral treatises, laws, educational practices, psychological theories, medical definitions, social rituals, pornography or romantic fiction, popular assumptions'. Foucault (1979) rejected the idea of fixed identities, gendered or otherwise, and emphasised that we have both space to engage in 'self-fashioning' and the opportunity to take on a variety of positions in relation to these scripts in the contemporary world.

Our choices are not, however, without constraints or consequences. One of the agencies which helps to construct our identity and subjectivity is the range of 'discourses' current in society.

> 'Discourses' are bodies of knowledge produced in a culture which have obvious links to regulatory apparatuses which have power over the lives and actions of individuals.
>
> (Holloway 1984: 223)

Discourses relating to sexuality have been examined in some detail in recent years (see Foucault 1981). Feminism has alerted us to the context of power in which our learning takes place, and postmodern feminists tell us also that the discourses within which it takes place are unequally laced with power. It is important to note that women are positioned differently from men in relation to discourses of the self and identity, especially where those discourses relate to sexuality; and this implies restrictions on their range of choices.[3]

Concerning masculinity, theorists argue that we need to recognise the shift towards a notion of *multiple masculinities* which has taken place in modern societies (Connell 1987; Brittan 1989). Masculinity is seen to comprise a set of positions and cultural choices from which the individual selects, 'rather than something which is unassailably and existentially rooted in an ontologically secure understanding of the world' (Morgan 1992: 12). Masculinity exists, theorists argue, in a plurality of forms. There is no fixed set of attributes which can be labelled as masculinity.

These insights draw our attention to the fact that the individual can shift between different forms and styles of femininity and masculinity. This alternation may not be consciously undertaken, and we need to be aware, says Morgan, of the flexibility of self, 'negotiated over a whole range of situations' (1992: 47). We are not seeking to argue that gender or, indeed, the underlying issue of identity are simple matters which are fixed in a once-and-for-all pattern. Morgan talks of a '"cafeteria" approach to masculinity, where there are a variety of forms of masculinity within modern society which men may choose from more or less at will' (ibid.: 81). The individual will choose to display different versions of the masculine or the feminine self in different contexts and under different pressures.

Young People and Gender Identity

We want now to consider the extent to which this range of choices operates in the early phase of adolescence. It seems that at this phase there are fewer choices of models available, and that young adolescents display traditional and stereotyped versions of gender identity. We are suggesting not that individuals are mechanistically positioned by this traditional gender script but that they are influenced by a range of social constraints which may vary at different points in the life cycle. The pressure to behave in traditionally masculine or feminine ways is, we suggest, strong at this stage largely because individuals are consumed with a concern to establish themselves as either feminine or masculine:

> Each sex, when educated with the other, is at puberty almost driven by developmental changes to find ways of signalling and ascribing its sex role.
>
> (Kelly 1981: 102)

The same processes are at work in relation to same-sex sexuality in adolescence. Judith Butler (1990) has introduced the notion of the 'heterosexual matrix'. She argues that in our culture heterosexuality is defined as 'compulsory', while other kinds of sexual expression are seen as marginal, dubious and, ultimately, unacceptable. The agencies and institutions of modern society, in Butler's view, all support this pattern of definition. In addition, however, the presentation of sexuality in these scripts suggests that gender identity is inextricably tied to the practice of heterosexuality. She claims that our understanding of gender is in terms of 'binary opposites', that male and female are defined as entirely different from and opposite to each other. The fundamental characteristic which maintains this difference between the genders is 'heterosexual desire' (Butler 1990: 21). In Butler's approach, the practising homosexual is challenging not only scripts which offer a pattern of appropriate sexual behaviour but even what constitutes appropriate gender behaviour.

Assembling and achieving a gender identity requires that the identity be communicated to the social world. Morgan writes that gender can be understood as part of a 'Goffmanesque presentation of self' (1992: 47). By this he means that individuals are concerned to signal their identity and what they are to the world around them, and that they use elements and objects from that world to achieve their objective. By focusing on the aspects of performance and activity in daily life, we can see more about the way that gender is 'done'. Symbol and interpretation are employed to make bids for masculinity and femininity.

This process is not a smooth and unproblematic one for successive generations of adolescents (Jefferson 1994: 13). In the section on psychoanalytic theory, we noted that Freud discussed the difficulties women experience in being socialised in the context of male power. In more recent psychoanalytic work theorists have begun to identify the difficulties that boys also have. Chodorow contends that the tasks of establishing and communicating gender identity are more difficult for boys than for girls. Female identity is seen to be ascribed, and what it is remains clear; but masculinity needs to be achieved and demonstrated on a daily basis. In these theories, masculinity seems to have a permanently defensive flavour about it. The presentation of self identified by Morgan involves a number of performance aspects for boys which, he suggests, do not come easily. As Norman Mailer wrote:

> Masculinity is not something given to you, or something you are born with, but something you gain, and you gain it by winning small battles with honour.
>
> (Mailer, cited in Morgan 1992)

Chodorow suggests that this demand to signal and achieve masculine identity gives an urgency to boys' activities as they come to dread all association with anything feminine. They try to achieve masculinity by making themselves different from women and all things feminine. Their subjectivity is to be marked as different from and in opposition to whatever is associated with the feminine. The two social categories of gender really exist only in relationship to one another. Masculinity can be clearly defined only in relation to and as distinct from femininity: masculinity requires femininity in order to achieve clear delineation.

We should recognise that whatever positive activities are involved in the acting out of masculinity, there are significant negative aspects, too. Chodorow argues that one of the ways in which boys act to assert masculinity are the devaluing and attacking of things 'feminine'. For Chodorow these activities are fundamentally related to the emotional task the child has of separating from its mother. The attachment between the child and its mother is strong because of the length of the time for which human children are dependent on their parents. Children are faced with the job of breaking this attachment and establishing themselves as 'separate' and autonomous individuals.

Feminist psychoanalytic work has argued that this task is more difficult for boys than for girls. 'For girls early development is more continuous and femininity can be easily understood in terms of motherhood' (Chodorow 1974: 24). Boys, by contrast, experience a constant need to construct their masculinity. We have already noted one strategy commonly employed: 'To develop a masculine identity young men need to disassociate themselves from all that is feminine' (Lees 1993: 300). This can involve depreciating and insulting women and things feminine. 'Boys need to denigrate girls in order to dominate them' (ibid.: 301). In recent years, feminist theorists have discussed the effects on men of their at-all-costs avoidance of the feminine. Jo Baker-Miller (1986) has stressed the destructive outcomes when, at a subconscious level, fear of the 'other' or anxiety about maintaining a separate and distinctively male identity drives men's actions and interactions (for more discussion of the issue, see Holloway 1984; Young 1990; Shaw 1995; and Raphael Reed 1998).

Young men may pursue ways of dealing with women which restrict and constrain women's opportunities and experiences. They may also repress and stamp on the qualities and aspects of themselves which they define as feminine. In recent years, male writers have interrogated the cultural definitions of masculinity in the attempt to understand some of the negative consequences that such definitions have for men. The negative consequences are usually seen to affect them emotionally, creating what Hearn (1987: 98) has termed a 'lessening in men by which they are limited in reciprocal and mutual living and loving'. For Hearn it means that men are both formed and broken by their own drive for power.

The new theories draw our attention to the cost to both men and women of the patterns of power that obtain between the genders. It is important, however, to recall one point that has been basic to the whole feminist project, namely: 'Masculinity, in all its various forms is not the same as femininity – it is after all a form of *power* and *privilege*' (Arnot 1984: 53). As Davies comments: 'The binary male–female, coincides with the binary powerful and powerless' (Davies 1997: 11). Theories of patriarchy make it clear that men have power over women. Some men have power also over other men. Chapters 5–7 will trace the implications of the gender-related patterns of power which operate in informal adolescent cultures.

Connell argues that '[d]ifferential masculinities exist with different access to power, practices of power and differential effects of power' (Mac an Ghaill 1996: 51). Connell's work on hegemonic and subordinated masculinities alerts us to the fact that structural factors of class and ethnicity position some men advantageously. Establishing hierarchies of masculinity is a life-time project which necessitates the day-by-day remaking of identity.

Earlier in this chapter we cited Chodorow as arguing that female identity is ascribed, and for girls involves fewer problems of definition than achieving masculinity does for boys. We wonder if feminine identity is so simple a matter as Chodorow suggests. Feminine identity may be ascribed but this need not imply that there will be no resistance to the guidelines given nor any negotiation with the principles on offer. We suspected that girls employ symbolic resources to contrive and signal gender identity, just as boys do and were interested to track this through the data.

If we return to the specific focus of this research, our argument is that we can discern pupils, girls as well as boys, actively using aspects of school life, including the curriculum, in their construction of gender identity. Pupils may well object to or resist aspects of the school curriculum which contravene their views of what 'proper' girls or boys should do. There is considerable evidence in feminist research of pupils reading gendered characteristics into activities and routines, and responding to them accordingly. Kelly (1981) and Haste (1981) have shown how girls reject the natural sciences in schools on the basis of gender identification. Measor (1983) looked at the effect of gender on girls' reactions to the 'hard' sciences and on boys' reactions to the domestic sciences.

Grafton and Miller (1983) showed how gender affects subject choice generally in secondary education. A gendered response to curriculum subjects serves to make clear to others a pupil's gendered identity. School provides a public arena for the acting out of feminine or masculine susceptibilities.

Pupils actively use aspects of school life as symbolic resources to construct their gender identity and their place in the hierarchy (Measor 1983 and Measor and Woods 1984). Schools and classrooms are places where pupils and their teachers do a great deal of cultural work on the construction of identity in a whole range of ways. Feminist research over the last twenty years has provided significant information about the gender socialisation which schools conduct. However we perhaps know more about the processes that have been at work on girls than those which affect boys (Delamont 1990).

Feminist work also offers insights on ways in which male pupils assert their entitlement to power and privilege over others in schools (Shaw 1980; Spender and Sarah 1982; Jones 1985; Lees 1986). More recently Connell (1987) and Mac an Ghaill (1994) have indicated the cultural work schools perform in the production of heterosexual and hegemonic masculinity.

Sexuality has a key place in the construction of gender and of identity, and therefore the sex education curriculum is particularly rich in resources for the 'weaving of a structure of symbolism and interpretation around natural differences' to which Connell (1987) draws our attention. The sex education lesson represents a particularly rich context for the acting out processes employed in communicating gender and sexual identity. While pupils actively use aspects of school life to 'do' masculinity and femininity in the way we have suggested, they are simultaneously engaged also in significant struggles about power, entitlement and identity.

Schools and the Socialisation of Sexuality

This theoretical discussion identifies some of the issues in the sex education work that we researched. Returning to the focus of this study, it is important to investigate locations where learning about and socialisation of sexuality take place. Schools comprise one agency involved in the social processes of learning about and construction of sexuality and gender identity. They may also contribute to the regulation of behaviour and its social control. Formal sex education in school is a setting for the formal socialisation of sexuality. Schools also provide a number of spaces in which informal social constructions of sexuality are forged. 'Behind the bike shed' may be one significant location for learning about both tobacco use and sexuality, but school corridors and buses to and from school are also important as learning locations.

If schools are important for formal socialisation, they also provide an arena and focus for the display of the symbolic resources we have discussed – for what Seidman has called 'adolescent self-presentation' (1992: 20). Adolescents can use schools for the acting out and public signalling of gender differences. Sex education sessions are particularly fruitful settings for the acting out of the symbolic and social construction of gender identity.

A Girls-only Lesson

A lesson on contraception was delivered in a very similar form in all the schools studied: teachers and health professionals displayed the range of contraceptive devices to the pupils, discussed the devices and offered written work on the topic. We first present data from a single sex, sex education lesson. The girls appeared actively interested, or at the very least conformist in their reactions to the lesson. Field notes give a picture of attentive interest: the girls were quiet and purposeful, there was no giggling and little apparent embarrassment. The girls made positive comments about the class in evaluations.

The lesson was part of the health professionals' programme at Gainton. It was given by a family planning nurse, referred to here as Anne. The account which follows is taken from our field notes. Anne divided the girls into small groups of about five people. She handed to each group an assortment of contraceptive devices and a worksheet on the devices. Pupils had the opportunity to handle and examine the devices – including condoms, femidoms, coils, diaphragms and 'the pill'.

> The groups set to work immediately, and there was a quiet buzz of discussion about the task. The girls seemed to find the activities interesting. There were muffled sounds of distaste when they got spermicide on their hands and mild objections to the condoms' rubber smell, but no signs that they saw any impropriety in the exercise.

We understood the girls' response to be an important element of sex-role learning and signalling. It implied a gendered code of behaviour, which the girls adhered to and accepted. They let it be known that they approved of what they were asked to do. Some clear gender messages were communicated about the activities and attitudes that 'proper' girls have.

> Anne circled the groups, giving further information. The girls worked carefully and conscientiously on the worksheets, sharing information with each other and taking great care to answer the questions fully. If a group of girls did not understand some item on the worksheet, they turned to Anne for help. After only a very few minutes of activity on the worksheets the girls began to ask the nurse for more information, indicating their interest in the subject. Anne encouraged enquiries by announcing: 'Feel free to ask questions at any time – just shout them out.'

The girls in this lesson signalled their concern to acquire knowledge of the range of contraceptives and how they worked.[4] The sex education lesson offered girls an opportunity to realise feminine identity in some new and, crucially, more sexualised ways. The curriculum was operating here as a positive resource for pupils to signal their view of themselves as feminine, but also as young women who are interested in their sexual identity.

After the girls had worked for about fifteen minutes on the worksheets, Anne drew the whole group together and discussed the contraceptives, using the worksheets. Anne added information which was in part based on the questions the girls had asked. She talked, for example, about the kinds of contraception that are most appropriate for younger women and offered advice about their effectiveness. The girls repeatedly asked for more detailed information:

> How long is it before the pill is effective once you start taking it?

> But how does the pill work, what does it do to you?

We believe that the girls' interest in the information indicated their recognition of its relevance to their future romantic roles as girlfriends and wives and to their nurturing roles as mothers. The sex education curriculum operated as a positive resource not only by offering them information which they needed but because of the opportunities it provided for acting out feminine sensibilities in a public setting. Sex education lessons provide a backdrop against which signals about feminine identity can be displayed.

> Towards the end of the session, Anne dealt with the condom as a form of contraception. She held up several types of condom and handed them round the groups. She explained how to open condom packaging and advised caution to any girl with long finger-nails when opening the packets. Anne then showed the girls how to put on a condom, using a plastic penis supplied by the contraceptive company. The girls continued to watch and listen attentively.

What was on offer in the sex education lesson fell into an allotment of gender interests with which the girls were at ease. The girls reacted in a positive way because the lesson sustained and supported their sense of gender identity and fitted into their gender codes. Their rapt attentiveness to the lesson was useful in demonstrating and communicating interest in 'proper femininity'. A positive response to the lessons signalled an affirmation of their femininity and was a means of building their standing and reputation.

The pupils remained attentive throughout the hour-long session and continued to ask detailed questions; pupils seated in corners of the room, whose view was less than ideal, craned their necks in order to see diagrams. At no point did Anne have to issue a discipline warning, nor was it necessary for her to strive to retain the girls' attention.

Recent work has furthered our understanding of some of the processes involved here. In her analysis of this sort of gender-related behaviour, Mason asked a familiar question about 'typical' female conduct: 'Do women have a distinctive morality and ethics based on care and responsibility for others?' (1996: 18). She suggests that an attitude of caring responsibility signals femininity or, more accurately, femininity appropriate to women. Mason developed the idea in some less familiar ways, arguing that such behaviour has an impact on the way women feel about themselves, and specifically about their own identity. Acting in a 'typically' female way serves 'to confirm their subjectivity' and makes them feel feminine. Mason introduces the notion of an 'internal feeling state' (Mason 1996: 39), and suggests that individuals act in particular styles because of the way it makes them feel and because they enjoy the feeling of fitting the role.

Particular behaviour feels 'safe': it is what the gender code prescribes, so that in the adolescent context the display of caring conformity shows that you are a 'proper' girl. This behaviour may have an additional pay-off, however: it can make the individual feel good about herself and the way she fits into the world.

There was a tacit acknowledgement of adolescent sexual activity in this programme. For example, Anne ended the session by giving the girls information about a health clinic for young people which she helped to run. She explained that girls could access contraceptive supplies there and that their confidentiality would be protected. While the girls would be encouraged to discuss the matter with their parents, the clinic would not involve either their families or their GPs.

Girls responded positively to this, appreciating that they 'were being treated like adults'. The provision of explicit and specific information, including how to access contraceptive supplies, the girls said, made them feel that this was an opportunity to signal a new maturity. The girls welcomed being spoken to 'like adults, and not as kids who know nothing at all'.

The field notes of the session indicated conformity, certainly, but also, we would argue, the girls' real interest. This was shown also by the questions pupils asked, their requests for more information and the close attention they gave to all that Anne had said. There appeared to be no resistance to the lesson, and the girls had worked co-operatively in small groups, conferring with each other without apparent embarrassment.

Data from the questionnaire evaluations supported this view. The girls were very positive in their evaluations of the sex education session. A typical comment was: 'It is important to know these things.' The material offered by the family planning nurse was seen by the girls as important at this point in their lives: 'You need to learn about it.' There was a telling number of pupils who commented with approval on the use of objects from the 'real' world, in this case contraceptive devices, in their lessons.

The activities in the sex education lesson supported conventional views of the interests and behaviour of 'proper' girls, and these pupils indicated their willing involvement. Their response made their sex-based identity clear to those around them. Pupils actively use aspects of school and the school curriculum to construct elements of their identity, in this case their feminine identity. They are not simply responding passively to gender stereotypes. None of the girls had a problem in indicating interest in this lesson, and even those girls who sometimes gave a deviant response to school work indicated conformity here. We suggest that sex-role learning plays a significant role in forming pupils' attitudes to sex education at school. The active nature of this process needs to be emphasised: girls come to evolve their own perspective on the 'cluster of attributes' they label *feminine*, and they select and use aspects of the school context to project their own feminine identity.

Conclusion

In the first part of this chapter we presented theoretical material relating to sexual and gender socialisation in adolescence. We aimed to indicate the tight connection between sexual and gender development to which the theory draws attention. There is controversy within this theoretical field, and our approach favours interactionist insights which focus attention on the way adolescents see and experience the cultural context in which they find themselves. The second part of the chapter has applied some of this theoretical material to the data in ways which, we hope, fruitfully extend understanding of adolescent responses and reactions to sex education lessons.

Chapter 5 presents data from lessons involving girls and boys, which were collected from all of the schools studied. The nature of the girls' reaction is thrown into sharp focus by an account of the boys' reactions to these lessons, and the data support our claim that boys react differently. It is significant that mixed-sex lessons did not much resemble the girls-only lessons. At the same time there is need to look in some detail at the reactions of the girls in the mixed-sex situation.

Notes

1   Sexuality has been studied by several academic disciplines. There are diverse perspectives from which to approach sexuality, including the social conditioning model favoured by radical 1970s' feminists such as Brownmiller (1975), social interactionism (Gagnon and Gagnon 1973) and the texts inspired by Freudian theory (e.g. Mitchell 1975; Chodorow 1978). The two leading schools of recent times seem to emphasise the social construction approach, although there have also been applications of cultural studies and discourse analysis to the study of the body which are influenced by postmodern thinkers like Foucault.

2   Current work in the social sciences has seriously questioned essentialist or biological explanations which view sexuality as 'natural'. In part, this questioning arose from research with a particular ideological framework. 'Both feminism and gay liberation question from different angles the idea that "human sexual behaviour" (Kinsey's term, 1948) or "human sexual response" could be treated as natural facts' (Connell and Dowsett 1992: 2). It is important to note that there is now widespread agreement on the issues among social scientists from different traditions and methodologies. There is agreement that 'rather than constituting a "natural and

private matter", sexual practices, desires and patterns of behaviour are socially made' (Adkins and Merchant 1996: 1). While there is wide general acceptance in the social sciences regarding the importance of social learning to the development of sexuality and gender, there are of course a number of different approaches to the matter (Vance 1984).

3   At this point the postmodernist approach perhaps comes close to the phenomenological in asking for careful attention to be paid to the notion of negotiation between the social structures which constrain us and the actions of individuals within those structures. Some theories have identified biology or genetics as the major determinants of these investments, but clearly such a view is unacceptable to much feminist work. An alternative view sees individuals as rational decision makers, making well-informed decisions about investment which guide our behaviour and our approach to sexuality. However, psychoanalytic theory, which has been closely interwoven with some branches of postmodernist feminism, demands that we take into account the intense emotional and sometimes unconscious factors that can influence our actions more powerfully than our rational choices. We need to recognise also the influence on our choices of discourses that we hear from birth onwards. Specific messages bombard individuals with precepts about 'normality' and guidance on how normal life should be lived; they become so familiar that they are taken to be self-evident and so not on the agenda for discussion.

4   We argue later that many of the boys displayed a very different reaction to the information they were offered on contraception, which seems to be identified as 'women's business' by young British males. There is some evidence that in Britain boys refuse shared responsibility for contraception, although this is not the case in other European countries, especially the Scandinavian countries where rates of teenage pregnancy are lower.

5 Boys

Sex Education and Sexual Difference

Introduction

We return in this chapter to one of the main findings of this study: we observed a gender difference in response to school-based sex education work. Boys displayed a different and much more hostile reaction to the sex education they received than did the girls, and we will demonstrate that *post hoc* written comments in the questionnaires were substantially more negative, too. The main focus in this chapter is on exploring the reactions of the boys to their sex education programmes. We use extracts from field data to illustrate the different reactions we observed. The data offer clear evidence of the high levels of hostility that boys but not girls displayed to the lessons and prompt speculation about the possible explanations for the gender differences in reaction in the light of the theoretical position outlined in Chapter 4.

In all five of the schools we researched, many adolescent boys objected strongly to the sex education programmes. Not all boys created problems: it is important to state that some appreciated the sessions. When there were difficulties, however, they were always created by male pupils; and boys created problems whether they were in mixed or single-sex classes.

There are several possible explanations for the boys' behaviour, which have been explored elsewhere (see e.g. Measor, Tiffin and Fry 1996). A full explanation of the boys' behaviour is difficult in our view. We suspect that the meanings the sex education lesson had for boys is a complex issue, and we can make only tentative suggestions about some of the processes involved. We appreciate that there may be methodological problems in this analysis of the data. For instance, we do not know how these same pupils behave in other lessons. What we observed, then, may not have been behaviour specific to sex education but rather the routine behaviour of difficult groups of boys in poorly disciplined schools. However, all five schools, which are set in three fairly affluent towns in the south of England, are relatively successful in league-table terms, and it is unlikely that the boys typically behave across all areas of the curriculum as disruptively as they did in the lessons we observed.

Quantitative research supports the view that gender affects responses to sex education and that boys disrupt sex education lessons. Woodcock's research (1992) provides a picture of the way adolescent males respond to the sex education they are offered. She found that about one-third of the respondents (with many more males than females) made comments on aspects of classroom behaviour during sex education lesson. The majority reported that boys had disrupted classes with jokes and laughter, and had specifically tried to 'wind up' their teachers.

We observed in the five schools mixed-sex lessons in which the focus was the use of contraceptives. In each lesson the teacher or medical practitioner had difficulty in maintaining discipline. It is important to note that in all of the lessons we observed, the teachers had some difficulties with discipline, even in Streamham School where the deputy-head taught the lesson. The majority of teachers were able to contain the boys' reactions to acceptable limits, but when the health professionals were in sole charge of a class real difficulties were experienced. This has a clear policy implication: where programmes use health professionals in the classroom, it is essential that they have received adequate appropriate training and that continuing support is provided.

As the researchers involved in observing these lessons, we have some concern that our gender made it difficult for us to gain a clear understanding of why these lessons provoked such strong reactions from the boys and that we have not fully recognised the anxieties the lessons provoked in them. We are nevertheless satisfied that one key element of the boys' reactions relates to gender codes: the data illustrate and add flesh to some of the theoretical issues about sexuality and gender socialisation identified at the beginning of Chapter 4.

We argued there that in order to understand the differences in reaction between boys and girls we need a better grasp of the way gender operates in adolescent informal cultures. We worked with a theoretical perspective that emphasised gender as difference and aimed to explore the ways in which gender, femininities and masculinities, is "done" in schools and classrooms (Griffin and Lees 1997: 6) through the 'routine of repeated social actions on a daily basis' (see Giddens 1991: 61–3). Chodorow's work is important to this analysis, for she explores the way individuals use symbolic resources to signal and express their sense of gender in daily life. Both Horney (1932) and Chodorow (1971) have suggested that a society places items, objects, styles, behaviours and values into categories that are gendered and read in a culture as masculine or feminine. We suggested in Chapter 4 that pupils actively use aspects of school life as symbolic resources to construct their gender identity and their place in the hierarchy.

It is important also to re-emphasise the work done on the different styles of 'masculinity' we discussed in detail in Chapter 4. Connell (1987, 1989) has suggested that males compete between themselves for status as well as seeking to establish power over women. We can discern relations of subordination and domination between individual men and between groups of men, as some are able to define their understanding of masculinity over others. We want to argue that it is possible to see competition for a high-status place in a macho hierarchy operating in the data which document the boys' reactions to sex education in school.

Boys' Reactions to Sex Education

We observed significant disruption in the mixed-sex education classes. The contrast with the girls-only sex education lesson documented in Chapter 4 was extreme. In mixed-sex lessons and in boys-only lessons there was noise, pushing and shoving, throwing of bags – and of the occasional punch; chair-legs were scraped along the floor, desks were rattled, and there was a sustained barrage of jokes and laughter. The jokes were made by the boys and were directed against a range of targets, teachers, girls and also other boys. The girls sat quietly throughout the disruption and noise, waiting to hear what the health professional or teacher had to say. The picture is a familiar one from a decade of feminist research. It is easy to ignore the girls' reactions altogether: even to researchers committed to understanding more about the girls' reactions, the boys' behaviour rendered the girls almost invisible in the classroom. The girls were not, however, entirely passive recipients, and we must attempt to offer an account of their reactions.

At Gainton school each small group of pupils was given contraceptive devices and worksheets. The family planning nurse held up a Femidom (a female condom). The room exploded into noise and raucous laughter, and jokes were shouted out by several of the boys:

Boy 1   It looks like a windsock.
Boy 2   What do you use that with – a submarine?
Boy 3   That's about big enough for my dick.

The boys reacted strongly to the sight, smell and feel of the devices throughout the lessons. The pattern that emerged was of boys objecting to the activities and making their objections very clear. We can make sense of the boys' behaviour in the sex education lessons by arguing that they were at pains to behave in ways that indicate their grasp of appropriate masculine behaviour and their ability to fit the blueprint. They are keen to be convincingly masculine to others and to indicate their legitimate membership of the culture of hegemonic masculinity. Other explanations are possible, however. The boys may feel they must behave like this out of fear of being unable to fulfil *proper* masculine sexual roles.

At Streamham School, when a school nurse showed diaphragms to the class, several of the boys shouted out comments expressing their disgust at the device:

Boy 1   It's disgusting, I ain't touching that.
Boy 2   Jesus, it's huge
Boy 3   Cringe, cringe. I wouldn't want to be a doctor.

When the health professionals passed the devices around the room, horseplay developed.

At Tonford School a group of boys bounced the Femidom's flexible ring around their table. In a class at Streamham School one boy bent the cap in two and flipped it around the classroom; it ended up in a dusty corner. Morgan (1992: 90, citing Roy 1960) talks of the opportunity for the display of masculine themes through 'horseplay, trading insults, sexual references and mock homosexual attacks' (see Collinson and Collinson 1989). There was clear evidence of all these gender-categorised styles of activity and behaviour in the sex education lessons. Throwing contraceptive devices around, telling jokes loudly enough for the class as a whole to hear them, and showing oneself unresponsive to the control of a woman – all such actions are designed to win status in the informal culture (see Measor and Woods 1984 for a longer account of informal culture and pupil behaviour).

In contrast, the girls seemed quietly interested in the sex education lesson. Their behaviour was the same as that described in the girls-only sex lessons: they were calm, attentive and quiet. They displayed the 'mild verbal and domestic' behaviours that Spender and Sarah (1980) argued were key feminine characteristics. Their willingness to engage with the material in the lesson revealed them to be obedient and 'passive, pliant and willing to adapt to a range of tasks and interests', again core feminine qualities (Lightfoot cited in Delamont 1990: 75).

The family planning nurse at Gainton handed an IUD around the room for the boys to handle. They felt the short ends of wire that emerged from the end of the IUD and made jokes about it:

Boy 1   It looks like a fish hook.
Boy 2   It looks like fishing line.
Boy 3   Fourteen-gauge to be exact.
Boy 4   Yes, to reel it in.

The boys drew on things that are familiar, like fishing tackle, to interpret the unfamiliar. They also drew on things that are male to deal with things that are female. They indicated their interest in, knowledge of and familiarity with items, like fishing tackle, that are associated with masculinity and that signal their distance from things that are feminine. There may be other issues at stake for the boys. Mac an Ghaill (1994: 56) draws attention to the possibility that adolescent boys resist any school practices which seem to emphasise pupil immaturity. In the situation we observed the boys' lack of knowledge was in danger of being revealed to the group as a whole, and their joking may represent an attempt to take some control over the classroom to prevent this exposure. Category maintenance work was undertaken in these activities where boys made reference to sets of signs which indicate 'that a person is a "man" or "not a woman" or "not a child"' (Hearn 1987: 137).

Boys and Jokes

Above the general noise individual boys engaged in joking behaviour which could be heard by the whole class. The boys continually competed to out-perform one another for masculine status. Connell (1987) suggested that one of the most significant ways of establishing hierarchies of masculinity is through sexual and other types of harassment. The horseplay and the teasing in the lessons may represent one arena where competition for status within groups of boys, and between groups of boys, was played out.

Kehily and Nayak (1997) have developed an analysis of humour and masculinity that is of direct relevance here. They suggest that it represents a discursive practice which plays a significant part in consolidating male peer-group cultures in secondary schools. It has a role in 'organising, regulating and policing heterosexual masculinities. within pupils' informal culture' (Arnot 1984: 48). Humorous exchanges between groups of pupils or between pupils and teachers represent a 'public performance of masculinity'. They suggest that boys who are the 'most skilled at employing sophisticated insults had higher status in the group' (Kehily and Nayak 1997: 73). The verbal sparring creates winners and losers in the competition and exposes some boys as vulnerable while others establish reputations as 'hard'.

The girls, in small groups of friends, exchanged some jokes, although not nearly so much as the boys. It seemed to us that there might be some gender-ruled behaviour occurring. Making public jokes which the whole class can hear seems to be exclusively a male activity, and bidding for a role as a whole-class entertainer is something that only boys do. There is significant research on gender rules for women speaking in public and the constraints they face, and such data do not contradict what we already know (West and Zimmerman 1975).

By contrast the gender code to which the girls subscribed demanded they show passivity, a gentle consideration for other pupils and a quiet, biddable quality in response to teachers, all of which they demonstrated in this lesson, while the boys played out the exchanges we have described. Those same gender codes also require girls to be co-operative and non-competitive. In this lesson girls chatted amicably, within their groups, about the pill, the diaphragm and IUDs, sharing information about the different devices in order to complete the worksheets they had been given. We are not trying to suggest that competition does not exist between groups of girls, but it is acted out in different ways.

At Streamham School, when the family planning doctor held up a speculum there was a strong reaction from the boys:

Doctor	What is it?
Jack	It's a metal sugar spoon.
Ken	A modern pair of chopsticks.
Robert	It's a dick pincher.

This last remark caused great amusement, and we suspect that the joker aimed to embarrass the female doctor. The use of a term like 'dick' is an intrusion of the vernacular into a formal classroom setting and is perhaps aimed to confound adult professionals. It is also possible to speculate that the joke reasserted an adolescent and male view of sexuality rather than a medicalised and distant model. Kehily and Nayak (1997: 73) talk about the way young boys employ 'acts of transgression' as part of the work of visibly conveying masculine identity. Language is one of the major tactics of 'transgression', and is used as a strategy to invert 'the rules of adult middle class society' and to 'violate social norms'. They suggest that young men celebrate 'vulgarity' in school classrooms and use language for its shock value. This transgression is treasured as a means of displaying masculinity and elaborating one of its themes.

Other joking behaviour we witnessed seemed to be intended as a bid for control over a classroom setting:

> At Gainton the family planning nurse handed out packets of contraceptive pills for the pupils to see. A couple of boys pretended to eat the pills, leading to others shouting out, 'Look at Joey and that lot'.

The boys shouted the comments in the classroom so that the nurse could not carry on with what she wanted to say. By their actions the boys for a short time gained control over the classroom. Researchers like Hargreaves (1967) and Willis (1977) have suggested that this is one of the objectives that some boys have in the classroom. Their research was more directly concerned with social class than it was with masculinity, but their data can be reinterpreted to offer insight into gender issues. Arnot (1984: 46) suggests that proving masculinity 'may require frequent rehearsals of toughness, the exploitation of women and quick aggressive responses'. Much of the boys' behaviour fits this blueprint, and can be understood as the public performance of masculine themes.

Boys reacted most strongly however to the sight of condoms. At Streamham, when the teacher produced condoms the boys could not contain their reactions. One boy hissed, 'Yeh' as the class exploded into male noise, laughter and disruption. Boys blew condoms into huge distorted shapes, one boy stuck a condom on his forehead, and others threw them around the room. During the laughter that resulted boys shouted jokes to each other:

Dan   Turn it into a water bomb.
Luke   Can I put it over my head? I've done it before.
Mark   Can you use Vaseline on them?

When the teacher advised him against doing so, another boy suggested:

Alan   Use WD 40 oil then.

In other schools the pattern was similar. At Tonford the nurse handed condoms to a small group of boys:

There was loud shouting and shrill screams, arms waved, legs jerked, heads circled and ogled. Boys picked up condoms and snapped them, like long elastic bands, threw them at each other or blew them up, and allowed them to float off like balloons. One boy put a condom on his head, stretching it around his scalp. He removed it and complained: 'It smells of inner tubes.' Another pushed a condom into his friend's face, and the friend responded loudly: 'Aghh! It stinks. It smells all pooey.' A boy secreted a condom in his pocket; another told the family planning nurse what he had done, and she retrieved it.

We have argued that in this sex education programme a number of 'new' messages were present. The programmes anticipated pupils having a sexual life rather than a merely reproductive life. Much school sex education has been criticised for denying pupils' sexuality (Wolpe 1987; Lees 1994). In this session there was no attempt to protect children from sexual knowledge – it was given openly. Morgan (1992) has suggested that when boys are presented with material which has a sexual component, the question of how to behave is highlighted for them. They need to show they recognise it as something sexually provocative and arousing. This may help explain the exaggerated responses pupils made to contraceptive devices and the displays of resistance to the lessons. Recent work has highlighted the difficulties which some aspects of the school system create for pupils. Mac an Ghaill and Hayward (1996: 56) discuss ways in which schools desexualise students and emphasise pupil immaturity, and suggest that male pupils may well take any opportunity they are offered to display their sexual awareness as an element of developing maturity.

In this context it is also important to contrast the boys' reactions with some of the girls'. The girls did not seem to have the same shocked reaction as the boys to the condoms in the classroom, although they did share some smiles and giggles with their friends.

There was a brazen resistance to female authority revealed in the lesson, which is in itself a display of one version of masculinity, especially when it is related to sexual material. The way boys experienced their performance of resistance – the way it actually feels to them – may be a significant factor in their motivation to behave in this way. Davies points out that we

> should not underestimate the desirability and joyful sense of power that boys can gain from being positioned within dominant forms of discourse which hand them ascendancy over others.
>
> (Davies 1997: 15)

We can here return to Mason's work, discussed in the previous chapter, and apply it to boys. She argued that displaying a particular kind of behaviour seen as 'typically' feminine has an impact on the way women feel about themselves and, specifically, about their own identity. We argue that similar processes are at work for the boys. Acting in a 'typically' male way serves 'to confirm their subjectivity', making them feel 'masculine'. The boys' behaviour in the lessons had emotional implications for them: to use Mason's concept (1996: 39), it produced a particular 'internal feeling state'. Acting in particular styles is agreeable because it allows the individual a sense of enjoyment and a feeling of fitting the role – he feels like a *proper* male. Mac an Ghaill has also explored this mechanism: 'Existing forms of masculinity and existing power relations are likely to "feel right" to the boys who inhabit them' (1994: 174). This, of course, also militates strongly against changes in gendered and sexual relationships, and is an aspect of which policy makers need to take account.

Another significant issue relates to teachers' power and surveillance of pupils. Dixon describes occasions when there was no surveillance by teachers, which allowed for an upsurge of pupils' informal culture and resistance. She suggests that we can see classrooms as a site for struggle over cultural values, and in her research found pupils taking opportunities offered by the absence of a teacher to bring 'cultural texts from outside the formal culture of the school into play' (Dixon 1997: 100). When the sex education programmes were run by nurses and doctors, this issue became significant. They did not have the teachers' level of knowledge about and familiarity with routines and practices that establish discipline over pupils. We suggest that the processes Dixon identified were at work in the classroom incidents we have documented. In the sex education lessons there was considerable group amplification of the processes of the acting out of masculinities and the policing of those who failed to match the blueprint for the status of 'proper male'.

At Tonford School boys joked loudly about the condoms. Some remarks related to oral sex:

Adam   Be sensible, please, and tell me, what flavour do you think this condom is?

Other jokes related to frequency of sexual activity (and claimed a great deal of it was going on). At Tonford a boy asked the nurse:

Ben   Will you give me three johnnies? I'm going to be very busy tonight.

Such joking involves hierarchical status among the boys. Claims to sexual knowledge and expertise, when substantiated, have a role in winning a place at the top of that hierarchy. It is argued that sexual success is one of the key aspects of achieving status in the hierarchies of masculinity. Giddens (1992: 9) commented: 'The reputation of boys depended upon the sexual conquests they could achieve.' Displaying a predatory sexuality appears to be one of the behaviours that successfully 'elaborates masculinity'.

The boys' reactions were in stark contrast to the girls' behaviour. In mixed-sex classes, girls sat quietly through the disruption and noise, waiting to hear what a doctor or teacher had to say. There were, however, things going on: they exchanged glances, for example, to communicate contempt for the boys' behaviour (in interviews the girls indicated how much they disliked such behaviour). The girls did not seem to have the same shocked reaction as the boys when presented with contraceptive devices. There were certainly no loud claims to sexual expertise made in a competitive way by the girls.

Many of the boys' jokes centred on the topic of the penis and specifically on competition between boys about penis size. Some joking was boastful and celebratory. At Gainton:

Doug	Which is the largest condom?
Stewart	That one will be for me, then.

At Streamham:

Doctor	What is the advantage of a female condom?
John	It is bigger than three inches.
Doctor	Condoms will stretch.

This exchange was greeted by general laughter from the class.

Not all the jokes had a celebratory tone. Boys frequently directed abuse at each other. Sexual success – or the lack of it – and sexual orientation were the most common targets for attack. Sexuality is not arbitrarily chosen as a target for abuse: it is routinely selected as a critical component in the constitution of masculinity. The other main topic for teasing concerned boys' penis size. At Streamham the doctor asked for a volunteer to demonstrate how to put on a condom. After much banter one boy agreed:

Jamie	What do you want me to do?
Jack	You can use a banana. You don't have to put it on yourself.
Ben	(*Sneering*) This is going to be good.

At this point, Ben opened his fingers to indicate the length of Jamie's penis, implying it was particularly small, and announced: 'It will be too big for him.'

Penis size is a key theme for adolescent boys, something that they discuss with great frequency. It is central to issues of masculinity and competitive hierarchical status. Nick Fisher, a journalist who writes specifically for young people, ran an 'agony uncle' column for boys for many years. He drew on letters he had received from boys to discuss this issue. He talks about the 'culture of the penis', which is characteristic of male adolescence. The penis is a 'key notion for masculinity, for definitions of masculinity and for achieving manhood' (Fisher 1994). But it is important to emphasise differences in reaction from different groups of boys. Not all behaved in the same way, or demonstrated equal ability to access and employ the 'culturally legitimised' styles of behaviour.

Some therefore began to establish and exercise power over other boys as well as over girls. We deal with relationships between boys and girls in more detail in the next two chapters.

Defending a Gender Code

The sex education programmes we studied aimed to be innovative and to present a relatively 'democratised' view of sexuality. The sex educators' programme offered access to information equally to boys and girls. The boys appeared to resent this as going against the values of their own adolescent culture (see Chapter 6). The information offered by the sex educators spoke of greater power and positive sexual entitlement for girls. The sex educators chose to offer practical guidance – for example, explaining the suitability of particular forms of contraception for teenagers. They aimed for an informal style, and this may have offended the boys' view of what is right. At Tonford School the family planning nurse offered tips on dealing with condoms, explaining how to get them to slide easily out of their packets and warning girls with long nails about the catastrophic potential of a damaged condom. She fitted a condom on a model of a plastic penis, and joked: 'So now, if you get some guy who doesn't know how to put one on, you can do it for him.'

More than information is being offered here: such material asserts a new positioning of girls in adolescent sexual encounters, one that offers power. It implies an independent female sexuality. Large projects like the WRAP study (see Holland *et al.* 1991) looked at the sexual practices, beliefs and understandings of young women. The research revealed sharp power differentials between the sexes in adolescent sexual encounters and emphasised the passivity at the heart of female sexuality, at least at this stage of the life course.

The sex education programmes challenged those patterns and contravened gender codes that concede sexual entitlement to men, but make it taboo for women, at least in adolescence. Such an approach threatened traditional power positions – the boys' interests were under threat, and in response some of the boys mounted an immediate challenge, warning the girls of their objections to the message. In the next two chapters we discuss in detail the teasing and joking directed at the girls. At the same time the boys continued to challenge the women teaching the session through the jokes and the teasing we have documented in this chapter.

These examples are typical of what happened in the sex education classes we observed. Our accounts of lessons given on topics other than contraceptives show similar patterns of behaviour, although it was the lesson on contraceptives that created the strongest reactions and responses from pupils. We are not entirely certain why this should be the case, and we suspect that male researchers may have greater intuitive understanding of the factors that motivated the boys' reactions. It is possible that contraception brought the boys into physical contact with 'objects' and so made the topic direct and explicit. With contraceptive devices the 'private' was made 'public'.[1]

An argument we forwarded earlier was that adolescents respond in culturally appropriate ways in order to elaborate particular gender themes. Girls indicated their interest in the material in the sex education lessons, which they defined as relevant to their future romantic roles as girlfriends and wives and their nurturing roles as mothers. The boys distanced themselves from this in the way that Chodorow identified, and elaborated masculine themes. Simultaneously they distanced themselves from anything feminine, signalling difference from feminine things and displaying aspects of traditional masculine roles.

The *new* messages in the innovative programmes contravened key aspects of the gender codes and regimes to which the boys were attached. Our speculation is that the sex educators' messages 'struck at the heart of stereotyped masculinity' and represented a public challenge to traditional patterns that could not be shrugged off and had to be resisted. Boys perceived a threat, and as a group mounted a robust defence of what they saw as core values and territory. While there has in recent years been considerable interest in change in gender relationships and sexuality (Giddens 1992), we consider that this behaviour reveals interesting evidence of the limits of change, 'the sheer intractability of gender relations' and the 'toughness and resilience of sexist stereotypes' (Connell 1987: xi).[2]

These ideas, however controversial, have one very useful aspect: they focus on the emotional aspects of the life of the male child–adolescent and they underline the involvement of feelings in the process of gender socialisation, as well as the purely cognitive or learning–thinking aspects of the child. The newer feminist psychoanalytic theories suggest that masculinity is essentially more precarious than is femininity. This work encourages us in the direction of developing a perspective on how boys see the world and what might lie behind some of their actions and reactions as presented in our data. The arena of sexuality will be a crucial one, and sex education sessions may allow us to gain a purchase on some of the important issues at work. Sex education is a key site in which the struggle over the symbolic and social construction and confirmation of manhood takes place.

Difference and the Erotic

The argument we advance is that boys and girls come to feel they *have* to behave in ways that differ from each other in order to be seen as either *masculine* or *feminine*. In order to extend our understanding of these processes we return to Connell's suggestion that the 'social patterns which construct gender relations do not express natural patterns, neither do they ignore them' (1987: 4). Individuals weave a structure of symbolic interpretation around natural differences which can exaggerate or distort them. Connell goes on to argue that it is these differences which constitute a large part of what gives erotic flavour to heterosexual relationships. What Connell is also suggesting is that at the heart of that difference is power, and that it and powerlessness are eroticised. A grasp of the way these different features are linked, whether consciously or not, is important to any attempt to understand the motivations and behaviour of young people. It may help explain also why boys offer so much resistance to change, and why any attempt to promote change results in challenge.

Gender and Identity

We discussed recent postmodernist feminist work in Chapter 4, and it is important now to return to some of that material because it raises a number of issues in relation to our analysis of the data. Holloway's essay on gender differences (1984b) has been taken as a key text here. Both women and men have what Holloway has called 'multiple positionings' in society. Women have multiple positionings in society as, for example, mothers, wives, consumers and workers. Holloway suggests that we might expect their subjectivity and sense of identity also to be multiple, and to shift and alter in the different contexts in which they find themselves: 'Individuals are fragmentary and positioned and repositioned from one moment to the next' (ibid.: 125). This theoretical position has implications for the present work. We need to shift our view of the nature of socialisation, for postmodernist theory argues that 'our socialisation is not a once and for all process: it does not create an immutable identity or subjectivity' (ibid.: 129). It implies also that we have fragmentary selves, constructed differently for different contexts. This means we can experience ourselves in some contradictory ways, an experience that can create difficulties for us.

Holloway has developed this analysis in interesting ways with her work on the notion of 'investment'. She argues that we make an active investment in a particular discourse, a commitment to a particular position. Gagnon and Simon's (1973) symbolic interactionist work on 'scripts' in this context makes a similar point. They argue that we recurrently invest energy in these approaches and positions, and this action makes the adoption of alternatives costly. These commitments exert an influence over our subjectivity that can counteract society's tendencies to fragment personality, identity and sense of self. The notion of investment carries within it an emotional element. Holloway suggests that just as the nature of our emotional commitment to a particular position in a discourse varies, so the nature of the pay-off varies. Adoption of some discourses confers power, while others may be supportive of our sense of continuity; other discourses again are hegemonic in that they carry the whole weight of social approval (1984b: 205). Mason's work (1996) also has implications here, because the individual may enjoy or feel safe in 'doing' a particular kind of behaviour and performing actions that are designated as suitable to her or his gender. The claim is that people make investments in taking up certain positions in discourses and, consequently, in relation to each other. There will, therefore, be some satisfaction or pay-off for that person in the decision.

We need to play-off the notion of investment against the notion of multiple positionings and, more importantly, against the notion of the self as fragmented. The investments we undertake and sustain make for coherence of personality, of self, of actions and behaviours, though postmodernist feminists assert that the commitment is not immutable, not once-and-forever. In particular situations, where specific pressures exist and specific interests come to predominate, we may repudiate one investment and adopt another.

If we apply such insights to the focus of interest here, adolescents and the social construction of sexuality, then adolescents will at this stage in their lives be positioned in a number of ways, hearing a number of different discourses, different messages from a range of sources including the media, their family, their school and their peers, about the construction of their sexuality and the meaning of their gender identity. The messages come weighted with different loads of power, and will have embedded within them references to different frameworks of knowledge, expert systems (Giddens 1992) and access to power. The question then becomes: in which of these discourses or messages, or indeed which fragments of them, will individual adolescents choose to make investments, and how permanent will those investments be in the face of forces of fragmentation?

We need a grasp of the messages or discourses that adolescents are hearing. But we also need a grasp of how adolescents themselves hear and respond to those messages in an attempt to understand the investments they are making. It is important to integrate with our earlier analysis the postmodernist point that the identity signalled in one context may not persist intact across other contexts. What we see pupils 'doing' in terms of the performance of gender in schools may be only one aspect of the selves they are constructing. They might show a different set of concerns or styles, a different identity in another location, for example at a club, or in the family. We need to remember that pupils are exposed to a range of discourses about sexuality and gender. Although girls, for example, invest in what appears to be a very traditional 'fashioning of self' as female and adopt a non-innovative set of attributes as feminine, there is no guarantee that this investment will survive into adulthood or even into their later adolescent years.

Conclusion

The sex education lessons need to be 'understood within a larger social context of reputations, faces and relative social status' (Daly and Wilson 1988: 128). At this phase in their life cycle, boys and girls are seeking to carve out a valued gender identity. For many of the boys a masculine identity is composed of stereotypical cultural values. Tolson (1977: 43) writes: 'Masculinity is a kind of performance, a style of feeling physical, of protecting oneself, of not revealing feelings.' The sex education lessons, through their content and pedagogic style, represented a threat to those identities. For the girls the lessons offered an opportunity to realise feminine identity in some new ways, crucially in some more sexualised ways. In addition, what was on offer fell into a traditional division of gender interests with which they were comfortable. The girls therefore resisted the lessons far less than did the boys. Girls responded positively because the sex education lessons supported and enhanced their sense of gender identity and fitted into their gender codes. Support for the lessons indicated an assertion of their femininity and a useful resource in building reputations.

Boys had a different set of reactions, and a different agenda to work with. Boys are often condemned for the kinds of behaviour detailed here, and the researchers have not offered a particularly sympathetic account of their responses. This may not be especially helpful if our interest is in developing policies to encourage change. It is important to acknowledge that we cannot simply condemn male children for their behaviour. As a society we encourage boys to be aggressive and assertive, and by condemning their behaviour and sympathising with girls we run the risk of simply reinforcing that discourse and failing to view analytically the pressure on all children.

Notes

1 We are grateful to Helen Charnley in the School of Applied Social Sciences at Brighton University for her suggestions on this topic, which are presented here.
2 This is not to deny the existence of factors for change. Significant economic and social changes have shaken the gender order. Hearn (1987), for example, has argued that occupational and educational change, and shifts in women's consciousness, have combined to 'displace notions of what it is to be male'. Willis has pointed to the impact of unemployment on this process, suggesting that we are moving toward a 'gender crisis' and cautioning that men may turn to 'one solution, which may be an aggressive assertion of masculinity and masculine style for its own sake' (cited in Lees 1994: 114). Others, like Goldthorpe and Lockwood, identify the 'dislocating effects of home centredness and consumerism' as playing the same role. But the process of change is not smooth, and a number of writers have argued that cultural forms have developed which seek to preserve and restate conservative ideologies of masculinity and class against the background of pervasive change. Within this 'crisis' Hearn, too, sees opportunity: 'Paradoxically in that lesser certainty and even in an increasing alienation we may find ourselves' (1987: xi).

6 Learning about Sex and Power

Introduction

In this chapter the analysis continues to focus on gender-related issues that affect pupil response to sex education programmes. In Chapter 4 we discussed the theoretical issues associated with the formation and signalling of gender identity during early adolescence. At the core of the approach taken there was the idea that at this stage of their life course, adolescents are driven to develop a clear gender identity and to signal that identity to their social world. The process, as Chodorow has argued, is particularly demanding for boys whose identity as *male* requires *performance* to indicate that they are not *female*. In Chapter 5 we considered male behaviour, and focused on the ways boys related to each other in processes of establishing patterns of status and masculinity. In this chapter we present data that shift the focus of attention and examine the ways male pupils behave towards girls, and issues of power, sex and gender in both sex education classes and in school more generally. The data offer a flavour of the nature of heterosexual interaction and relationships in schools in early adolescence.

In Chapter 4, we noted Chodorow's claim that one of the ways boys act to achieve manhood is by devaluing and attacking things that are feminine. As Arnot (1984: 53) expressed it: 'Masculinity, in all its various forms, is not the same as femininity – it is after all a form of power and privilege.'

In this chapter we examine the language and practices of boys and girls, in their daily lives at school, for evidence of the signalling of sexual and gender identity that we have discussed. We need also to understand more about the ways that boys, or at least some boys, make a claim for a gender identity which grants them the power and privilege to which Arnot refers. We need insight into the ways that this power and privilege are exercised and a grasp of the processes of policing and regulation involved in maintaining the gender–sex order visible in sex education classes and school interactions between male and female pupils.

Some of the themes from the data presented in this chapter are familiar after several decades of feminist research on daily life in classrooms. We document the way adolescent boys 'talk' to and behave with the opposite sex, and offer a picture of the struggles over power and privilege that occur. We move from this relatively well-known material to data relating to issues of gender and the body, gender and knowledge and gender-defined patterns of responsibility for sexual matters. This material helps develop insights into patterns of gender and sexuality in adolescent informal culture. The values and attitudes characteristic of that informal culture can involve difficulties for the teaching of sex education.

We look first at a set of data describing interactions between pupils in mixed sex education lessons. It is important to note that one element of the adolescent culture we describe is that boys acted with significant aggression towards girls in the schools we studied. This aggression could be expressed verbally. Chris Haywood (1996) has explored the issue of 'talk' and has argued that in both style and content 'talk' has a role to play in relation to power. She suggests that 'talk' between men and women can operate as a technique to police and regulate assumptions about gendered sexualities (ibid.: 241). We observed boys joking and teasing girls about a number of matters, but particularly in relation to their bodies and appearance in ways which alternately enraged and defeated them. The aggression was also expressed in behaviour: boys looked, touched and harassed girls. There was in schools, then, considerable evidence of male pupils seeking to exercise the power and privilege we have discussed.

We consider the jokes and teasing we observed boys engage in in sex education lessons. We have already considered jokes directed to other boys in Chapter Five. We focused on interventions directed at girls in the lessons and to a lesser extent to the female professionals delivering the lessons. In the previous chapter we discussed Kehily and Nayak's (1997) suggestion that teasing and joking are related to competitiveness between boys for power and status. We consider whether, in a number of complex ways, they represent a discursive practice which is involved with establishing male power over girls.

Girls' Bodies and Appearance

In our classroom observations we recorded a number of jokes which involved male pupils commenting on girls' bodies and appearance. They showed some of the implications that male views of female bodies have for girls. The girls found the teasing unpleasant and denigrating; we observed girls looking very uncomfortable in response to it, and in interviews they complained about it. As we spent time in the schools we heard frequent male commentary on bodily matters, such as breast size. Boys would walk through school corridors admiring 'the size of her knockers' or disparaging 'her little tits'. They also discussed 'the size of her arse', commented about whether a particular girl had 'good legs' or spoke in judgement about a 'pig-ugly' face. Girls could be placed into the categories of 'fit bird' or 'fly bird'; they could be 'tasty', a 'dog' or a 'log'.

These interactions related directly to girls' having an 'appropriate' body image (discussed in the next section), and illustrate the difficulties that can arise for girls if they are seen not to fit this image, as well as the public commentary and judgements that boys make about girls. The atmosphere is competitive, aggressive and sexualised. Recent feminist research has drawn our attention also to issues of the male 'gaze' in relation to women, which we discuss in more detail later in this chapter. We gain a glimpse here of the way men 'gaze' at women and then judge them.

We collected data from girls at Tonford School that made clear their fear and resentment of the boys' actions:

Sophie   Paul said to this girl, 'I don't want to go out with you', because she'd got small tits.
Paul   I did not! It was Steve, my brother.
Jack   That's all Steve ever talks about.
Paul   He didn't like the girl. She asked him out, and he only said it as an excuse not to go out with her.
Sophie   It's a bit immature to say that.
Paul   My mum said if she had been the girl she would have punched him in the face.

It is important to recognise the different perspectives expressed within the data. Paul is keen to disassociate himself from his brother, and Jack does not entirely approve of what Steve has said. It is also interesting that Sophie feels willing to discuss this incident with her teacher, perhaps hoping for some support from her. Paul's comment about his mother's reaction also indicated the support that older women can offer in resisting some of the messages about bodies generated by young males. There are, we suspect, policy implications to the exchange, for it indicates the impact that sympathetic teachers can have by offering support to girls in these contexts. This is an issue which will be discussed in more detail in the final chapter of the book.

A girls' focus group at Streamham School discussed the issue of male teasing, and agreed there were problems. Janie, for example, said:

Janie   Girls get harassed by boys about chests and periods, and if they are not experienced. The lads reckon they know everything, and take the piss out of girls if they don't have a big chest, or having to use tampons or if they aren't experienced.

This is the sort of information we are used to reading in feminist literature: boys taunt girls about their periods and breast size. We have a large amount of data on this sort of verbal teasing, and we know how much girls fear and dislike it and how threatening they find it (see Jones 1985; Halson 1989; Herbert 1989). The interactions relate to having an 'appropriate' body image, and show the difficulties that can arise for girls if they are seen not to fit this image. Sociological theory has drawn our attention to the significance of the 'male gaze'. Foucault's work has played a key role in developing the notion of the

86

'gaze'. He used the expression *le regard* to imply not just the act of looking but the employment of research, language and discourse to construct the body out of all those elements of the gaze (Foucault 1979). What the body *should* be is then sustained and constrained by a number of discursively constituted institutionalised settings (Hewitt 1991: 235).

Male and Female Bodies and Puberty

In this section we introduce data from sex education classes conducted with younger pupils, which we consider allow us insight into some of the background factors that influence the behaviour and attitudes of adolescent boys and girls in this context. The data describe some of the underlying differences in boys' and girls' perceptions of their bodies and the body's relation to their sexuality.

Data collected in a Year 7 class (with pupils aged 11–12) seem to suggest that girls and boys have significantly different views about their bodies. The body has become an important area of research in the social sciences (Foucault 1979). Sociology of the body suggests that we cannot simply see the body as a *natural* entity: 'it is heavily endowed with meaning' (Waterhouse 1991: 108). Coward (1994: 66) suggests that we should look at the body as 'a surface of inscription – a text on which the social is written'. We gain access in this data to the views of young people on the verge of puberty, who were developing an adolescent gender identity. The data indicate something of how these young adolescents read a set of social meanings and disclosed a number of messages about their bodies and the different implications of male and female bodies.

The body is clearly of interest in a study concerned with gender. However, there are areas of more specific relevance because research draws our attention to the connections between the body and sexuality: 'To think and talk about sexuality is first of all to think about and talk about bodies' (Valverde 1985: 29). We want to speculate about the impact that gender-differentiated views of the body may have on adolescent sexuality, and of course the implications for sex education.

Data from Streamham School illustrates a number of themes, in particular the different perceptions boys and girls have of their own bodies and the changes their bodies undergo; and the significance changes in physical maturity and the move towards sexual activity have for the different genders.

We present a long extract taken from a lesson led by Janice Letts, a Personal and Social Education teacher, who was working with her own form in the summer term of their first year in the comprehensive. The topic was changes in the body at puberty. The teacher had drawn gingerbread figures of a male and a female body on the board. She asked the pupils to list the changes in each body form, which she then drew on the figures:

JL   So what happens to my gentleman gingerbread man?

Sean	His voice changes.
JL	What?
Sean	It goes high and low sometimes.
JL	What else happens and changes?
Dean	Muscles grow.

The teacher then shifted the angle and asked about the kinds of feelings likely to be associated with these physical changes:

JL	What might the boys' feelings about this be?
Dean	It's cool!
Aran	I think he'd feel good about that.

There was substantial agreement with this assessment from other boys around the room. What is significant, of course, is the fact that the boys see these body changes as positive, and they offer them an unalloyed welcome. The teacher then went on to develop the list of physical changes:

JL	Right, so what else happens?
James	Hairs on his chest.
John	Hairy armpits.

Janice Letts again encouraged the pupils to discuss the feelings they experience as accompanying these changes:

JL	How might that feel?
John	Might be warmer – sweaty.

Pupils then began to list other changes that accompany puberty:

Tim	(*Very quietly*) The willy gets longer and hairier.
JL	(*Addressing the class*) Yes, the willy gets longer and hairier.
Matt	Yes, the willy grows.

The teacher followed the same pattern of asking pupils about feelings in response to the new data they provided:

JL	How might he feel about that?
Tim	Well, it's embarrassing if you have to shower or get changed together for sports.
Jack	Facial hair.
Ben	Spots.
JL	Feelings?
Boys	(*In unison*) Embarrassed.... Needs to shave.... Proud ...

It is necessary to analyse these reactions. Here we see the pupils displaying a number of responses to the impact of physical changes at puberty. There was, to be fair, a mixture of reactions: some embarrassment is present, to be sure; but we need to note the pride identified by the boys in their experience of developing muscles, and the marking event of having to shave as a signal of incipient manhood. There is in this data a glimpse of the importance for boys of the male 'gaze'. When boys are getting changed in a public situation, and are therefore exposed to the 'gaze' of other males, there is real potential for embarrassment. It was interesting that only male pupils responded to the teacher's request for information about physical changes, and it was only male pupils who offered accounts or definitions of the emotional reactions to changes in the male body at puberty.

The full significance of the male reactions perhaps becomes clear only if we compare them with the responses pupils made to the same questions about female development. Janice Letts followed the same pattern for the female figure as for the male figure:

JL	So what happens to my gingerbread lady?
Sophie	Hips widen.
Tamara	Breasts get bigger.
JL	How might that feel?
Sophie	Embarrassed, because she has the biggest ones in the school.
Jack	Yeah, the biggest bombs!

The girls' account of their emotions in this exchange about bodily development at puberty are distinctively different from those of the boys. There is no reference to pride in the physical developments; instead it is the potential these changes carry for embarrassment and for humiliation that is highlighted. The girls seem to view the changes in their own bodies through the eyes of male viewers. It is how boys will react to their bodily changes that is discussed: it seems almost that the female body is socially composed through male gaze. This study is exploratory, as we stated in the Introduction, and we would suggest that this area would be a fruitful one for further research.

It is interesting that a male pupil intervened in this discussion to offer the viewpoint of the male 'gaze' and to define the feelings that accompany the bodily changes for girls. The girls had not made any comments about the boys' bodily changes. It was significant also that Jack chose to use language that is vernacular rather than biological in tone, referring to 'the biggest bombs'. In Chapter 5 we referred to Kehily and Nayak's analysis of male vernacular language and suggested that the latter represents a strategy to invert 'the rules of adult middle class society' and to 'violate social norms', which 'is part of a strategy to visibly convey masculine identity' (Kehily and Nayak 1997: 74). It is, of course, significant too that what the boy says is derogatory, and that it immediately draws attention to the sexuality implied by the development of breasts.

The teacher and the girls ignored what Jack said, and the offering of information continued:

Cathy   Periods.
JL   How might that feel?
James   Embarrassed, because she's the only one who has had them.

It is again interesting that a male pupil chooses to intervene, not purely on a point of information, but in an attempt to answer or define what girls might feel about having periods. The teacher encouraged the class to think more about the issue, and asked for more reactions:

JL   Any more feelings?
John   Moody. Girls get moody.

Again a male pupil answered, delineating the feelings that girls have in relation to menstruation. Alice then offered a comment which agreed with and expanded on John's comment, again emphasising the dangers and difficulties of these female experiences:

Alice   You lose friends by being moody.

Other girls went on to identify the difficult and embarrassing set of changes that being an adolescent female seemed to them to involve:

Charlotte   Spots on her face.
Gemma   Hairy armpits and legs.

Janice Letts attempted to elicit feelings from the pupils about these experiences, and again the pupils dwelt exclusively on the negative:

JL   How might that feel?
Kate   Worry about getting sweaty.
Gemma   And smelly.

At this point, 'BO' was shouted from all over the room. The teacher went through the other body changes, ensuring that pupils had a comprehensive list, and then returned to a discussion of the feelings involved for adolescents in these changes:

JL   So, we said 'cool' and 'proud' were some of the feelings for the boys. What about the girls? Do they feel proud and cool as well?

The answers the teacher received to this question simply repeated the feelings of embarrassment, anxiety, shame and fear. The girls made it clear that one of their major concerns was that the difficulties they have in coping with the physical changes meant their friendships are endangered.

This is interesting information, but before aiming to analyse its content we want to consider the pattern of classroom response in this mixed-sex lesson. Girls remained quiet when asked about changes in the male body, but boys seemed to be willing to offer their views about the impact of changes in the female body. This may relate simply to the pattern, familiar from feminist research (Shaw, 1976; Serbin, 1978), of boys being dominant in school classrooms when public discussion is happening. We wondered, however, if there was something important about the right assumed by the boys to suggest or identify what girls feel, or to interfere in defining the significance of girls' feelings in relation to their bodies.

We now turn to the content of the comments. There was a dramatic difference in gender reaction to issues of physical development. The data indicate that boys at puberty were able to express pride at the bodily changes they experienced and welcomed the developments, happily anticipating the new status they could bring. In the classroom there was no indication of a diversity of feelings experienced among the boys, but some may have had considerable anxiety about aspects of their own development. We must acknowledge that in this informal adolescent culture there may well be strong gender taboos inhibiting boys' discussion of 'body' matters or indeed admitting to any anxiety in a classroom setting.[1] Gender codes mean that girls are more willing to discuss their anxieties, which are read as having a different meaning; but we do not consider this is an adequate explanation for the tone and character of the boys' comments. Girls had a very different set of responses from the boys'. The girls' anxieties about their bodies were clear: they seemed concerned about the way their bodies were perceived by others and they were aware that the changes in their bodies could result in embarrassment and teasing from boys.

There was, perhaps inevitably, a significant weight of data on the issue of appearance and the presentation of an appropriate body image. The girls were immediately concerned with the way their bodies were viewed and received by others. They worried about having spots or having BO. The boys did mention that puberty for them can bring spots, but the girls seemed more concerned. The boys did not, for example, admit to anxiety about BO, although it was a key issue for the girls. Feminist work has alerted us to the importance of the issue of appearance for women. Simone de Beauvoir (1988: 49), for example, argued that a woman's identity is intimately linked with her physical appearance, which is viewed as a measure of her intrinsic value. Loss of beauty means loss of both identity and worth.

Work on the sociology of the body has expanded our knowledge of some of these areas (Bourdieu 1978; Foucault 1979; Baudrillard 1988; Featherstone, Hepworth and Turner 1991). Holland and Adkins (1996: 3) talk about 'appropriate femininity' as 'embodied'. The material has become familiar and has even passed into the mass media and general discussion in Britain. It is clear that there are body shapes and styles that signify femininity and attractiveness, and they carry a high emotional value for women. Failure to meet these models can be a cause of great distress throughout women's lives, but the distress is particularly acute in adolescence.

There are direct connections to sexuality in reactions to body images. Research suggests that the physical body needs to be presented in a particular way in order to be read as sexual, as sexually attractive and available (Featherstone *et al.* 1991; Coward 1994). The view of Featherstone *et al.* is that the release of the body's expressive capacity is dependent on the achievement of an acceptable appearance. In our study the girls seemed to be constructing a conventional female identity, which is passive and concerned with appropriate appearance. The female body is portrayed as a quiescent thing, available for male scrutiny and the male gaze, and accessible as a topic for male commentary.

It is perhaps not surprising that young adolescent males and females should see their bodies in different ways. Feminist work has emphasised that the male body is given value in our society in contrast to that of the female. Bourdieu (1978: 265) developed a notion of 'physical capital', according to which the body is seen to create and possess value. There are issues in our culture about the way the body is constructed so that there is a particular relation of maleness and male power to genitalia and sexuality. But sexuality is not the only issue: Connell (1983: 19) has developed the idea, pointing out that 'to be an adult male is distinctly to occupy space, to have a physical presence in the world'. Male precedence can be expressed in a range of 'bodily' ways. Body posture is one example, as also is the overt physical deployment of the body. There are issues for young adolescent boys about learning to present their bodies in appropriate male postures at this point in their lives.

The discussion of masculinities in recent research offers insights here into the connections between power, masculinity and rationality (Frank 1991: 75). Morgan (1992) points out that in some models of masculinity men are portrayed as reasonable beings who are clearly identified with rational activities and are less emotional than women. It is interesting that in our data about the girls' bodies, the boys target the issue of emotionality. They reveal a line of thought suggesting that girls' bodies and bodily processes cause problems for their emotional well being and their ability to be rational. They see this as a cause for judgement.

It is important to question what young males are telling other adolescents, both other boys and girls, about bodies. There is evidence of a distinctive set of messages, one for males and another for females. Feminists have begun to identify the strategies by which masculine discourses have historically valourised and universalised male bodily experience (Gatens 1983). It may be possible to relate this material to the ways the boys talked about the girls' bodies. There was criticism of girls' bodies and of their bodily processes because they are different from those of the male. The development of the female body in the boys' view is lacking: it produces breasts, which are a source of teasing, and periods, which are a source of embarrassment. Female development yields spots and hair and smells, unlike boys' bodies, which produces an enviable male form, a form that creates a sense of pride and secures precedence.

French psychoanalytic theory may offer important insights here. It has been particularly concerned with the fact that the male is regarded as the standard, as the reference point – the female is treated either as being the same – hence not existing separately – or as lacking, and therefore inferior and subordinate to the male: 'The male is the norm against which she is measured and found wanting' (Connell and Dowsett 1992: 94).

Wood (1984) researched young male adolescents' views of girls, and offered a similar picture. He describes in his research how the 'reproductive and excremental aspects of the female body were constantly referred to by the boys in a fixated and disgusted tone edged with nervousness' (ibid.: 54). The boys seem to work with a notion of the male body as an ideal type, and women's bodies by contrast disappoint because they fail to meet the standard of the male. Wood worked on how we can identify male discourses of difference. If men portray themselves as the norm, as the way bodies and ways of being in the world ought to be, then women can only be second-rate copies. Men will be the ideal type and women will be the 'other'. The male discourse of difference involves a negative representation of women: the difference is not simply difference, but implies hierarchy, so that the male takes precedence over and is superior to the female.

The male 'gaze' does not, of course, fall only on female bodies: it can be directed towards other male bodies, which too can be found lacking and failing to match up to whatever a particular culture counts as the 'proper' representation. Not all male bodies are seen as having equal value: 'some bodies may be seen as more masculine than others' (Morgan 1993: 80). This can give rise to competition between males about bodily form and appearance, and for the physical presence that Connell has discussed.

There are suggestions in the data of a fundamentally different set of feelings about the body and about body image on the part of young male and female adolescents. It is possible to suggest that the social meaning of bodily change for girls is different from that of boys, leading to different social consequences and perhaps even a different relationship with one's own body. Simone de Beauvoir noted this pattern and commented:

> Puberty takes on a radically different significance in the two sexes because it does not portend the same future for both. It is true enough that at the moment of puberty boys also feel their bodies as an embarrassment, but being proud of their manhood from an early age they proudly project towards manhood the moment of their development – they joyfully assume the dignity of being male.
>
> (de Beauvoir 1988: 340)

'Looking' and the Male 'Gaze'

It is important to note that harassment is not always expressed verbally. Research into sexuality has begun to examine the issue of the male 'gaze', discussed earlier in this chapter. Lees (1986) alerts us to the difficulties girls in schools experience with a particular style of male gaze. Girls discussed their objections to the 'leers blokes give you. The leering sort of look. You know, they make you feel like an object for a bloke to look at and touch … just for their satisfaction' (ibid.: 106). In their research, conducted in the east Midlands in the 1980s, Measor and Woods found a similar problem, of boys 'looking' in ways the girls found very difficult:

Jenny	You have to do PE in the hall in shorts and everything, all up on the climbing frame.
Interviewer	Don't you like doing PE in your shorts?
Jenny	Yes, but the boys sort of take the mickey out of you.
Amy	Yes, they all come up and start whistling and everything. And they all come round and look in the windows and knock on them.
Sally	You expect boys to be a bit crude about things like that.

(Measor 1989: 48)

In the current study, completed ten years later, the issue remained important to girls. We have already presented data suggesting that boys look at and judge girls' bodies and appearance. There seem to be occasions when boys put their desire to 'look' into practice and exert their perceived right to 'gaze' in ways the girls found entirely unacceptable. At Streamham School for example:

Caroline	Boys drop things and then bend down right in front of us to pick them up.

In a sense, sex education lessons provoke the male gaze, because they focus on female bodies and reproductive systems, and often involve the study of visual images of female bodies and reproductive and genital organs. This offered boys the familiar activity of 'looking', and placed them in role as someone who has the right to look. This often produced a sexualised response from the boys, and it embarrassed and offended the girls:

Carole	It is awful, the boys say stuff like 'Corr! Look at that!'
Julie	The boys just laugh.

Sociological and psychoanalytic work in heterosexual patterns of interaction has alerted us to the importance of 'looking'. Freud 'considered the gaze to be a largely phallic property, arising from a desire to master the subject of the gaze' (Waterhouse 1991: 112). Feminists note that there is a split between those who look and those who are looked at. The argument is that women become passive objects of a scrutinising male 'gaze': 'It is male desire which is prioritised, the right to look, to 'gaze' has become a male prerogative' (ibid.). Theweleit (1987) argues that it is male desire that is signified in the 'I' of western culture, where women are placed as the object, the 'other' (cited in Edwards 1993: 96). The role of women is to *provide* pleasure, not to *feel* it. Rich discusses pornographic film in a way that illustrates Theweleit's point and effectively draws our attention to the way sexuality is constructed to privilege and focus on male desire and need:

> How much space has the film preserved for men? We have been forced to watch always from the seat of a male buyer: the positioning of women is in the light of male desire.
>
> (Rich 1979: 351)

In this approach men are the 'I' and women are 'the object of the male gaze' (Waterhouse 1991: 110). The male does not carry the burden of sexual objectification. His role, both on the screen and off it, is an active one; it is distinct from the female role, and the difference is not benign – it is equated with power. Gender is constructed around difference and around dominance and submission.

It is important to identify a number of 'embodied practices, signification practices and behaviours and actions' that signify maleness in the way Chodorow has described. 'Doing' them signifies masculinity to the world, but also allows the individual engaging in them to 'feel' male. Pollock (1998) writes of the *flâneur*, a character or type who moves about the urban world voyeuristically feasting his eyes on anything he cares to view. Pollock comments that the *flâneur*'s sense of self, his very subjectivity, depends on his ability to devour with his eyes. This is conceptually interesting: it is by carrying out these actions that the individual comes to feel his identity. Performing the action makes the individual, in this case the adolescent boy on the threshold of acquiring a sense of his masculinity, feel right, feel himself to be a 'proper' male secure in his masculinity.

Touching

Looking can be associated with touching. Other forms of harassment in our study involved physical contact, which caused problems for girls who were exposed to it. As we spent time in the schools walking with or near pupils moving between classrooms, we became aware, as have other researchers, of the amount of physical harassment that boys enact on girls (Mahony 1985; Lees 1986; Herbert 1989). It is impossible to remain unaware of the significant extent of uninvited touching that occurs in crowded corridors and staircases within a co-educational school. Boys do walk behind girls and attempt to lift their skirts; they do touch hair and pull bra-straps.

Janie was walking up the stairs. Alan repeatedly touched her, and then moved rapidly away before she was able to respond.

On one occasion in the school grounds we witnessed physical harassment accompanied by verbal teasing. The role of researcher was useful here because pupils recognised us as being adults but not teachers, and this allowed us a view of pupils' informal culture:

> As two of the researchers walked through Whitefarm School a group of Year 8 pupils was standing in a huddle, and one male pupil hugged a girl. Two other boys walked towards them and began to tease, noisily and aggressively. 'Put each other down!' 'What you doing with her?' 'Are you gonna get in her knickers?' 'She'll let you shag her!' 'Don't shag her. She's had half the school.'

The boys' stance was aggressive and malicious, and their insults nasty. This was not a simple joke intended to amuse and introduce humour into a boring school day. It seemed to the researchers that this was an important incident because it alerts us to the nature of the adolescent informal culture in which a display of physicality can result in insults and aggressive teasing.

Boys do harass and tease girls and other boys in the context of sex education, as well as other lessons. How are we to make sense of all this? It seems to represent an assertion of male power over girls, and of some males over others. Halson, for example, wrote of the teasing and harassment she observed in schools that they represented 'a product of and a reproduction of power differences between women and men' (Halson 1989: 139). They are visible evidence of power differences between young men and women. Such actions are also an example of gender 'work'. The boys' actions play an important role in the creation of gender identities, signalling a certain set of interests that a 'proper' male has and also, perhaps, testing out what they consider are their 'rights' over the girls among whom they find themselves.

What goes on in many schools amounts to sexual harassment. Sedley and Benn (1982) provide a definition of sexual harassment. It covers 'repeated and unwanted comments, looks, suggestions or physical contact that might create a stressful or intimidating working environment'. There are policy implications here for the establishing of sexual harassment policies in schools (these are discussed in detail in the final chapter).

We now turn to the area of controversy in the sex education classroom over the issue of sexual knowledge, which reveals a number of the same themes but may offer further insights into the processes at work.

Gender, Information and Knowledge

Our observation of the five schools revealed boys and girls acting in accordance with gender codes to which they were attached. We can discern in their reactions to sex education a traditional picture of what it means to be a *proper* boy or girl. There is evidence also of boys, and to a lesser extent girls, policing these gender codes and acting on infringements. A similar process appears in relation to information. It is a significant symbolic resource in the process of gender 'work', of establishing and signalling a gender identity.

There was a gender difference in the responses to the information offered about sexual matters. It seemed to represent a problem for boys, who were keen to assert that they already knew all they were offered in the sex education programmes, and did not need the information. We have already presented participant observation data, which showed boys resisting sex education lessons. Boys made jokes ridiculing any suggestion that they might need to know any more about sexual interaction. In evaluation sheets from all the schools, the boys were dismissive of the sex education work, insisting that they already knew the information:

- 'I knew most of it already.'
- 'A waste of time.'
- 'Not a lot was tort.'
- 'The activities were childish.'

We thought it significant in this context that all of the spoiled questionnaires returned to us, and those with jokes written on them, came from boys. In the Streamham evaluation for example, when asked what their opinion was of the health professionals' session, one boy answered simply 'Crap'. Another wrote 'Shit', and a third 'It woze crap'.

There was a lack of serious application on some forms, which seemed to the researchers to represent a kind of cynical rejection of the sessions the health professionals had run. Again all these forms came from boys. Some of the boys from Gainton made silly jokes:

Q   What did you like best in the session?
A   Femidom.
Q   Why?
A   It's big.
Q   What did you dislike most in the session?
A   Femidom.
Q   Why?
A   It's big.

Other evaluation sheets, also completed by boys, rubbished the efforts of those providing the sex education programmes: 'I'm staying selabot and becoming a monk' and 'My mummy said not to have sex till I'm married'.

Other data from questionnaires provided evidence that backs up a point we made earlier in relation to masculinities: boys are keen to show that they recognise material is sexual or has a sexual connotation, and they therefore want to respond to it in this way. When asked to evaluate the health professionals, sessions, one group of boys answered: 'Not good. They should ask prostitutes to teach us, they work for sex for a living, ha ha!' Other boys, when asked for an opinion about the sessions, replied: 'Later mate! Later maybe!'

We argue that such data reveal an important element in adolescent culture concerning the taboo on revealing ignorance about any aspect of sexuality (see the final chapter for a more detailed discussion of the policy implications). The data suggest that sex educators will gain a better response from male pupils if they eschew strategies that require pupils to reveal the extent of their ignorance about sex. Ignorance about some aspects of sex seems to have greater implications for male status than for female. Any admission of needing information will likely betray a lack of knowledge and hence a loss of face. Instead it is important for adolescent males to demonstrate the possession of knowledge, claim to be fully informed and able to retain a place in the hegemonic masculine culture.

Other authors, however, have suggested a different explanation of male resistance to sex education work, arguing that adolescent cultural codes suggest that boys do not want to know about some of the matters discussed in sex education lessons. Matthews (1992) has suggested that boys may rule sex education to be a feminised sphere and reject it as a result. She argues that *young* adolescent males make it clear that they do not want to know about sexuality; in fact not knowing is part of their identity work as heterosexual males. Showing interest in sexual matters is defined as feminine and threatens the presentation of self as 'masculine'. This process may well be going on, but we argue that the pattern is more complex. Our data offer further insights into some of the underlying issues. It seems that there is a gender division of information. Boys reject some areas of information, because their gender indicates that they should have nothing to do with them. There are, however, some other kinds of information boys consider crucial, and from which females should be excluded. We contend that there are gender-based rules about who should know what.

Adolescent informal cultures in the schools we studied ruled that boys and girls should have different levels of information about sexual matters. Boys had a view about the level of information appropriate for girls, and they seemed to resent any situation where girls appeared to have knowledge about sexual matters, or more knowledge than the boys deemed appropriate. Data collected from Whitefarm School indicates that the boys would attack girls in such a context:

Diane	Could you use both a Femidom and a condom at the same time?
Cathy	How safe is the Femidom?
Sue	It can't be as safe as the condom!
Cathy	How do you take it out without getting sperm everywhere?

Diane	That would be a bit fiddly. They are about that (*demonstrating*) long. They look really weird.
Teacher	(*Answering a question from another part of the room*) Condoms are easily available and relatively cheap.
Cathy	Pack of three is about £1. 27.
John	(*Working with a group of boys*) How come you know all of this about condoms and Femidoms and that?'

His comment is the prelude to a barrage of teasing from the boys about Cathy's sexual proclivities. When the teasing began, Cathy looked uncomfortable and made no attempt to reply. The teacher, who was at the other side of the room, was unaware of the boys' tirade and did not intervene. We suggest that this is an example of one of the ways boys attempt to define the situation: girls will be teased and subjected to verbal attack if they reveal too much knowledge about sexual matters in a classroom setting. Attack is also an effective form of defence, deflecting attention from what may have been John's own ignorance in this respect.

Such data and their explanations are familiar from feminist work, but why should this be the case? Why is the possession of information a controversial matter among adolescents and a problem for boys? We gathered data that may offer additional insights into the vital processes involved for adolescents in the task of 'doing gender'. It is important to make it clear that the data we collected relates only to heterosexual relationships: adolescents did not in our hearing say anything about homosexual experiences or identity development, and therefore we have not attempted to develop equivalent understandings of the gay pattern of experiences. There are some important underlying principles at work here regarding gender-based divisions of responsibility for sexual knowledge and expertise; there is also the perspective that codes of masculinity require adolescent males to take on responsibility for particular areas, while adolescent females take on others.

Sources of Information and Gender

We became aware of these social and gender constructions in relation to data on the sources of information about sexual activity that adolescents use, rely on and prefer. While girls discussed the importance of friends, magazines like *Just Seventeen* and their families, particularly mothers and sisters, as major sources of information, boys stressed pornography as one source they felt was important, as well as their peer group.

At Whitefarm School we interviewed the school nurse, who had asked pupils to say where they gained information about sex, as part of her own research. She was surprised and shocked when 39 of 62 boys said 'hard pornography' was one of their major sources of information:

Adam   Try switching to channel 34 and 35 on Cable on Saturdays.

The school nurse also collected interview evidence that the boys download pornographic material from the Internet. It is, of course, possible that the boys recognised the high shock-value of this comment for their audience, and we should be cautious of merely accepting it. Nevertheless, we consider that the comments need serious attention.

Other data aided our understanding of this matter, since similar information was collected from all of the schools involved in the research. We observed a Year 9 class at Whitefarm School led by a PSE teacher, Miss Magges, who was trusted and liked by her pupils. In all the focus groups and interviews we conducted at Whitefarm in this research and in a second research project a year later (Measor and Squires forthcoming), pupils discussed this teacher in very favourable terms. The following is an extract from field notes written in Miss Magges' class:

Darren   Film, videos, porn does help.

The girls sitting near him collapsed into giggles, which angered Darren and the group of boys sitting around him.

Matt   It's a sensible answer.
Darren   In class you only get what happens explained to you, whereas in porn you can see exactly what is going on. You must feel stupid going into a sexual relationship when you don't know what to do, which you wouldn't from only hearing what happens at school and looking at diagrams in the text books you are given.

The boys went on to explain that they valued pornography because it provided the opportunity for acquiring specific and explicit information about sex. It is possible that the boys were simply enjoying the shock-value of their comments. We consider that Darren in this context was not speaking in an attention-seeking or deliberately shocking way. He spoke quietly and seriously about his anxieties, and about the solution that he had found. We wonder to what extent his solution is the preferred one for many boys. Clearly, further research would be necessary to establish that.

In the Streamham evaluation boys commented on their levels of anxiety about 'first-time sex'. They were critical of the fact that in their sex education 'we were only told what to use, not how to do it'. At Tonford, pupils judged their sex education to be:

OK, it could be more personal.
My school is quite open, but it never discusses very intimate things. We discuss contraception and sex but not what to do when having sex. We don't know.

A boy at Ferryfield School spoke of the need for more detailed pictures in the sex education material they used in schools: 'The pictures are all sketches. Make the pictures more graphic.' There are indications that some boys have high levels of anxiety about knowing enough about sex. Their way of handling this was to turn to pornography: its explicit detail apparently eased this anxiety.

Social constructions of adolescent sexuality and of heterosexual masculinity are exposed here. Knowing what to do in a sexual encounter is defined as a male responsibility, not as a shared concern for two young partners who can mutually explore and experiment. In matters of practice, of experience, girls are defined as not needing to know or needing to know less. Shame, however, is likely to befall any boy who cannot take charge and does not know exactly what to do. The shame is not mutual: we collected no evidence of girls feeling the same anxieties and responsibilities. Core aspects of the self are involved: masculinity and femininity are again constructed through difference, and again the power differential is clearly present, as well as constructions about gender.[2]

We can perhaps discern in this information some of the gender differences in relation to sexuality being played out in interactions between adolescents in their informal culture, and pick up evidence about the price males pay for their dominance in the gender regime. It allows us to explore some of the insecurity and anxiety that may lie behind the behaviour of the boys, and may represent the price they pay for the power and dominance they claim. The data offer further insight into the 'conceptual knot of power, anxiety and desire' Holloway (1984: 238) identifies in the gender regimes that are currently established. Connell (1987), writing in this same vein, draws our attention to the costs of social advantage for men.

Gender, the Family and Sexuality

It is important to investigate some of the underlying issues about the ways that boys obtain not only information about sex but their attitudes and stances to sexual encounters. There are significant issues about the nature of sexual social-isation, and gender differences within the family in particular, that are important for our understanding of adolescent responses

Our data suggest that boys and girls received their information about sex from different sources and this may affect their preferences for different sources of information. Our questionnaire results suggest that boys and girls have rather different attitudes on this matter.

One of the most significant issues relates to gender differences in the way parents behave towards sons and daughters in relation to information about sex. The general picture that emerges from research in the UK over several decades is that many parents do not offer their children sex education, but where it is given girls are likely to be offered much more information than boys (Farrell 1978; Miller 1986; Allen 1987; Carlson 1987; Frankham 1993). Our evidence is that girls generally gain a substantial amount of their information from their parents, or more accurately from their mothers, and many of them feel able to talk to their mothers about problems they experience. In the questionnaires returned to us 62 per cent of the girls said that they would talk to their mothers if they wanted more information or were worried about something; 38 per cent of girls did not feel able to discuss such matters with their mothers. In contrast only 42 per cent of the boys felt able to consult their mothers about any worries or requests for information. It is interesting to note another set of figures in this context: only 13 per cent of the girls and 22 per cent of the boys said they felt able to discuss things with their fathers on matters of this kind. This means that more than 50 per cent of the boys felt cut off from maternal help and support in connection with sexual and relationship matters, and that the majority of both boys and girls felt less able to consult their fathers.[3]

Observation data supported the information given in the questionnaires. In interviews the boys tended to state flatly: 'Boys don't really go to their parents to talk about sex.' Their sense was that girls are much more likely to do so. In participant observation at Tonford School tutors constructed a lesson where pupils discussed the problem pages of *Just Seventeen* magazine. When the teacher asked who they would consult if they felt they had a problem, only one group of boys stated: 'We would speak to our parents first, and then best friends.' The boys in other groups in the class did not agree: 'None of us would ask our parents if we had a problem.'

Many more girls than boys seemed to feel closer to their mothers and more linked in a confiding relationship with them. Another significant point relates to adolescent perceptions of the different roles, aptitudes or indeed attitudes of fathers and mothers. Both boys and girls expressed this, and we discuss it further in the next section.

Objections to School Sex Education

We identified a number of pupils who actively objected to schools and teachers attempting to address sex education at all. They considered that it was not quite 'proper' to discuss sexual matters in school. It is important to note that these objections came exclusively from a small minority of the *girls*. They were not representative of the girls across the five schools, but their views were strongly expressed and related to what seemed to be deeply felt principles.

For these girls sex was something that belonged to a realm beyond that of the school, and specifically to the private realm of the home. Learning about sexual matters was something that belonged within the family. It was parents, most usually mothers or other female family members, who should be involved. In response to the sessions the health professionals conducted with girls at Gainton School, the following comments were made:

Anna   I haven't really enjoyed our work very much because it is hard to talk about it at school.

Lucy   I would rather talk to my sister or my mum about it than at school to strangers.

These girls objected to talking about what they see as some of the most intimate areas of life and experience to people they categorise as 'strangers'.

There was a similar response from a minority of the girls at Tonford. One commented: 'I didn't like this little "to do" we had with [the health] visitors.' The objection was not just to the health professionals' input but to teachers' attempts to address sex education:

Laura   They teach well, but some teachers didn't want to tell you much when you asked something. They didn't say it as clear as your mum or sister would.

This is a theme encountered in research in the Midlands in the 1980s (Measor and Woods 1984). There, some of the girls objected to school sex education:

Amy   Well, me mum's already told me about it anyway.

This pupil went on to suggest that the home and her mother were the proper territory for these discussions. Debbie made this even clearer with an evocative description:

Debbie   My mum told me about periods when she used to wash me in the bath. I had long hair, it got really tangled, and my mum used to do it and wash it out for me, and used to tell me all about it in the bathroom.

For Debbie, it was at such moments of shared mother–daughter intimacy that sexual information should be exchanged. Sally had a similar account:

Sally   I just went into my mum's room first of all, and she goes, 'What have you come to see me about?' and I goes, 'Nothing', and then she just told me. She just got this little book out about marriage and things like that.

Jenny, too, had the experience of talking to her mum about sex, and she contrasted it sharply with her experience at school:

Jenny   Like Sally, my mum told me about periods and that while I was in the bath, but in my old school we did a film on seeing babies born and I

remember looking at it and not thinking at all … not really understanding.

The warmth and confiding character of the home as the context for learning about sexual matters was compared with what these girls perceived as the cold and impersonal approach of school sex education. From a feminist perspective there are some areas of difficulty here, as we do not know what these mothers told their daughters. Girls are a captive audience for mothers to pass on romantic ideals of traditional feminine roles without having to offer any broader analysis. We did not collect similar accounts from the boys, and this needs further analysis. It is important also to note that not all of the girls had these positive experiences, and we will look at this material in the next section.

Many pupils across the different schools complained that their parents had not discussed sex with them at all, and these complaints came primarily from boys. At Streamham, James pointed out that school sex education 'is a good idea for people whose parents don't talk about it'. At Whitefarm, a group discussed the issue in an interview:

Pete   Some mums get embarrassed. You're lucky if you've got a mum who
        will tell you.
Matt   From my family I haven't learned anything – exactly, it's a waste of
        time.

It is important to contrast the boys' accounts of their parents' failure to discuss sexual matters with them with the girls' accounts, which to varying extents tended to emphasise intimacy and inclusion.

Girls, too, can face problems in this context: 38 per cent of the girls in our survey said they could not discuss sexual matters at home. Other data made it clear that girls can face specific problems with sex education given at home: some girls said, for example, that their fathers could be prohibitive about the amount of detailed sex education they received because it was felt likely to encourage girls to grow up too quickly:

Hannah   My dad's found it really hard to accept that I'm growing up and
         having relationships.
Ellie   It seems difficult for men to accept daughters growing up.
Lisa   Yeah, I do find it difficult with my dad, because I'm like his little girl.
         But if I was to say to him, 'Dad, I'm sexually active. Where can I get
         some condoms?', he would go, 'Get to your room, don't talk about it.'
         But my mum and I could talk about it quite openly.

Sources of information and counselling about sexuality varied with gender. Boys and girls were exposed to different kinds of experience, in which information about sexuality and messages about desire also vary. Home and intimacy with parents, especially mothers, is important for many, although not all, girls in a way it is not for boys. There are important questions to be asked about those social contexts in which, it appears, mothers feel free, or even compelled, to tell their daughters about sex, but not their sons. There are equally important questions about those discourses in which there is the suggestion that fathers should not tell daughters but should tell sons about sex, but that they do not do so. These family patterns indicate a picture of boys learning about sex and sexuality in ways that by and large do not include adults, or more especially trusted adults, and where there appears to be some element of exclusion from the family. This has important implications for sex education programmes, and may offer us insights into why the boys resist sex education work.

We have dwelt on the fact that many, perhaps the majority, of the boys had not gained their information about sex from trusted adults inside their families. The different family experience of the girls 'primed' them to access and accept information from teachers and other adults, like health professionals. This may offer a partial explanation for the negative and disruptive behaviour of boys when they are offered sex education in school. We speculate that boys obtain a significant mass of their information and knowledge about sex from what might be termed 'illegitimate' sources. We do not suggest that these sources are in any *real* sense illegitimate, but they are to some extent taboo and hidden. Boys do not gather their information from parents or teachers or biological textbooks. Their major sources of information are their friends and perhaps pornography, although clearly much more research is necessary to establish this. We feel it important also to raise the question of the effects on teenage boys of this feeling of being excluded from a certain kind of family intimacy. They seem to respond by creating an independent space in which their friends and commercially produced material take on the role of prime information givers.

For boys, the role of pornographic discourses about female sexuality is also important. What varieties of desire do the women in those films express, and what kind of sexual behaviour and attitudes are displayed? Academic research on pornography suggests that women communicate passivity, permanent receptivity and a set of erotic practices directed towards male pleasure rather than being located within female pleasure (Rich 1979; Theweleit 1987). There are, then, doubts over the messages boys get from these films about how they ought to behave and how they can expect their partner to behave.

Conclusion

The first section of this chapter provided an account of the nature of gender interactions in a school setting and indicated some of the patterns of power play between male and female pupils. Boys teased girls verbally, by a way of 'looking' and by touching. We offered insights into some of the ideas relating to male and female bodies and, by extension, the identities that underpin behaviour and attitudes. In the second section we looked at gender-based blueprints about knowledge and information, and sought to develop a purchase on some of the cultural practices and ideas within families and society that produce such blueprints. The sex educators' programme seemed to create more problems for the boys, because it implied that they needed information and therefore threatened the careful construction of 'reputation, face and relative social status' (Gilmore 1990: 185) that seems to be an important element in their construction of masculinity. This offers an explanation for the boys' objections to the sex education programmes, and their attempt to rubbish and undermine their significance.

In 1984 Arnot wrote an article called 'How shall we educate our sons?' that looked at the problems created for both boys and girls by contemporary codes of masculinity. The question of how sex education is provided for boys in particular is a crucial issue. We have argued that a well-intentioned attempt at innovation touched on core aspects of the adolescent masculine self, and was therefore resisted. The Sex Education Forum (Lenderyou and Ray 1997) has recently published material asserting that most programmes fail to provide subject matter that engages the interest and meets the needs of boys. The liberal position is that a policy challenge remains, which is to develop programmes of sex education that avoid these affronts to male and female pupils and manage to offer opportunities to both genders for developing an understanding of aspects of sexuality and sexual behaviour about which they are curious. However, the data we have discussed reveals configurations of the informal cultures of boys in relation to masculinity and sexuality indicative of the considerable difficulty involved in creating programmes to accomplish this liberal objective that do not simply privilege male sexual entitlement.

Notes

1   Nick Fisher wrote an 'agony uncle' column in magazines intended for teenage consumption and also wrote a number of sex education books based, in part, on the letters that he received in his role on the magazines. He has discussed the very high levels of anxiety that boys expressed about particular aspects of physical development. His work with boys, together with material the Sex Education Forum has recently published, entitled 'Lets hear it from the boys' (Lenderyou and Ray, 1997), indicate that boys do have a range of anxieties which they do not find it easy to discuss.

2   In her 1991 research, Hall documents twentieth-century changes in attitude to sexuality and to sexual performance, which she traces through an analysis of letters sent to Marie Stopes (the family planning innovator) from the 1920s onwards. She comments: 'Much of this new phase of writing about sex (in the 1930s) can be seen as replacing one set of anxieties with a new set. There was a new performance ethic, with emphasis on getting it right' (1991: 74). Hall suggests: 'In order to get a woman to submit to him in this new eroticised way a man was also under pressure to do all sorts of things' (ibid.: 82). The new sexual relationships, Hall suggests, laid much more of an obligation on the male to be sexually competent, and this probably remains the case today. Hall found that men had written asking Stopes for information about techniques, for example: 'can you not tell me of any literature on the subject which goes into details of the techniques, etc., of the sex act' (quoted ibid.:

105). This is echoed in our research in the boys' expression of their need to know 'exactly what to do'.

3   Our figures correspond with statistics of national research conducted on the issue of teenagers' feelings about consulting their parents. In 1997 the Health Education Authority study suggested that 61 per cent of the young people surveyed could talk to their parents about these issues; 19 per cent, a substantial minority, however, stated that they do not find it easy to talk to their parents, or do not talk to them at all about matters sexual. Girls seem to find it easier than boys. Turtle, Jones and Hickman's 1997 research supports this picture and suggests that girls found their fathers much more difficult to confide in than their mothers. More boys than girls could confide in their fathers (39 per cent of girls found talking to their fathers difficult compared with 27 per cent of boys). Ingham's 1998 work offers some insight into this situation. His results showed that over 90 per cent of the parents surveyed felt they should discuss various topics with their children, but only half reported actually doing so – even to a very small extent. There is some evidence of variation according to social class, with lower socio-economic groupings being less likely than higher groupings to offer sex education to their children. There is some evidence that parents will talk to their teenagers about some topics more readily than they will others. There seems a particular reluctance on the part of parents to deal with STDs, which perhaps is based on their perception that they do not possess enough information to offer their offspring.

7   Gender, Sexuality and Power

Introduction

In this chapter we focus on gender-related issues that affected pupil response to the sex education programmes. The aim remains the same: namely, to understand more about the ways that gender and sexual identity were signalled by adolescents in the school setting. We continue from Chapter 6 the task of documenting the nature of adolescent heterosexual interaction and relationships in the school settings we studied.

We need to emphasise again that, as Arnot (1984: 53) has said: 'Masculinity, in all its various forms, is not the same as femininity – it is after all a form of power and privilege.' Women have a subordinate role in society, which means that they face a range of different kinds of inequality. The inequality has implications for women's relationships with men, and permeates their experience of sexuality. Some feminist thinking has gone further than this, arguing that heterosexual sexuality does not simply share the cultural values of an unequal society and therefore reflect them, but that it is one of the most significant agencies by which inequality and oppression are shaped and generated.

Mitchell (1972) was concerned to distinguish the different structures which construct and maintain male power, and sexuality figured in her theorising as one of the most significant. For Mitchell, and for other feminists, sexuality required serious analysis in any attempt to understand the subordinate role in which women found themselves. Mackinnon, too, considered sexuality to be 'the primary social sphere of male power' (1983: 281). Sexual relationships, or more accurately, heterosexual relationships, are identified as one of the key sites that confer power on men and remove it from women.

We begin this discussion of sexuality and power with an account of male teasing and joking behaviour which relates to female sexual behaviour and sexuality. We pursue the analysis begun in Chapters 4 and 5, where the language and practices of pupils were examined for evidence of signalling of sexual and gender identity. We go on to explore ways in which male and female adolescents view sexuality, and aim to develop an understanding of the codes of sexual behaviour appropriate in adolescent cultures. The issue of the double standard is important in this context: it lays down quite different codes of sexual behaviour for male and female adolescents. This discussion links to that of Chapter 6 because we continue with data that offer evidence of how boys, or at least some boys, make a claim for a gender identity which grants them the power and privilege to which Arnot refers. It is important to understand more about how boys employ this power and privilege; and to track the policing and regulation they undertake to maintain the gender or sex order in classrooms and schools.

It is clear from the data that girls were under considerable pressure to construct their identity as feminine in relation to that of the heterosexual male. Boys were also under pressure to develop and signal their masculine identity in relation to the heterosexual model. We explore some of these processes in more detail throughout this chapter. It is important to reiterate that we collected no data about homosexual relationships from the young people we studied. We cannot therefore offer any insight on how young people with a same-sex sexual orientation deal with such pressures and issues.

Male Jokes and Female Sexuality

We have discussed the fact that boys teased and harassed girls on a number of issues. In Chapter 6 we concentrated on data relating to the body, appearance and knowledge about sexuality. We now focus on the issue of sexuality and sexual behaviour. Boys aggressively challenged the girls about their sexuality and sexual behaviour, and we need to examine this information to develop a sense of the gender codes operating in the informal culture. The picture of boys treating girls with disrespect and contempt, seeing them as a source of amusement and entertainment, and asserting their control over them is familiar from twenty years of feminist research in classrooms, and we have offered only a few examples here (Shaw 1976; Mahony 1985).

The family planning doctor at Streamham discussed emergency contraception and the morning-after pill, and passed packets of pills around the room, explaining that a girl at risk of pregnancy must take two pills, the second after a given interval. Some boys began to joke and suggest that particular girls were in immediate need of the pills:

John	I saw you eat one, Denise.
Aran	Why did you ask me to nick one for you?

Girls who are suspected of being sexually active become targets for teasing from the boys. At the same time the jokes mounted a challenge to the women teaching the session, in the way we outlined in Chapter 5, interfering with their ability to pace the lesson as they chose.

In their jokes boys identified particular girls as interested in sex, and taunted them. In Streamham the doctor discussed the age of consent, asking pupils for their views:

Tammy	I think it should be 14.
Doctor	Why?
Ben	Because she wants to give it a go.

Ben's joke provoked considerable laughter in the classroom, and considerable embarrassment for the girl involved. The data indicate the risks that girls face if boys suspect them of being interested in sexual activity. They indicate also the public badgering that boys directed to girls when girls answered questions and participated in open class discussion, which again we are familiar with from feminist research (Spender and Sarah 1980).

The WRAP study (Holland *et al.* 1990) was a large project that looked at the sexual practices, beliefs and understandings of young women. It revealed sharp power differentials between the sexes in adolescent sexual encounters, and emphasised the passivity at the heart of female sexuality, at least at this stage of the life course. Our data support the view developed in the WRAP project that girls have a problem if they appear to be interested in sexual activity and a problem if they want to say 'yes' to male invitations.

Teasing was directed not only at girls suspected of being sexually active or interested in sexual activity but at girls suspected of being insufficiently interested in sex or unwilling to accede to boys' definitions of acceptable sexual behaviour. At Whitefarm school, in a lesson on contraception, the idea that celibacy is a way of avoiding pregnancy and STDs was raised:

Lisa	Celibacy is the most efficient way. You can just say 'No'. You can't get AIDS or a STD.
Cary	You can't get a virus.
Lisa	That's what I say.
Darren	Yes, but you're just a prick-tease.

The joke produced general amusement among the boys in the classroom, and again revealed the discomfort that girls feel, as Cary and Lisa both blushed and complained angrily to their friends. In the first set of jokes, the girls were teased for being too sexual; in the second, the girls were made to feel uncomfortable because in the boys' eyes they were not sexual enough. Sue Lees' treatment of the names defined as 'slag' and 'drag' (1986) documents this paradox. 'Slags' are too sexual and 'drags' are not sexual at all. Lees indicated how girls are faced with negotiating a path carefully between the two polarised images.

Seidman (1992) argued that men define women's sexuality in a way that leaves women powerless. In adolescence, girls appear to be damned if they are interested in their sexuality, and damned if they are not. We suggest that there is again gender 'work' going on here: boys and girls signal different orientations to sexual expression. There is evidence of some boys policing the boundaries of youth culture, and handing out social judgement about those girls who seem to have overstepped the mark. Seidman sees this kind of activity as a 'political tactic by men to define and regulate their sexuality' (1992: 79). The policy implications for classroom practice of these considerations are addressed in detail in the final chapter.

The data may provide a partial explanation of girls' reluctance to ask and answer questions in open classroom discussions, and illustrate one of the factors that feminist research has identified as constraining girls' progress in school (Shaw 1976; Stanworth 1981). Our account of the single-sex lesson (Chapter 4) indicates that the girls both answered the family planning nurse's questions and asked questions of their own. Girls did not tease or harass other girls in the way that they are teased by boys; nor did they comment about male sexuality and judge levels of sexual activity or interest appropriate to males.

Gender and Sexuality

Our data indicate that boys and girls in the schools we studied seemed to express very different views about sexuality and sexual behaviour. Clear codes about sexuality and sexual behaviour appropriate for boys and for girls were stated. We found evidence that adolescents of both sexes considered that male and female sexuality were very different. Girls suggested that the reasons why boys engaged in sex are somewhat different from girls' reasons for sexual activity, and that sexual encounters meant different things to boys and to girls. Girls read strong emotional content into sexual encounters and saw them as an expression of emotional commitment within a relationship. Girls in our study saw boys as interested in sex either as a simple physical pleasure, or because of its status-giving potential – and they were resentful of the boys' attitude on either count.

Girls perceived boys as sexually predatory, and disliked the way they heard them talking about sexual partners. Cathy, at Ferryfield School, said:

Cathy   Oh yes, some of them, the boys, say: 'Oh, I laid six this week!' They say of this girl or that: 'Oh, she was four star.'

Girls suspected that for boys a sexual encounter was important and valued in part as something that they could brag about to their mates. It is possible that many girls saw this kind of male behaviour as 'normal', as if it was taken for granted that this is the way that boys behave. They saw this behaviour in essentialist terms – this is the way boys are, as if their nature is a fixed and given entity deriving from their biological or even their genetic make-up. There was, in the comments we collected from the girls, little sense that they have power to stop the boys talking like this, or to change their attitudes and behaviour.

Interviewer   Do you think relationships and sex are different for boys and for girls?

Lisa   I think it is different because of the maturity gap, because girls mature faster than the boys. People who are about 14 – this is the boys – it seems all they want is sex, to put it bluntly: 'Yes, I'll go out with a girl to have sex and see what it's like.' But if you go out with someone older, then they've got over that stage.

This reveals something of the way in which different social meanings and significance are attached to expressions of sexuality in the behaviour of men and women (see Connell and Dowsett 1992: 100). It seems that being successfully predatory sexually is one of the major strategies of boys for signalling gender identity. Showing a clear and constant interest in sexual matters, and displaying success in a number of sexual conquests, makes clear that one is a *proper* male with a place in the hegemonic masculine hierarchy. Being a *proper* girl, 'doing femininity', requires a very different expression of sexuality and a different code of behaviour, and it is to this area of the 'double standard' that we now turn.

The Double Standard

In adolescent informal culture one of the strongest set of rules concerns sexual behaviour appropriate for the different genders. There is a substantial body of research offering the picture of a robust double standard operative in adolescent culture. The double standard means that it is fine for boys to amass sexual experience, but unacceptable for girls to do the same thing (Willis 1977; Lees 1986). Empirical research provides abundant evidence of the persistence of a culture in which young men set the agenda for sexual activity and pleasure in a way that young women can not (Willis 1977; Wilson 1978; Griffin 1985; Lees 1986; Wallace 1987). It is clear from the research that sexual expression for women, in adolescent, and probably many adult, cultures, is possible only in some rule-bound and restricted patterns. Any transgression of these rules can bring unpleasant penalties to girls, from both boys and other girls. It is acceptable for girls to be sexually active only if they are in well-established and long-term relationships in which a high degree of commitment is publicly displayed. The other condition is that they should not have too many partners. 'Women's sexuality is rendered safe only when confined to the bonds of marriage or wrapped in the aura of "love"' (Lees 1986: 28).

It rapidly became clear that in all five schools we studied the double standard for sexual culture was alive and well. Our data support the view of adolescent sexuality discussed in the research literature on the double standard. Here we present only a brief account of our observations.

At Ferryfield School, a PSE teacher encouraged pupils to discuss their attitudes to the double standard. He read out a statement and asked pupils to respond to it:

Teacher	Teenage boys get a good reputation if they are sexually active and have lots of girlfriends, but girls get a bad reputation if they do the same thing.
Sandra	If a girl does that – like especially when they're under-age – they do get a reputation, they're a bit slaggy and that.
Lee	(*Laughing*) Matthew knows a word to describe it.
Teacher	What is it Matthew?
Lee	(*To Matthew, who is giggling*) Go on say it.
Matthew	'Lucky bastard' is what the bloke would be called.
Sandra	I think it is more important for a girl than it is for a boy.
Gilly	You're just going back to that 'different for girls and boys' thing again.
Sandra	Yes, but you just get back to that slag thing.

The double standard in adolescent culture has messages for both male and female behaviour. Sexuality is a key aspect in the 'performance' of gender. For *men*, the demand is that they be sexually active and sexually successful: 'It is through their sexuality that men are expected to prove themselves' (Lees 1993: 132). To achieve hegemonic masculine status men are under pressure to respond sexually and to amass sexual experience. Penalties can be attached to men who are unable to prove themselves in this way, as they are assigned a subordinate status in a group. Sexuality offers men also the most significant opportunity to create the feeling that they are *properly* masculine: 'It is against women's sexuality that men are motivated to measure their masculinity, and because they must prove this at each such encounter, their masculinity never rests assured' (Morgan 1992: 121).

For *girls*, the message is very different: research has made it clear that penalties attach to breaking the cultural constraints on sexual expression for girls. The penalties, according to Willis (1977), relate to 'getting a reputation' and being known as a 'tart' or 'slag'. Boys place girls in two categories, and while they are prepared to use 'slags' for casual sexual encounters, a stigma attaches to them which means the boys did not consider them *people* with whom they have relationships. The data from our study support Willis (1977) in indicating that the boys perceive girls to be one of two sorts: one is the kind you have as a 'girl-friend'; the other is a 'tart'. The language of adolescent culture has changed in the twenty years since Willis' research, but the values have not. In our research the boys made it clear that once a girl was known to be sexually active – what they termed a 'spunk trough', a 'skank' or 'a filthy muff' – they refused to view them as potential girlfriends.

In research undertaken by Lynda Measor with Peter Woods in the 1980s, interesting evidence of the importance of 'reputation' came to light. Some insight was gained into the extreme penalties that can attach to a complete loss of reputation. Donna, for example, was considered to have completely transgressed the limits, and her behaviour was seen by both boys and girls as inappropriately sexual. It was said that she had had a large number of casual sexual partners, and that she had fallen pregnant and had an abortion in her first year at secondary school. Donna became a victim of sexual harassment and abuse once this reputation was fully established. At a local disco, a group of boys surrounded her and removed almost all the clothes she wore. This was widely discussed in the school, which further sullied her reputation. At the end of the summer term a group of boys took Donna to a lonely part of the school grounds after school hours and subjected her to sexual abuse. It was brought to an end by the surprise arrival of a teacher (Measor and Woods 1984).

In adolescent culture, sexual reputation is of considerable importance. Male and female adolescents stand in different relations to sexual responsibility and expression. Reputation for women is based on sexual abstinence, while for males it is based on sexual profligacy or, more accurately, the possession of 'experience': 'In journeying into adult sexuality, young women seemed to be under pressure to safeguard their reputations, young men under pressure to demonstrate theirs' (Holland *et al.* 1992: 239). In sexual contexts where the woman is the object of male desire, masculinity consists in making a conquest.

It is not only behaviour that is seen to be at issue: notions of male and female sexual desire are constructed differently. 'Masculine desire is constructed around a sexual object that is attractive because it is untouched, discardable once consumed' (Lees 1986: 108). Lees suggests that girls who are thought to have had a number of partners are placed in a category that is to be avoided by boys: 'At least the girls we go out with ain't second hand' (ibid.: 96). Lees argues that once a girl is known to have had a number of sexual partners 'the language of consumer society emerges, [and] it cheapens a girl if she sleeps with a boy'. Girls bodies are seen as commodities: 'the value of them depends on their attractiveness but also on their purity' (ibid.: 46).

Female desire, by contrast, is built around a sexual object valued in part for its experience and presumed expertise. The romantic novelist Barbara Cartland expressed this value: 'A man should not be a virgin on his wedding night. You want one person who knows what he is doing.' Sexuality is therefore defined as distinctively different for boys and for girls, and it is a key element in defining gender identity.

Female reputation is based on the practice of restraint, and femininity is indicated by abstinence from sexual encounters, by displaying strict levels of personal control. It is also possible that such a *proper* femininity is based on a lack of desire, which makes this restrained sexual behaviour a simple matter for girls. It seems that we can observe male attempts to intervene in female sexuality in some complex ways, by defining not only how it should be expressed but actually how it should be experienced. Male reputation, on the other hand, is based on the practice of an actively expressed sexuality: masculinity is indicated by conquest, which itself is indicative of a high level of sexual desire. The binary divide, which according to Davies (1997) characterises gender, requires opposing behaviour (activity–passivity).

Male Pressure and Sexual Encounters

This style of masculinity, which values sexual conquest highly, seems to mean boys having to put pressure on girls to become sexually involved with them, and this can prove very difficult for young women to resist. Research conducted with large national samples indicates that this is a common problem throughout Britain.[1]

We have commented on the sexualised informal adolescent culture characteristic of the schools we studied. One element of this culture was pressure to have sexual relationships. At Ferryfield School, Year 9 girls discussed the issue in a focus group. Alice was the only girl to query the force of this pressure:

Alice   Well, it depends. If you are a weak person, then you could be influenced into it by what other people say.

The remainder of the group agreed that there was significant pressure, although some of them did not approve of it.

Julie   Now, when you get to 16, if you've not had sex, it's like a shock to some people.

Katie   A friend in my class came up to me and said that someone else had said: 'Well if you haven't had sex by the time you are 16 then you're chicken.'

The other girls stressed that the pressure on them to have sex from boys with whom they were involved was the real difficulty.

Lynn   But it also depends on the pressure as well – there are different types of pressure. There's jokey pressure and there's hard-sell pressure. If you're out somewhere and all your friends are talking about it, well that's one thing. It depends where the pressure is coming from. If it's coming from a boyfriend, then it is usually a lot harder to cope with.

The girls here point to the difficult and contradictory issues confronting them. They discuss the pressures that come from their peer group, from other girls and from boys with whom they are involved to be sexually active, and the difficulties of dealing with this. The girls reflected on what the issues were:

Lucy   The peer pressure can be so difficult, and it's also about confidence – how to stand up for how you feel, to have sex when you are ready for it.

Katie   Saying 'No' to sex, that is the most difficult thing to do.

A number of issues arise from these comments. Girls mention pressure from boyfriends to enter into sexual relationships with them, and they define it as difficult to deal with. They itemise the issues of confidence and assertiveness, and state that behaving in ways that exemplify both qualities is a most difficult thing to do. Feminist research has pointed to the contradictory situation in which young women find themselves in heterosexual encounters. Matthews (1992) argues that gender codes for girls lay down an obligation that they should not be assertive; nor should they initiate sexual interactions. Yet they are supposed to be able to say 'No' in the face of considerable male pressure. We examine this issue in more detail in the final chapter, which discusses the policy implications of the data.

A number of writers on sex education who have considered these issues have assumed that the problem is one of a lack either of confidence or of communication skills, making it difficult for young girls to be assertive (Lenderyou and Porter 1994). Matthews instead demands that we look at those social and structural characteristics of our culture that 'place women in a powerless position' (1992: 25). Feminist work points to the power that men, even young men, have in these situations. This derives from the power they have to define female sexuality, female reputation and what counts as being a *proper* girl. Adolescent informal cultures lay down a number of obligations for ways of feeling and behaving sexually. The implications of this culture for the construction of sex education policy will be discussed later, but the implications for gender codes are important as well. The culture, Matthews suggests, presents itself as 'the truth of femininity as well as the truth of sex'. By following the blueprint given to girls by their informal culture, by exercising restraint and indicating an absence of desire, girls come to feel that they are moving into adult femininity. 'There are no other available obliging relations which call her into adult femininity' (Matthews 1992: 28).

Morgan extends the argument about the nature of *gender performance*: 'Masculinity is not about the possession or non-possession of certain traits. It is the maintenance of certain kinds of relationships between men and women and between men and men' (Morgan 1992: 67). This draws attention, in our view, to some of the crucial aspects of gender identity. Both genders inhabit the same social world and do not develop clear boundaries in isolation, one from the other: rather, male and female are defined in terms of an antithesis, an opposing couple in a force field.

Gender identity and gender characteristics are assembled from resources which come into play as a result of social interaction. Each gender needs the other to contrive and illuminate the distinctions between them. We have 'a binary code of masculinity and femininity' (Giddens 1992: 190). Femininity comes into sharp focus only when set against masculinity. Masculinity is defined in a sharper silhouette against femininity. The two categories make sense only when defined together: one core element of being a man is that that individual is not a woman; and vice versa. 'A sense of being a man or less than a man comes to the fore in relation to women. Being typically feminine for example does not make sense except in a heterosexual relationship to its binary opposite the "masculine"' (Morgan 1992:. 41). Sexuality is at the centre of the processes involved in constructing and 'doing' gender in the way we discussed at the beginning of this chapter. Connell and Dowsett, for example, argue: 'Sexual power is the key to masculine control over every sphere of life' (1992: 81).

Female Sexuality

There are implications for gender identity in this kind of research, but there are in addition implications for sexuality, and we focus now on female sexuality. What is interesting about the data we have presented on the double standard and male pressure is that the girls at no point acknowledge the pressure of their own sexual desire in the situations they face. They are silent about whether they equally want the sexual experience into which they say boys are pressing them. The girls are willing to discuss *male* pressure and *peer* pressure to have sex, but throughout all of the data we can discern what Fine has called the 'missing discourse of female desire' (Fine 1988).

An important piece of empirical research into adolescent sexuality has been published since our data were collected. Its conclusions on the 'missing discourse of desire' connect with our research. The WRAP research (Holland *et al.* 1998) looked at the nature of adolescent sexuality in the context of HIV/AIDS and studied 496 young women in Manchester and London. The research suggested that young women in Britain in the 1990s have little language to discuss their own sexual feelings, and express little sense of their own sexuality:

> We were struck by the limits of pleasure and the absence of female desire in the young women's accounts of their sexuality. Achieving femininity is constructed in relation to masculine desires in ways that subvert young women's control over their bodies.
>
> (Holland *et al.* 1991: 240)

It is important to understand some of the reasons for this 'absence' of female desire. Given what we have said about the nature of adolescent culture, there are good reasons why this should be so. Adolescent girls operate within the confines of the double standard which indicates that female sexuality should be restrained in its expression. We have indicated something of the problems and penalties which can confront girls who express their sexuality.

We collected other data that may offer insights into the way this situation comes about. These concern the development of male and female sexuality in adolescence, and offer some understanding of the sources of the 'missing discourse of desire'. At the heart of this matter are data on boys and masturbation. In all of the schools we researched, we heard constant jokes and comments about 'wanking', 'tossing' and 'tossing off' – from boys. We heard no comments on the topic from girls. At Tonford, for example, we observed a lesson with Year

9 pupils which focused on *Just Seventeen* magazine. A group of boys opened the magazine and said: 'Let's turn to the bit about wanking and read that.' On another occasion, in the middle of a lesson on contraception a group of boys began to joke: 'You can beat an urge but you can't beat a wank.'

We know very little about adolescent male masturbation, although a number of researchers have suggested its importance, and there is a wealth of fictional literature alerting us to its centrality in the life of male adolescents, of which *Portnoy's Complaint* is perhaps the best-known example (Roth 1971). Gagnon and Simon (1973: 13) argued: 'A detached, discreetly managed male sexuality is learnt through masturbation-centred childhood and adolescent games, which focus the male sense of sexual feelings or desire in the penis, giving the genitals centrality.' As a result of these practices, boys learn about their own bodies and have detailed knowledge of the nature and pattern of their own physical and sexual responses.

Kinsey's research supports Gagnon and Simon's view that masturbation plays an important role in male adolescence, and adds to our knowledge about the issue. He reported that observation of older boys masturbating was common for boys prior to their own masturbatory experiences. Other research agrees with this view: 'Most knowledge about masturbation for boys comes from their peer group' (Moore and Rosenthal 1993: 4). The suggestion is that boys share a culture of masturbation, and that in groups boys learn about ways to masturbate. They therefore share a culture of knowledge about physical strategies for ensuring their own sexual satisfaction. Their own sexual responses are known to them and they understand something of the nature of their own desires. It is important to note that this is an area about which we know very little, and, about which it is, we suggest, difficult for female researchers to collect data. It needs male researchers to develop our knowledge of the area.

The other issue which is significant for our purposes is that this behaviour belongs to boys and to groups of boys. It is gender-specific, and it seems to be the case that girls do not have a similar culture. We never heard any girls speak in a similar way in any of the schools we researched, and there is no supporting research evidence to suggest that girls have a similar shared culture of learning about their own responses, or their own bodily reactions, desires or needs. By contrast, there is evidence that within adolescent informal culture there is a tightly constrained register of pleasure for women, and a code that denied much sexual feeling to 'respectable' women. One implication of this code of sexual restraint for women is that it affects not only the expression of their sexuality but actually their experience of it.

These different experiences of learning about sexuality are not surprising given some of the cultural codes in adolescence. The double standard locates the site of female sexuality and desire in the 'slag', and defines and denotes it as bad. It means that only 'bad' women, females who do not behave as *proper* women, feel much sexual desire. Images of women are split into the innocent and the guilty, the virgin and the whore, the wife and the mistress. Only the latter in each pairing is supposed to be guilty of sexuality (Lees 1986: 131). Female sexuality is still located to some extent in the 'other', who is a marginalised outsider to the society. Women who would be non-slags therefore must restrain their sexual activities, but also should reserve their feelings and reactions; they should not really feel sexual. The double standard and the creation of the 'slag' category therefore are involved with the suppression of an overt sexuality in girls, and the way they experience sexual desire is constrained by assumptions that are made about the nature of male and female sexuality.

There are definitions of human sexuality implicit in the adolescent informal culture, and they indicate a subordinate role for female sexuality, in comparison to male sexuality. Adolescent girls in the 1990s in Britain still express traditional views about sexuality and femininity; there is little evidence of real female sexual autonomy: they retain a 'masculinised' sense of sexuality. Feminist theory has argued that sexuality is 'masculinised' in that it is defined by men in ways that prioritise male sexuality and sexual pleasure, and for 'respectable' women includes no discourse of female desire. It is worth developing a grasp of some of the central arguments here, as they have policy implications as well as significance for our understanding of adolescent sexual culture.

Masculinised sexuality makes female sexuality invisible, and it is important to note that it makes it invisible not only to men but to women themselves. It means that women traditionally give pleasure rather than receive it. As Macintosh wryly comments: 'It seems that innately women have sexual attractiveness, men have sexual urges' (1978: 54). In this blueprint, women's own sexuality gets lost – for both men and women. Mackinnon comments: 'Sexuality is to feminism what work is to Marxism, that which is most one's own and yet most taken away' (cited in Hearn 1987: 19). Delphy traces the implications of this for sexual behaviour and expression in saying: 'Women discipline their own bodies and pleasure to suit men in ways their partners are unlikely even to be aware of. In doing so, they concede to men's definitions of what is pleasurable' (1993: 3).

A process of fundamental *alienation* takes place where women lose touch with their own physically and emotionally felt responses. Recent French theoretical work has also developed these ideas. Irigaray, for example, writes of the effects of these processes for women:

> Such pleasure is above all a masculine prostitution of her body to a desire which is not her own, and which leaves her in a familiar state of dependency upon man. Not knowing what she wants, ready for anything, even asking for more, so long as he will 'take' her as his 'object' when he seeks his own pleasure.
>
> (1985: 88)

The WRAP research team found girls expressing such 'masculinised' versions of sex. They discovered that young women were not confident about taking part in a discussion which emphasised the physicality of sex. Rich (1979) and Theweleit (1987) have argued that it is male desire which is signified in the 'I' of western culture, and this is clearly in evidence in the data collected from these young women. The girls had no specific set of desires of their own, but were able to talk about sex only from a male perspective. We have in adolescent informal culture no 'scripts' for active or indeed overwhelming female desire. We want to suggest that when young women discover in relationships the strength of their own sexual desire, they are not well prepared to accept it. It confounds their ability to make good quality decisions for themselves about what they want from relationships. It also has implications for their abilities to deal with issues of contraception and safer sex practices, issues dealt with in detail in the final chapter.

Conclusion

In the last three chapters, we have presented data which reveal something of the values that persist in adolescent informal culture in relation to what counts as *proper* behaviour for male and female. Appearance is important; having the right body image is crucial; and possession of knowledge is also of great significance. Sexual behaviour, however, is the key component, and female sexual behaviour is formed in the context of adolescent male views of what counts as appropriate, and indeed as 'right'. In summary, we can conclude that the ways in which sexuality and gender are constructed in adolescent culture mean that there is pressure on young males to make 'conquests' and to develop sexual experience. It is an essential element in gender work and in establishing identity as masculine. The same culture confronts young women with a difficult double message. On the one hand there is a demand for abstinence in order to establish an appropriate reputation as a 'nice' girl. On the other hand the same girls confront pressure from boys with whom they may feel emotionally connected, and we suggest that it is important to emphasise the pressure they face of their own desire to be sexually active. The codes for behaviour which are laid down in the adolescent informal culture place very severe pressure on young people. It is in this context that sex education programmes must operate.

There are of course other discourses in our society relating to sexuality and appearance and knowledge, but the evidence of this data is that they do not permeate the informal culture that characterises the early years of adolescence. Young people embarking on their first sexual experience must travel into unknown territory guided by what they have already absorbed of masculinity and femininity. The territory is unknown because of adult abdication of the responsibility to provide maps and signposts to young people. There are complex reasons for this that are not dealt with in this book, which is focused on adolescents, but we consider it important to indicate some of the implications for young people. The actively desiring woman, the woman luxuriating in extravagant sexuality, the woman seeking out men for her own sexual pleasure, is constituted as a wholly negative subject, and these are some of the dominant images with which young adolescents grow up.

Note

1   There was clear evidence of this male pressure resulting in girls becoming sexually involved before they really felt ready to do so. Research conducted with large national samples suggests that this is a common situation, and it is the case, for girls at least, that early sexual experience is more likely to be associated with regret. The younger the age at which intercourse first occurs the higher the percentage of girls who feel that they had sex too soon. It is crucial, however, that we take account of gender in this context. In a survey (Wellings *et al.* 1994) of people who had their first sexual experience before the age of 16, it was found that over half of the women felt regret, whereas only one-quarter of the men did. Qualitative data suggests that young men are more likely than young women to perceive their first sexual experiences as positive (Thomson and Scott 1991). This may relate to the fact that for men there are cultural pressures that prohibit expression of dissatisfaction or disappointment.

8   The Failings of School Sex Education

'Teachers Tried to Avoid and Slip Over It'

Introduction

In this chapter we consider pupils' views of the failings of their sex education programmes. They expressed resentment about a number of issues. Pupils had a strong sense that school programmes had failed to offer them sufficient explicit information. They felt also that sex education had failed to offer help with problems they encountered which they found most difficult to handle on their own. These often related to conflict between the sexes. We look first at the question of information, and then go on to consider issues relating to gender. A persistent theme in this analysis is the request from adolescents for help and support from trusted adults.

Information – 'What Adults Didn't Tell Us'

Innovative sex education programmes had been developed by the schools we researched. All had taken steps to ensure that pupils were given unambiguous information about reproduction, conception, contraception and sexually transmitted diseases. This nevertheless failed to satisfy pupils' perceptions of what they needed, as we have indicated in earlier chapters. While pupils welcomed the explicit and open approach to work on contraceptives and STDs, they perceived a number of gaps in their sex education in other areas – and this provoked the repeated criticism: 'I thought there could have been more information.'

Pupils considered that information was lacking in two main areas. The first relates to emotional content: 'They talked about what would happen to your body, not about your emotions.' The second complaint concerns the lack of explicit information on a wide range of topics: 'I thought it wasn't really good enough for information about sex, oral sex, gays, bisexual people, etc.' Young people were critical that sex education did not deal directly with sex and with the experience of sexuality. It failed to give them explicit information about a number of topics and did not discuss alternative sexual orientations.

Including Emotions

One of the main areas of criticism we encountered in school sex education programmes related to the lack of time devoted to discussing emotional aspects of sexuality. We collected data on this topic across all five of the schools we researched. Gender, unsurprisingly, had a strong effect on this issue. It was, almost without exception, the girls who complained about the lack of attention given to emotional issues. The sex education programmes presented by health professionals came in for particular criticism in this connection.

At Streamham, pupils objected to the clinical way in which information was presented to them. School sex education for some girls was, according to one, 'poor because they taught you about the parts that made the baby and that, but not the emotional side of sex'. Another girl said: 'It's all about contraception, and no emotions, etc.' At Gainton the complaint was: 'There was no chance to talk about the feelings' side, it's all just the biology and the facts, and about what goes where, and that.' At Tonford, female pupils commented: 'They need to go into the emotional side of a sexual relationship, and not just the physical, if they are going to teach it.' And again: 'I think emotions and feelings about sex should be taught, and not so much of the facts.'

It is important to emphasise that the majority of boys in the study did not comment on the fact that emotional issues had been ignored in their sex education programmes. There were a very small number of boys who agreed with the girls' views on this matter. One boy from Streamham commented on his school sex education: 'It is alright in that it shows all the equipment, but it doesn't tell you how to have good relationships.' Another boy from Gainton said: 'It's too factual, not enough depth into feelings.' We emphasise, however, that there were very few comments of this kind from boys.

The sex education literature has, for a number of years, indicated that complaints from female pupils about the lack of discussion of emotions are widespread (Lenskyj 1990; Buchanan and Ten Brinke 1996). Girls in the recent Buchanan and Ten Brinke survey said that in sex education the exploration of emotional relationships is treated like 'a well kept secret' (1996: 26).

This lack of information from school sources left young people with a number of difficulties. Girls from Gainton recognised this when they said: 'People write in to *Just Seventeen* with problems that they haven't really been taught about at school.' Adolescents recognise that exploring the world of sexuality is complex, and can be fraught with difficulties, and ask for help from those adults they trust. Adolescents do not seek to exclude adults, at least trusted adults, from their world. The health professionals' programmes were highly regarded for their ability to offer up-to-date information about contraception and STDs. They faced criticism, however, for their lack of attention to emotional issues. This links back to the point we made in Chapter 7 about adults abdicating responsibility for tackling all of the issues relating to sexuality.

There was evidence that pupils considered some, although by no means all, teachers better prepared than the health professionals to provide effective input about emotional issues in sex education. The PSE departments at Whitefarm and Tonford Schools had put considerable resources and effort into developing programmes that dealt with a range of emotional topics relevant to adolescents. We will return to this issue in a later section of this chapter. At this point, it is worth stating that in these two schools where pupils had *expert* PSE teaching, the complaint about lack of emotional content was encountered less frequently. Whitefarm pupils made such comments as: 'I think it is good'; and 'PSE gives you some emotional ideas, which biology doesn't'. At Tonford School the PSE staff worked closely with the health professionals. After the health professionals' visits, the teachers extended the work into areas of emotion, and pupils welcomed this:

> I definitely would not ask a question in there, with the visitors. PSE is a more relaxed environment and you are all in the same boat. Anything you aren't sure of gets confirmed in there.

This model seemed to be the most effective of those studied, and gained higher levels of pupil approval than did the others.

Including Sexuality in Sex Education

In Chapter 1 we discussed the picture of sexuality presented in sex education programmes, and identified this as an area of controversy. Jackson, for example, argues: 'What passes for sex education is in fact education about reproduction rather than sex education and is rarely about sexuality in its broader sense' (1982: 22). Pupils in all of the schools we researched echoed these criticisms. They complained that their sex education had not included any explicit discussion of sex or sexuality. At Streamham pupils said:

Janie	They never actually talk about sex. Some teachers will only talk about contraception, AIDS and STDs, and never actually talk about sex.
Ken	If a teacher isn't straight enough to talk about sex, then they should not teach you the subject. I think some teachers shouldn't teach this subject.
Matt	It's not been very good, until Year 10 teachers tried to avoid and slip over it.

Sex education programmes run by both teachers and health professionals at Gainton and Tonford gained praise for many aspects of their work, but did not escape pupils' criticism on sexual content. A typical comment was: 'I do not think we had enough information about sex. Contraception – yes, and that's about it.' There seem to be a number of different aspects to the complaints. The sex education programmes failed to present sufficiently detailed information about the experience of sexual feelings and desire, especially for women; and pupils complained that the information they were offered was neither detailed nor explicit enough about the full range of sexual behaviours.

A discourse of Desire

Fine (1988: 3) argued that within sex education there is no 'discourse of desire'. She suggests that we need to observe the contexts in which messages about sex education are given, and listen to what *is* said in them, but also to what is *not* said, and to observe the silences very carefully. In this way we can start to build up a picture of what is defined within the school setting to be safe, good and even sacred and what is positioned as taboo, bad and dangerous in relation to sexuality. There is, Fine points out, a silence about desire in general and female desire in particular. In Chapter 1 we pointed out that sex education which excludes any mention of desire is in marked contrast to the other discourses relating to sexuality in modern industrialised society.

Female Sexuality

Fine argues that female desire and sexuality find no place in school sex education; school sex education is silent on the subject of *female* desire. It transmits a number of messages about the dangers of desire for women: sexual activity, and hence sexual feeling, is seen to have a number of potentially bad consequences for women. Pregnancy, abortion, STDs, and social and economic vulnerability are some of the main 'dangers' spelt out. Fine states that in the American school sex education programmes she studied the message is clear: that the only safe way of expressing desire for women is in married, and of course, heterosexual relationships. We have already discussed (Chapter 7) the feminist claim that in our society sexuality is 'masculinised', and have pointed out that there are few clear models of female sexuality.

We found that young people expressed resentment about the lack of information about and assistance in such matters. We interviewed a group of 17-year-old pupils at Streamham School, who looked back on the sex education they had been offered earlier in their school careers. They considered they had 'needed more information about the actual feelings of desire and lust.' They were critical of sex education's silence over the powerful feelings that accompanied sexual activity. Pupils had been surprised by 'the number of feelings you experience, such as "[being] scared", "insecurity", "[being] unsure of things". Neither the discourse of sexuality in the media nor sex education had offered effective preparation. Younger pupils also spoke, perhaps less clearly, about the lack of discussion of the 'really intimate things', which had left them wanting more. A girl from Year 9 at Ferryfield School said that the sex education provided was 'OK, but it could be more personal. My school is quite open, but it never discusses very intimate things. We discuss contraception, but not sex.'

Danger and Desire

In the crisis-based response to HIV/AIDS a discourse developed that for boys links desire with danger. It was clearly present in the sex education programmes we studied. For boys, the message is that desire is now inextricably mixed with danger. The dangers of contracting HIV/AIDS were graphically spelt out to adolescents. In Chapter 3 we presented data indicating that pupils welcomed this information. On the one hand pupils were pleased that they had been given explicit and relevant information about sexual matters that affected them. On the other boys had to recognise the dangers of a free and untrammelled play of desire:

> You'll have to be careful now you know you can get AIDS.

> The thing I disliked most was knowing it's not impossible to get AIDS.

> Just thinking about it and worrying about it, if I ever get these diseases, because I need a life.

There were indications that for some of the boys the new messages produced the beginnings of resentment. A 14-year-old boy from Streamham said:

> All they ever do is talk about the dangers of sex and that, and nothing about the pleasure.

Boys from Whitefarm commented:

> It's alright but all we get to know are the dangers.

> They tell us about the danger, never the love and enjoyment.

Boys from Tonford were resentful that sex educators 'never talked about the love and enjoyment – what is nice about sex'.

This link between desire and personal danger is a new one for males in our society. It positions males in new, unfamiliar and unwelcome ways in relation to their sexuality and sexual behaviour. The message contravenes a number of other messages with which males are more familiar, and which position them in a way they prefer.

Including Explicit Information

The lack of direct and explicit information about sexual practices also provoked pupil resentment. In Chapter 5 we discussed boys' negative reactions to the sex education programmes. They objected that sex education failed to offer them information that was explicit enough, and explained that they turned to pornography in order to obtain this information. We want to pursue this theme in the light of other data we collected. Pupils made it clear that they resented the lack of 'nitty gritty' information about sexual behaviour. At Streamham, pupils commented:

> We were only told what to use not how to do it.

> We weren't told what to do when having sex. We don't know about these things.

We collected responses from both boys and girls which indicated their feeling that the sex education had not been anything like explicit enough.

A Variety of Sexual Behaviour

The main problem concerned what pupils considered a narrow definition of sexuality – as intercourse. Pupils felt that sex education programmes had not dealt with a wide enough variety of sexual behaviours and, as a result, had not met their needs. This criticism related partly to same-sex sexuality, but pupils also wanted more information about the range of heterosexual behaviours.

Homosexuality

A small number of pupils requested that school sex education should deal more directly with homosexuality. They wanted discussion about sexual orientation that would develop understanding and tolerance:

> Understanding that being homosexual is OK, and things in reality, instead of always being so scientific.

> I also think that homosexuality should be taught and not banned because of the legal age which is 21, and then we will be able to understand more about homosexuals and their feelings, and not to treat them different.

Individual teachers explained the nature of government legislation on this topic. They discussed why they considered Section 28 limited their ability to discuss the issues. Young people expressed considerable resentment about the legislation and judged its prohibitions to be unreasonable. Some pupils identified the issue of sexual orientation as important and were critical of sex education programmes that failed to include information on the matter. We must acknowledge, however, that within the secondary school contexts we witnessed a substantial amount of homophobic behaviour, mostly among boys. Jokes were frequently made about homosexuality, and epithets like 'puff' and 'poufter' were routinely used as terms of abuse. Tolerant attitudes were not noticeably widespread among pupils.

Heterosexual Behaviour

Pupils considered also that their sex education had not dealt in enough detail with the range of heterosexual behaviour. Pupils at Ferryfield requested more discussion 'about the sexual activities leading up to sex'.

Data on this issue were collected at all of the schools we researched, and it seemed to be an important issue for adolescents. A pupil at Whitefarm School commented that they needed information on 'different ways of having sex'. Some pupils expressed a wish for information on sexual practices 'other' than sexual intercourse, and specifically asked for information on oral sex: 'Teachers teach enough about normal sex. They should go into things like oral sex.'

One girl at Streamham School made it clear why the topic was of interest to her as an adolescent experimenting with sexuality:

> The session was quite interesting, but she didn't really say anything about oral sex, and maybe people want to have oral sex with their partners but are not ready to have sex.

Pupils wanted information about ways of interacting sexually that could be exciting and even satisfying, but which stopped short of intercourse. This girl asked for more information about sexual practices which are alternatives to traditional heterosexual intercourse. It is possible that she had been influenced by discourses around 'safer sex' and that oral sex was categorised in her mind as one of the safer sex practices.

Issues that Were Avoided – 'They Dropped the Subject'

Young people were resentful that their sex educators were unwilling to meet their requests in this context. In data collected from all five schools, there was evidence of pupils feeling negative about teachers and health professionals who would not 'answer questions fully'. There was resentment when sex educators 'always changed the subject when difficult questions came up'. Objections came from both boys and girls:

> It was good, but not really detailed. They told you but then dropped the subject.

> She was not very helpful. She did not answer my question properly.

> I thought it was very helpful and interesting, but they didn't take some of the questions pupils said seriously.

> They pushed some questions aside.

> She was very brief in her answers.

The pupils made accurate observations about the sex educators in their written evaluations. The questions that were 'dropped' always seemed to relate to oral sex. We observed a sex education session conducted by a family planning doctor at Streamham School. The doctor was very open and willing to answer questions; she joked with pupils and showed little embarrassment. What follows is taken from field notes on a question-and-answer session.

Pupils had written anonymous questions, to which the doctor gave answers; pupils then asked supplementary questions. The doctor read out the question 'Are flavoured condoms safe?' There was laughter around the room, which the doctor joined in before replying: 'All condoms are safe if they have the kitemark.' She reached into her bag and fished out a couple of condoms:

Doctor	What flavours have I got here?
John	Have you got strawberry?
Doctor	Um, no. Only minty!
Dan	Can you get thrush from them?
Doctor	No, that shouldn't happen.
Mark	Yes, but why do they make flavoured condoms? Aren't they just for oral sex?
Doctor	(*Ignoring the question*) Does everyone know what Thrush is?

A very similar situation arose in a sex education lesson at Whitefarm School. The lesson dealt with contraception, and the teacher was discussing condoms:

Peter	We did a condom test once to see how strong it was.
Jill	You can have flavoured ones.
Diane	And different coloured ones. On the pack it says that they're only for vaginal sex, and then why are they flavoured?

Again her question was ignored.

Pupils were angry with the lack of response they had from adults on the matter of oral sex: 'Teachers should be ready for pupils asking about sex and oral sex.' Some other girls reflected the same viewpoint: 'Yes, I think they should be prepared to take questions seriously and not ignore them because they thought it was silly. I think they should talk more about oral sex, e.g. "69", etc.' The adolescents made the point that as they were already sexually active, in their view they needed information that related to the sexual experimenting in which at least some of them were engaged:

Julie	They should take all the pupils' questions seriously, however funny they seem, because they are serious and teach pupils how to do oral sex, e.g. playing with each other's parts.
Jim	Pupils might want to know how to do it, if they've done it wrong and why not to do it. These should be told by an experienced person.

129

The pupils' response to the issue of safer sex practices was similar to their response to contraception: there was an assertion of their rights to make decisions about their sexuality, and a resentment of adults who shut their eyes to the realities of adolescent life. One pupil said:

> What these teachers don't realise is that we need to know about safe sex, AIDS/HIV, contraception, etc. It's no good just scooting through the subject, because we need to know all the facts and figures.

The health professionals' programmes came in for the same criticisms as did other sex education provision in the schools we researched. One girl at Streamham pointed out:

> It was OK when the nurse came in, but she talked about what most of us know. She should have talked more about oral sex.

The session done by the health professional at Gainton was appraised by one pupil thus: 'The lesson was good, and she answered any questions we had, but she should've talked about oral sex.' We have already suggested that pupils approved of sex education that offered information that was new to them. In this context, the information fell into the too little, too late category and met with disapproval from adolescents. Pupils endorsed sex education that gave access to the information they wanted, and offered that information explicitly and openly. Whenever sex educators close down that access, adolescent objections begin.

We need to raise a number of questions about these data and how we are to interpret them. It is possible to dismiss all such comments as simply attempts to embarrass those leading the sessions. The data relating to oral sex were collected not long after the media had focused attention on the school nurse in Leeds who had answered the questions about 'Mars Bar Parties' asked by 9-year-old boys in a school sex education lesson. The issue of oral sex as a topic for classroom sex education had received an enormous amount of media attention at this point, and pupils knew their power to create disruption for sex educators, and may have been tempted to use it. We cannot know really what the motivation for these requests from pupils was, or even if they are genuine requests for information or simply evidence of a wish to embarrass health professionals and teachers.

Research suggests that young people are engaging in a wider variety of sexual behaviours than before with more partners. The practice of oral sex is now widespread among adolescents. 33 per cent of British adolescents reported they would engage in oral sex outside of a steady relationship (Ford and Morgan 1989). When 18-year-olds were asked the same question, 46 per cent of boys and 28 per cent of girls stated they had engaged in oral sex with a casual partner, 56 per cent and 50 per cent with a steady partner. Some of the professionals we researched were fully aware of the issue, and recognised its importance to adolescents. One of the HIV/AIDS advisors stated: 'Kids talk about oral sex all the time.' In other research one of the present authors completed in 1996 and 1997, evidence was found to back up what the HIV/AIDS advisor said: 'Patterns of sexual activity seem to be changing. Young people's attitudes toward oral sex seem to have shifted dramatically in the last ten or fifteen years' (Measor and Squires forthcoming). For example, in interview one girl commented:

> Well, you are much more likely to give someone a blow job than to have full-scale sex with them. It is something which has changed since your generation.

There is also evidence of gender differences making their way into this behaviour:

> Girls will do it for boys.

> Yeah, [girls] will admit to having given blokes a blow job.

> But it is much rarer for a girl to get a bloke to do it for her.

This is highly controversial, and once again we are aware that there will be adults reading pupils' comments and feeling very disturbed that young adolescents are discussing this issue. We considered it important to gain a grasp of their point of view, and to reflect it. This was the reality of adolescent discussion; the question of the appropriate adult response to it remains open.

School sex education dealt with contraception and with condom use; it therefore focused on a particular definition of 'safer sex' practice. We will discuss this issue in detail in the final chapter of the book. What is important is that the 'safer sex' practices that adolescents are being encouraged to adopt are not those they want. The messages from school sex education about the overwhelming importance of condom use in pupils' views paints only part of the picture of safer sex practices. School sex education messages are at variance with those received from elsewhere by this AIDS generation. In our treatment of the legislation, we discussed the conservative approach that has had a constraining impact on current sex education policies in schools. At the same time young people are hearing significantly less-restrictive messages about sexuality from HIV/AIDS campaigns. Both of these tendencies have been in circulation for some time, and young people have now picked up on them only to express the confusion created by hearing two different discourses.

Pupils talked about the gaps left in their knowledge as a result of the limitations of school sex education. Adolescents pick up information from a range of different sources. Young people are aware of the publicity given by the tabloid press to a range of sexual scandals involving well-known 'soap' series' actors and prominent political figures. In the Introduction we made the point that young people live in a highly sexualised culture. It is possible for adults to *wish* that young people were not exposed to this information, and suggest that adolescents *should* not be exposed to it, but the reality is that they are. They may well be left curious or anxious about the information they glean from the mass media, and this is an important issue for the agencies which have responsibility in respect of young people.

For those involved in sex education the question is complicated by media reactions. The tabloid press has pilloried the actions of a number of teachers and health professionals who have worked with under-age adolescents. Sex educators talked constantly, and entirely reasonably, of their anxiety to avoid a similar fate. We do not intend in this discussion to offer personal criticism of the actions of individual professionals caught in a very difficult quandary. Sex educators in the schools we researched faced situations in which pupils asked for information about safer sex practices, and in at least some of those cases the requests seemed to be genuine: it *was* information that was sought. This places an adult attempting to provide effective and responsive sex education for adolescents in a very difficult position. We have said that our objective in this book is to present the viewpoint of adolescents on the sex education they receive. At the heart of the issue is the fact that, as the evidence shows, young people know about such practices as oral sex. They have heard about it in the playground, from their peers and, if from nowhere else, the tabloid press. Nevertheless, they are not receiving from their schools the information and guidance to match their current knowledge, and perhaps their own experience.

We unearthed further evidence relating to the issue in another research project dealing with young people. It seemed that 'children' first heard about oral sex when they were 9 or 10 years of age (detailed in Measor and Squires forthcoming). We know that this is a controversial statement, and that many parents and sex educators will not be at ease with the idea that 'children' of this age have contact with this kind of information. We are not attempting to make a judgement on whether it is 'good' or 'bad' that children know about such matters. The problem facing sex educators is that children *do* know, and we need to make a considered response to this situation.

Media interest in the Leeds' 'Mars Bar Parties' incident began because parents objected to what the school nurse had said to their children about oral sex. It is possible to argue that parents need to be more in touch with what their children know and are discussing. The parents involved in Leeds might then have been less shocked that their children had raised the issue in school. We have already discussed research establishing that many parents choose not to offer their children, especially their sons, any sex education. The problem is how adults should respond to the mixture of knowledge, half-knowledge and confusion which is the hallmark of sexual information picked up in the playground. Another issue is adolescent exposure to information from the media. If parents are unhappy about the information their children glean from the printed media, then an effective strategy would begin by campaigning against the sensationalism characteristic of the tabloids and other gossip-sheets. A simpler strategy would be a refusal on the part of families to buy newspapers that publish such material.

There is evidence that adolescents already feel they know 'the basics', and that their request is for more advanced information. Many adolescents in our study had a level of sexual knowledge that would count as 'sophisticated'. This is perhaps inevitable given the publicity and propaganda surrounding the safer sex messages about HIV/AIDS:

> One of the striking effects of the HIV/AIDS epidemic is that by increasing public willingness to discuss homosexuality, it also allows permission to discuss sexuality in general.
>
> (Altman cited in Connell and Dowsett 1992: 32)

Our data shows pupils asserting their 'right' to information about alternative sexual practices, which they see as no different from their 'right' to information about intercourse, contraception or pregnancy. The values of at least some adolescents are out of step with those of the adults who teach them and plan their curriculum. There is a need for new government policies that will clear some of the confusion in the area of sex education.

Policy Implications

The policy implications are clear. Adolescents in our research requested that formal sex education programmes should deal more with the implications of sexualised cultures in the modern world. Much sex education has sought to discourage and prohibit sexual activity in adolescence, and has tended to focus on the negative outcomes of sexual activity to achieve this objective. It has linked desire with danger, especially for women and increasingly for men, in some of the discourses which have resulted from the HIV/AIDS campaigns. Sex education could usefully offer space for the kind of considered thinking that we discussed in Chapter 3. Personal and Social Education teaching is beginning to encourage pupils to look critically at some of the messages of a sexualised mass media. We observed effective work on advertising campaigns that use sex to sell, for example, a range of consumer goods. An escort through the 'carnal zone' that Roberts (1998) identified would be useful to young people living in a sexualised culture. A sexualised popular culture is not the only issue: there is also a need to tackle some of the pressures which arise from within adolescent informal culture too, an issue to which we now turn.

Gender Issues

The adolescents in our research were critical of their experience of sex education because they felt the schools had not dealt effectively with the gender issues that arose. Both boys and girls commented on this failing, although there were a greater number of issues for girls. Girls requested that teachers and health professionals should tackle a number of controversial topics related to gender. They objected strongly to the boys' behaviour in sex education lessons. Girls in all of the schools we studied asked for intervention to reduce the disruption to their learning, and the teasing and harassment to which they were exposed in the lessons. The girls' objections were not limited to boys' behaviour in the classrooms, but extended more generally into heterosexual relationships. Girls asked for adult help in finding ways to deal with some of the sexual tensions arising from adolescent informal culture. They specifically wanted to discuss the difficulties of dealing with the double standard and with the pressures boys placed on them to engage in sexual relationships.

Gender issues, too, were important to some of the boys in this research, although the gender issues for boys were rather different from those which affected girls. Boys did not seem to object to the girls' behaviour in sex education classes, or girls' ways of treating them in the same way. There is nevertheless a growing body of evidence to suggest that many boys are being poorly served by sex education programmes and that this is a real problem. In our view, some of the issues involved relate to gender.

The View from the Girls

Girls resented boys' behaviour in sex education programmes, and they requested teacher intervention to improve the situation. Girls frequently told us that they felt extremely uncomfortable in mixed sex education classes. We have described in detail (Chapters 5–7) the atmosphere in these mixed classes. Girls were acutely aware of the disruption that the boys caused to their sex education. Much of their comments showed a deep sense of offence and affront. They resented the boys' laughter and shouting, their stupid behaviour and their annoying and immature comments.

The girls also resented the way boys behaved towards them in sex education lessons. In mixed-sex lessons girls remained interested and engaged by the work, and very frustrated by the boys' disruptive actions. They were equally frustrated by the sex educators' inability to control and curb the disruptions – and their failure to tackle classroom issues of gender.

Gender Inequality and Teacher Intervention in Classrooms

Girls wanted teachers to intervene directly in some displays of male behaviour. We presented data in Chapters 6 and 7 relating to boys' jokes which had girls as their target. It was interesting that the teachers involved did not choose to challenge any of this behaviour towards the girls. Teachers did not confront boys about the jokes which focused on girls' bodies, appearance or sexuality. Girls objected strongly to the teasing. Occasionally they would try to retaliate by making jokes in response to those of the boys, but this was fairly rare. One girl at Ferryfield School raised the issue in a focus group. Kelly discussed the way 'boys really put the girls down'. She complained that 'teachers never really do anything about it', and she considered it important that they should do so. There are policy implications here for individual teachers about the extent to which it is important and useful for them to confront boys in such interactions with girls.

In Chapter 6, we presented data on the body and puberty, and indicated the gender differences in response to this work. Boys took a dominant role in these lessons and revealed their negative views of girls. The teacher involved did not question the boys' answers when the girls were asked to give descriptions of the feelings accompanying their bodily changes. Nor did she challenge the sexist language the boys used or discuss the fact that gender differences were so clear. Girls considered there was a case for doing so, and wished that teachers would intervene more firmly. It may be that the teacher in question knew very well the pupils she was working with, and knew that a challenge – for example, to the kind of language they used – would simply have ended the discussion. Pupils would no longer have been willing to open up and discuss the issues. The issue is not an easy one, even for an experienced teacher. There is a case for reflecting on appropriate ways of handling the difficulties that result from gender regimes in training programmes for sex educators.

Girls also asked for adult help in dealing with gender interactions outside of the classroom and the school context. One significant theme in the data relates to girls' views of the sexual situations in which they found themselves, and their perspectives on the power differentials that existed between them and their male counterparts. We were interested to find that many of the girls requested the support of adults, including their teachers, in handling these difficulties at this stage in their lives. Girls were resentful when they considered that teachers were failing to make effective interventions on their behalf, and they made a number of suggestions about what teachers could most effectively do.

The issue of the double standard and male pressure was particularly significant in their view. A girl at Ferryfield said:

> I wish we could do some work on other ways with relationships and how you feel in certain situations, like that idea of role play on dealing with pressure from boyfriends. That would be a good one.

At Streamham a similar feeling was expressed, by a female pupil:

> I wish they would talk more about peer pressure and confidence – how to stand up for how you feel, to have sex when you are ready for it.

When teachers did offer opportunities for work on this topic girls welcomed them. At Whitefarm two girls commented:

> I think it has been good and we've been able to talk freely about things like not to be pressured into having sex.

> I think it's been good to be told that we can say 'No' to sex because that is the most difficult thing to do.

Pupils did not reject the help and intervention of adults in this context: they actively wanted it, and made suggestions for ways the work could be extended. A pupil at Streamham suggested teachers should deal, for example, with how 'the effects of a sexual relationship are different for different people'. Another commented: 'I think they should have asked about how we feel about relationships we are going through.'

When adolescents discussed the PSE approach to sex education, where well-trained teachers dealt with issues found to be of real concern and difficulty in pupils' lives, then the help of adults was welcomed and appreciated. Advice on developing the skills of assertiveness and communication was recognised to be important and relevant.

It is also important to note that it was this area for which the health professionals' programmes gained most criticism. Pupils were aware that these programmes had not dealt with controversial gender issues. This underlines the importance of tightly integrating health professionals' programmes into the wider curriculum programmes of sex and health education in school. The Sex Education Forum recently published guidelines about effective sex education (Thomson and Scott 1992) pointing out that effective programmes share a number of characteristics: they focus on recognition of social influences; they address the pressures on young people, and include work to help them understand and negotiate those pressures.

Pupils consistently requested more help and more time on this area of their lives and experience. They wanted explicit, relevant work to be carried out which could address their current concerns. The data raise the more general matter of how sex educators can deal with issues of male power in theory and with boys in the classroom. Much of the writing on innovation in sex education that we have researched deals with the issues in purely liberal terms. Sex educators are encouraged to foster assertiveness in girls and to build their confidence. In dealing with boys, the advice is for educators to appeal to their rationality and sense of responsibility. 'Remember to talk about teenage fatherhood as well as teenage motherhood' (Biddulph 1998: 3). Woodcock stresses the importance of discussing issues of 'responsibility' with boys (1992: 521). The liberal approach includes no suggestion that boys need to be confronted or challenged about the pressure they exert on girls. It does not address the reality of the male hierarchy and issues of inequality in power between boys and girls in informal adolescent cultures. The liberal view does not fully acknowledge that any attempt to intervene to produce change will invariably imply conflict.

Policy Implications

Single-sex classes

The girls' experience of boys disrupting classes, teasing them and making it difficult to discuss issues involving gender inequality led girls in Gainton school to take action. They asked that the health professionals should talk to them in single-sex groups, a request that the (female) deputy-head granted. In other schools we saw girls making similar requests which teachers did not always grant, although Tonford experimented with the strategy. In Chapter 3 we presented data from the single-sex lessons that resulted. In that setting girls were able to find out what they needed to know, take the initiative in asking for information, and indicate their interest in having an identity as a sexual person. In mixed-sex classes they had considerable difficulty in doing any of these things. Adolescent informal rules about appropriate gender behaviour placed blockages on girls engaging in such activities, and boys policed any infringe-ments of the adolescent culture. For example, in Chapter 6 we looked at the difficulties girls faced when they discussed the reliability of different contracep-tives. Girls recognised the great difficulties in overcoming this informal culture, and opted for separate teaching.

There was clear evidence from our study that relationships between the sexes were not easy in the early years of secondary school. Research about informal pupil culture indicates that boys can, and do, make life difficult for girls. Girls are exposed to harassment and teasing by boys in relation to sexual issues (Clarricoates 1980; Spender and Sarah 1980; Stanworth 1981; Walkerdine 1981; Delamont 1990). The studies offer us a picture of the differential power relations which exist between the genders, and the ways they are acted out in the daily lives of some boys and girls. Our knowledge of this situation means that some of the taken-for-granted notions about it being a good idea to teach boys and girls together for sex education may need to be questioned (Measor 1989).

We argue that this information backs the case for providing at least some sex education work to single-sex classes, though we are aware that many sex educa-tors, both teachers and health professionals, are opposed to this.[1] Girls at Streamham and Tonford asked for single-sex work in sex education, but this was not offered to them. Research into the provision of single-sex work has made a number of issues clear to us in recent years. The work of Stanford High School in a single-sex setting for maths has made it clear that the best results in an academic subject are achieved by single-sex classes for the first two years of secondary school. In the later years co-educational learning provides better results. It is possible to argue that a similar structuring of sex education provision might work. We believe that there is a case for delivering sex education programmes to single-sex classes in the early years of secondary school, and that this case disappears later on in the pupil's career. This fits with the data we have on the topic from pupils. Up to the end of Year 9 and the beginning of Year 10, the majority of pupils welcomed the idea of single-sex lessons for sex education. However, after that point the majority seemed to want co-educational provision. One other option tried out at Streamham school in the years after this study was completed involved the development of 'gender days'. Teachers and youth workers suspended the Year 9 school curriculum for one day. They took groups of pupils into the youth work facility attached to Streamham School where they spent the day working on personal and health issues with pupils in single-sex groups. Their evaluations suggested that this option was popular with pupils.

Small-group teaching

Other strategies to tackle some of the gender issues involved in delivering sex education might include the use of small-group single-sex teaching. A number of the girls made the request that sex education in schools should be taught in small friendship single-sex groups. This was seen as an alternative if single-sex provision was not possible. One girl at Streamham commented

> It was OK, but difficult to ask questions in front of the whole class. I think that the nurse should've talked to girls and boys separately as I think the boys get embarrased and the girls can't talk openly.

A similar request came from Tonford: 'I wish they would make the lessons more confidential and let us work in friendship groups.'

A move towards sex education provision in small friendship groups might also help in the solution of problems arising from the issue of differentiation where there are within the same class young people at very different stages of maturity. Large classes can be split into smaller groups of pupils for teaching. If pupils are allowed to divide up on the basis of friendship, this might ensure that adolescents of similar levels of maturity cluster together. A teacher or health professional could then work with the smaller, more homogenous, group. Ingham has written about the advantages of this method (1994: 6). There are significant resource implications to providing larger numbers of qualified adults to work with the small groups. Ingham comments: 'A cost-effective way of presenting at least some of the curriculum in groups may be to use peripatetic advisors or youth workers' (1994: 6).

Girls stated their difficulties with boys in sex education classes. We had a commitment to recording pupil perspectives on sex education work. It is important we record their extreme discomfort, their embarrassment and sense of being involved in an activity they did not feel was quite right. As adults we would not tolerate being placed in such a position, and we consider that this question needs some consideration by sex educators. At the heart of this matter is the issue of the extent to which we should listen to young people in this context – or, more accurately, the extent to which we should listen to girls, and allow them to be the decision makers on this issue.

A number of researchers have sought to identify school strategies that best foster increased equality of opportunity on gender issues. Whyld (1983: 25), for example, has argued that sexism is more likely to be reduced in schools where there are organised groups of teachers committed to tackling gender issues, a sympathetic head and an awareness that eradicating gender issues is a priority. Girls are best placed to resist the range of pressures they find themselves under in schools where they have a sense that they can rely on a supportive teacher or more generally a supportive school context.

Whole-school policies

The teasing, jokes and physical harassment that we have documented in the schools we researched have a number of implications for classroom work and strategies, as well as addressing broader issues. Sexual harassment policies, for example, have a role to play. It is clear that while some schools have developed such policies, not all have done so. If we want to create change in adolescent sexual culture, we need to tackle routine daily behaviour between the genders. Whole-school policies which relate to equal opportunity issues need to be in place. We cannot focus policy efforts only on sex education. In fact any attempt to create effective sex education will involve a consideration of sexist behaviour in other areas in schools.

Lees argues that

> even more important than changes in the curriculum are changes in the social relations of the school. It is no use changing the curriculum if girls are being harassed and abused and rendered subordinate to boys in day to day interaction.
>
> (Lees 1986: 148)

The ethos of a school plays a major part in determining the quality of sex and personal relationships' education. A whole-school policy that recognises this can contribute to change (Thomson and Scott 1992: 8). The Sex Education Forum considers it important that the aims and objectives of a school's sex education policy relate to other school policies such as the equal opportunities policy (ibid.: 7).

Boys and Sex Education

We said earlier that gender issues are important also to some boys in sex education programmes. Boys did not seem to object to the girls' activities or reactions in sex education classes in the way that the girls did to the boys' behaviour. They did not ask for girls to be excluded from sex education programmes, or see any advantages to single-sex teaching. Neither did boys ask for any adult help or intervention in the way that girls did. Nevertheless, by their disruptive activity in sex education lessons, boys made it clear that they disapproved of the programmes. We suggested in Chapter 5 that this was based in part on gender grounds. The sex education programmes contravened some significant elements of masculine culture. Innovative programmes speak of greater sexual entitlement for girls and offer girls knowledge equal to that on offer to boys; and we have already argued that this challenges codes of masculinity.

We know that one reason boys object to their sex education is that they judge the factual information offered to lack depth (Woodcock 1992: 517). While we do not in any way disagree with Woodcock's conclusion, we suspect it may be only part of the picture. Boys in our study made it clear that they wanted what they considered to be 'male appropriate' information. Boys in our research said they found sex education embarrassing and boring. The health professionals' programme was devised and presented by an all-female team. Boys considered that material was selected to appeal to girls and meet their needs, while it failed their own. Boys expressed such grievances as the following:

The session dealt more with girls than with boys.

I felt embarrassed because most of the contraception is for women.

I didn't like it when it was only about women.

Boys in our study said they wanted information that was appropriate to them. We have speculated that what they wanted was more explicit information about sex. In Chapter 6 we argued that there were hints in our data that boys discuss sex in much more explicit ways than do girls. By this we mean that within their own groups boys discuss and perhaps experiment with sex in an outspoken and physical way. To reach boys, sex education needs to maintain something of that direct and explicit tone. Boys resented sex education when it failed to do so, and it is clear that more research needs to be done on this issue.

Male Responsibility

Sex education programmes need strategies to reach out to boys and encourage their sense of responsibility in relationships generally and about contraceptive use and safer sex in particular. From the data we presented in Chapter 5 it seems that the boys saw themselves as being responsible for knowing what to do in a sexual encounter, in terms of physical actions. They did not, however, see themselves as being responsible for contraceptive or safe-sex practices. The boys had an oddly asymmetrical construction of what count as their areas of responsibility – but what may be important for policy in this context is that the boys saw themselves as being responsible for *some* aspects of the sexual encounter. This may offer sex educators a starting-point for work more generally on the issue.

Boys and Emotions

The data indicated also a sexually predatory attitude on the part of young men. Sexual relationships were a matter of status and simple physical pleasure for many of the boys in our research. The emotional aspects of sexual involvement were not given priority. 'It is now a commonplace that men have difficulty expressing their feelings and emotions' (Morgan 1992: 78). Government programmes have begun to highlight some aspects of importance, and to develop specific models for working in this area. Tessa Jowell, in February 1998, stated the importance of encouraging teenage boys to talk about the emotional and physical aspects of their relationships with girls. Speaking about a national programme launched in May 1999, she declared that the government wanted schools and community groups to work with young people to focus on relationships 'in their whole sense. Boys tend to judge relationships by sex, if we can get them to be more in touch with their feelings and talk about them it would be a marker for progress' (*Guardian* 9 February 1998: 8).

In Chapter 5 we discussed how boys acquire information, and suggested that many boys are given little information at home. Whatever the origins of this pattern of non-communication with adults, we want to draw attention to the difficulties it creates for boys – and for the adults who attempt to offer them sex education. Many boys are excluded from a confiding connection with sexual knowledge and counselling at home. There are questions about whether boys carry this pattern into their relationships with other adults, seeing the development of sexual knowledge and attitudes as something which is done in isolation from trusted adults. We suggested there that this pattern of male experience makes it difficult for boys to accept the formal sex education done in schools. In this study there are no examples of boys asking for adult input or support on issues they found difficult. Girls by contrast asked for teachers' intervention in a number of areas relating both to classroom interaction and to sexual relationships outside of school boundaries. This male isolation needs to be addressed, and parents could play a major role in creating change.

Policy Implications

Gender issues are of significance to young people in secondary schools. We probably know more about the impact they have on girls' lives and experiences than on boys'. New initiatives that aim to improve our knowledge of the way boys see sexuality and sex education are under development. Programmes that seek to match their preferences and styles of learning more effectively have been devised, and we look in detail at some of these programmes in the next chapter. We have discussed the need for programmes to overcome the isolation of boys from trusted adult help. Peer-education strategies may be able to play an important part in overcoming the problem.

There has been considerable development of peer education programmes in recent years, where a group of young people are offered training to work with others who are usually slightly younger than them. No systematic evaluation has been done of peer education programmes, and this is badly needed. What evidence there is suggests that peer education can be effective in communicating information and in affecting both attitudes and behaviour. The work we saw done by peer education groups in Streamham school and youth centre impressed us a great deal with its ability to communicate with young people.

Gender of Teachers

There is another area of controversy relating to gender which needs discussion: the gender of the teachers involved in sex education work. Male teachers were, by and large, unaware of the intricacies of this issue. PSE teachers at Ferryfield were complacent, as the following comment indicates:

> I think anyone with a bit of sensitivity and understanding can teach it, basically, to anyone, so I think it just requires careful handling and also a lack of embarrassment.

We collected data suggesting that this is an issue of some sensitivity for young people. There is evidence that these young adolescents had a preference for being taught by someone of their own gender in the first years of secondary school. At Gainton boys complained about the gender of the team of health professionals: 'all women'; 'no men'; 'there were no men to talk to us man-to-man'. They were uncomfortable with the idea of female-only health professionals:

> I'd find it difficult to go to a woman school nurse. A man knows what you're on about, and he's experienced and knows what's what.

Girls were aware of the boys' difficulties. At Streamham, a female pupil said:

> It was good she wasn't shy, but I think some of the boys were a bit embarassed about the fact it was a woman talking.

One explanation of the boys' objections to the health professionals' sessions is that they were reacting to the provision of sex education by a female. All of the health professionals we observed in schools doing sex education work were women. One policy implication is that it would be useful to recruit male workers to the health professionals teams and, of course, to sex education more generally.

Many girls also stated they found it difficult to cope when sex education was given by a male teacher:

Amy   You want to ask questions, but we have a male science teacher and you can't.

Debbie   With a male science teacher you think twice about asking a question.

There was a further issue: girls objected to the *behaviour* of some male teachers. It is important to note that, by and large, it was not the behaviour of the PSE teachers, most of whom have been trained to deliver sex education, that provoked this criticism from the girls; it was the behaviour of some male teachers drafted in at Gainton to take responsibility for classes when the health professionals came into school. Girls from a group at Gainton said in their evaluations: 'I didn't like Mr. Jones' jokes, he's not funny'; and 'I was angry because the teacher took the piss out of virgins'.

Policy Implications

We suggest that the data have significant implications for policy and for the practices of sex educators. At the moment, schools do little to challenge the dominant discourses of femininity and masculinity, and the differences in power and opportunity to which they seem to lead. One question relates to the extent to which sex educators should be challenging some of these ideas, and pressing for change. There are issues about the most effective way of organising sex education, and the claims of single-sex classes need to be considered.

There are also policy implications relating to the gender of teachers in sensitive curriculum areas. It is important to recruit adequate numbers of male teachers to work in PSE generally and sex education in particular. There are important issues about equal opportunities and sexism in the male teaching force to which many researchers have drawn attention and that continue to need attention (Sikes 1986).

Conclusion

In this chapter we have looked at what young people told us was missing in sex education programmes and attempted to develop an understanding of what they considered the failings to be. The data suggest that young people want, and indeed expect, access to explicit and sophisticated information about a wide range of sexual activity. They want the support of trusted adults in those areas of their lives they find difficult. In addition, some young women want the adults responsible for them to intervene in controversial areas of their lives, including issues that result from gender inequalities.

Sex education currently operates within the paradoxical situation we documented in Chapter 2, when dealing with the legislation. One motivating force behind the development of policy has been the pressure exerted by the moral Right, which has led to tighter definitions of what sex education should be. At the same time, however, HIV/AIDS has exerted an opposing – broadening – pressure. We can see something of the impact of the contradictory forces and policies in classroom practice.

A number of researchers have argued that HIV/AIDS has altered the public discourse around sexuality in general: 'For good or bad HIV infection and AIDS has brought sexuality into the forefront of public discourse' (Altman 1992: 32). The effect of the panic over the virus has been to change some of the traditional inhibitions relating to the discussion of sexually explicit material. The claim is that the HIV epidemic 'has acted as a solvent at least in Britain on the legitimation of traditional moral ideas' (Mac an Ghaill 1994: 169).

Radical theorists see sex education as having the potential to be involved with social engineering. They point out that, historically, sex education was designed to protect society: 'The dispensing of social knowledge as a prophylactic for the unwelcome consequences of freewheeling sexual behaviour is the cornerstone of modern sexuality education' (Sears 1992: 17). This motivation seems to persist in current sex education policy and practice, much of which seems to offer a limited perspective on sexuality while attempting to constrain sexual experimentation and protect 'innocence'.

Permission to take control of and responsibility for one's sexuality, and depictions of the life-enhancing features of sexual expression, are important messages to adolescents, along with the usual warnings. Warnings have their place, 'but are often the only features of adult to adolescent communication about sex' (Moore and Rosenthal 1993: 201). A number of individuals and organisations have expressed their concern about this state of affairs. Thomson and Scott (1992: 51), for example, have stressed that it is important that the positive aspects of human sexuality and sexual relationships are also included:

> Sex education should be treated as a positive opportunity for young people to understand and be in control of their emerging sexualities. It is important that we do not approach the teaching of sex education from a position which treats sexual knowledge as dangerous and potentially corrupting.

There is value in encouraging in the young person a sense of personal worth and a sense of the value of health. The development of skills in personal relationships involves enabling adolescents to make decisions for themselves and not simply to respond to peer pressure or the influence of the media.

Note

1   Despite the opinions of the young people, we found that there was significant controversy among sex educators about the issue of single-sex classes for sex education, with a high percentage declaring themselves opposed to it in principle. The health professionals' objection seems to be that they find boys-only groups very difficult to teach. We have shown how boys objected to the sex education sessions and made their objections very clear, and disrupted lessons. There is a direct conflict between the needs and expressed wishes of the girls for single-sex lessons and the wishes and needs of health professionals who want the girls in classes with the boys because it makes the boys easier to handle. PSE teachers often were very committed to running sex education classes with both sexes present. They considered that sex education was one topic among many that they dealt with where there was a possibility of embarrassment and difficulty, but that good teaching could exploit the potential of the situation. The PSE advisor attempted to persuade teachers at Streamham to undertake some experimentation with the strategy of single-sex classes, discussing research which indicated its strengths. She was unable to change the views of male teachers, particularly the older teachers.

9 Conclusions and Policy Recommendations

Introduction

In this chapter we tease out the policy implications of the data we have presented. We do not by any means deal with all of the policy issues relating to the teaching of sex education. A substantial literature exists, which deals with a whole range of issues that we have not tackled in this study. In Chapter 1, we stated that the two major controversies we intended to focus on relate to generation and gender. They have formed the two central themes of the book. In this concluding chapter we seek to draw out the policy implications of the data for the two features.

The first section of this chapter looks at issues relating to the controversy over *generation*. We focus on the legislation that has shaped sex education in Britain and examine the case for change. We also consider calls to improve consultation with young people about their sex education (Tones 1986). Work with parents is also considered in this section, since they can have an important impact on what is acceptable in a sex education programme in a given location.

In the second section we turn to some of the *gender* issues that arise from the data. We focus on the issue of differences in power between boys and girls. We argue that any attempt to improve rates of teenage pregnancy and STDs in the UK will involve change in the gender and sexual cultures of young people. We outline new approaches for working with gender issues, and look at some of the strategies with which schools can experiment. We return again to the fact that we collected very little information on homosexuality in our research. We consider nevertheless that it was important to offer some recommendations for practice and policy in schools on this issue, but these are based on the research of other people.

In the third and final section of the chapter, we look briefly at the views of young people on who should be responsible for their sex education.

Generational Issues

Policy and Legislation

We began this book with a consideration of the controversy over sex education in the 1980s in Britain. We outlined the arguments in the bitter debate between liberal opinion and 'moral majority' groups in the context of HIV/AIDS. The debate resulted in sex education legislation being put into place by a succession of Conservative governments. The legislation restricted sex education provision in schools. At the same time, however, pressures from HIV/AIDS campaigns opened up discussion of sexual behaviour and attitudes in public health work. The result has been a confused mix of messages for adolescents about sexuality.

The lack of a clear national policy has had a number of negative effects. Perhaps most significantly it left the way open for pressure groups to affect policy making and practice at all levels from individual schools to government departments. Concerned agencies with substantial expertise in adolescent sex education, like the Family Planning Association and the Brooks Advisory Centre, stepped into the vacuum. They have been left to put forward the case for liberal or radical agendas and to allow the voice of young people to be heard. It cannot be right that decisions and policy making over a crucial part of young people's development are left to the efforts of independent bodies like the Sex Education Forum. They are no substitute for action at a national level.

Sex education practitioners do not feel the current policy framework is appropriate to the needs of young people in Britain (Scott and Thomson 1992; Lenderyou 1994). Young people in our research expressed only resentment about its provisions and its view of their entitlements. A number of policy recommendations arise from this dissatisfaction. At the very least there is a clear need for improved, detailed, local and national guidance on sex education. This should be updated to clear the current confusion and offer more positive leadership to governors, teachers and parents.

New Initiatives

In the light of pupils' views about the sex education they receive, it is interesting to look at initiatives proposed by the Labour government. There are indications that the administration elected in May 1997 is evolving new policies. Questions remain as to whether adolescents' views are being considered to a greater extent than during the previous Tory administrations. At the time of writing there was no new legislation actually proposed. A number of commissions to look into the issues had been established, but publication of their reports is delayed. This is the position as of April 1999, but it is clear that there are likely to be changes soon.

PSE initiatives

The development of PSE generally and of sex education in particular has been highlighted by the consultation paper *Excellence in Schools* (DfEE 1997). The consultation paper highlights the role government wants schools to take in tackling what it terms 'our most pressing public health problems including

147

teenage pregnancies' (DfEE 1997). A National Healthy Schools' Initiative and an Advisory Group on Education for Citizenship and the Teaching of Democracy has also developed alongside the consultation paper.

The Qualifications and Curriculum Authority (QCA) has started to review the National Curriculum. It is considering the inclusion of PSE within the new provision. The QCA will be advised by a DfEE and Department of Health (DoH) Health Education in Schools group. Innovations in spiritual, moral, social and cultural guidance are being piloted with support in ten schools in a number of areas including Rochdale, Hampshire and Birmingham, and without support in 150 other schools. The DoH sent all schools and health promotion offices a sex education pack in March 1998. The DfEE has promised to produce guidance on confidentiality in schools in collaboration with the DoH and others.

Health of the Nation Initiatives

The DoH has published a consultative Green Paper on public health, *Our Healthier Nation* (1998), proposing a national contract for better health. There is a focus on healthy schools and on children and young people, but sexual health is not emphasised at all in this document although it does recognise the need for local initiatives for reducing teenage conceptions. A separate strategy for dealing with unintended conceptions as well as a strategy for HIV/AIDS are planned.

Teenage pregnancy initiatives

An *Action Plan on Teenage Pregnancy* was recently launched by the DoH. Tessa Jowell, the Minister for Public Health, speaking at the Brook Advisory Centre's annual conference in 1998, announced that the government has set up four task groups to tackle the problem of unwanted pregnancies, particularly among the under-16s. The four task groups have the titles:

- Sex and Relationships Education
- Commissioning and Providing Family Planning Services
- Vulnerable and Hard to Reach Groups
- Research and Development and Data Collection

A national strategy was to have been launched in May 1998. This was delayed, though a national programme to reduce the rate of unintended teenage conceptions has been developed for launch in the summer of 1999.

Homosexuality

While in opposition the Labour Party promised to repeal Section 28, but it is clear that the House of Lords will block this legislation. The government has postponed the promised repeal of Section 28 until legislation is passed changing the power of the House of Lords to block. Gay activists have protested against the delay, and allege that so long as existing legislation remains on the statute books teachers are deterred from tackling homosexual bullying and providing effective AIDS education. They point to a suicide in Britain in November 1998 of a 15-year-old boy that was connected with homosexual bullying. The Queen's Speech in November 1998 moved to equalise the age of consent for gays, lesbians and homosexuals at 16.

The 'moral framework'

In addition to these legislative initiatives there has been a welcome change in the moral framework. Teenage magazines were heavily criticised by MPs in 1996 for carrying sexually explicit articles. Ministers have made approaches with a view to enlisting these publications in the fight to stem the rise in teenage pregnancies. Tessa Jowell met with editors of magazines like *Sugar*, *Bliss* and *Just Seventeen*. She concluded: 'They have an important role to play in communicating with young people in their formative years' (*Guardian* 20 April 1998). There are also indications that some of the gender-related issues may now be tackled. Ms Jowell stated that it was important that boys were made as aware as girls are of their responsibilities in relation to contraception and sexual health. She commented: 'This means cultural change' (ibid.).

Evaluation of the New Initiatives

There has been a general welcome for the new initiatives, and some dismay at the delay of reports commissioned and in the publication of new policies. On the basis of the views of the young people in our research there is a case for change in the legislation. Changes that would allow sex educators in general and teachers in particular to develop programmes to meet the requests young people are making of adults for help and support. A political fight will probably be necessary to defeat the 'moral majority', and there is perhaps no other option than to ask the Labour government to take on that fight. As Anne Weyman, chief executive of the Family Planning Association, said recently:

> Above all we need the Government to signal its willingness to put the needs of young people for education and advice first, and to disregard pressure from the minority who believe that children should be kept in ignorance.
>
> (*Guardian* 20 March 1999)

Polly Toynbee has argued (*Guardian* 16 March 1998) that a political battle is necessary to win back the ground taken by the 'moral majority' groups in the last decade-and-a-half and to develop the services that young people want and need. She made the point that our research has made clear to us: what is required is sex education provision that works effectively. Programmes in The Netherlands and Scandinavia have reduced rates of teenage pregnancy and STDs. There are skilled practitioners working with creativity and commitment in the UK to forge effective relationships with young people and develop programmes that will meet their needs, too. The requisite knowledge, skills and commitment are available. The political will to take on the 'moral' majority and redress the balance in respect of what is deemed acceptable in sex education is what is now needed (ibid.).

Consulting Pupils

A second set of policy recommendations in relation to 'generational issues' concerns the importance of consulting with pupils. Health education professionals argue that sex education fails in part because the adolescents' own concerns are not sufficiently considered by those who plan the programmes. The critique derives from developments in the health promotion field in recent years. There is increasing emphasis on the importance of consultation with the groups targeted for health promotion, so that participation is achieved. The Sex Education Forum published guidelines on effective sex education (Sex Education Forum 1994). It recommends that young people be consulted about their own sex education, and comments that this is something that is rarely done. Our research would support the importance of consulting pupils. It could help achieve a match between the curricular requirements and the audience's needs. Teachers must, however, be given greater freedom to respond to the findings of such consultations, and this implies changes in the policy framework and in the training provision for sex educators.

In the sex education programmes we studied there was very little consultation with pupils about the content in advance. Little attempt was made to discover what pupils most wanted to know. Whitefarm School was the exception. It had taken part in a multi-agency programme funded by the local health authority to set up a council of young people. The youth council was consulted about a range of provision for young people. It managed to introduce a number of improvements in local schools. This is another example of a 'healthy alliance' and one which seemed to have considerable potential. In the other schools adults decided what ought to go into the curriculum, so that adult views of what is important in a sex education programme were imposed upon pupils. Health promotion principles emphasising consultation to achieve participation were not employed rigorously in this case, and it is possible that the results would have been more effective if they had been so employed.

There were particular implications for young men in the programmes run by the health professional teams. One blueprint of sexual behaviour was presented in the formal sexual socialisation, its content having been decided by a team of adult females. It is possible that the programmes took too little account of the boys' existing knowledge, interests and preoccupations. We considered (Chapter 5) that this could have been a contributor to the boys' disruptive activities in the sex education lessons. In addition, little account was taken of the informal culture of these adolescents, or of the ways sexuality and relationships are viewed within adolescent culture. There are inevitably gaps in perception and life experience between teenagers and adults, and they are particularly acute in the field of sexuality. This gap becomes harder to bridge when adults are working with constraints of the kind currently imposed by legislation in the UK.

For many years young people have evaluated sex education programmes negatively. They have made it clear they consider sex education offers them too little information too late in their lives (Farrell 1978; Allen 1987). There is little evidence that sex educators have been able to make effective use of these evaluations and so create more effective programmes. Kenway and Fitzclarence (1997) argue that it is not only sex education that is negatively affected by the way adults think about young people. They suggest that children are schooled in an education system permeated by 'poisonous pedagogy', by which they mean that children 'suffer from both powerlessness and violence in relation to adults' (ibid.: 121). Iris Young suggests that we should understand this situation in terms of social justice, and has argued for new ways of looking at the concept. Traditionally definitions of social justice have focused on material goods and resources, and on their distribution among people in a society. Some theorists have also 'considered the distribution of such non-material goods as power, opportunity or self respect' (Young 1990: 16).

Achieving social justice means the elimination of institutionalised domination and oppression. A conception of justice provides 'in the first instance a standard whereby the distributive aspects of the basic structure of society are to be assessed' (Rawls 1971: 9). Young argues for a wider definition:

> I wish to displace talk of justice that regards persons as primarily possessors and consumers of goods to a wider context that also includes actions, decisions about actions and provision of the means to develop and exercise capabilities.
>
> (Young 1990: 16)

Young's perspective is that dignity and respect can also be distributed. Raphael Reed agrees: 'Oppression and domination should be the primary terms for conceptualising social justice rather than adopting distributive paradigms' (Raphael Reed 1997: 27). It can be argued that young people face social injustice in Young's terms. Schools do not prioritise a curriculum and a set of practices that open opportunities for young people to learn control over actions, or decisions about actions: they do not always maximise the scope for developing and exercising capabilities. Change in sex education is probably part of a wider campaign against this 'poisonous pedagogy' and includes wider aspects of social justice. Raphael Reed states: 'There is a need for greater democratic principles of participation, active citizenship and decision making for students in schools' (ibid.: 23).

Work with Parents

One issue that arises from this research relates to the importance of sex educators working with parents. If a school implements a new policy, it is important to bid for time and resources to offer consultation sessions with them. Several of the programmes we researched had done this and found it worked to good effect. Health professionals at Gainton commented:

> We like to train the parents as well. There's a growing number of parents' evenings. A couple of days before we do the workshops for the school, we do a workshop for the parents so they know what is going on.

The importance of funding for programmes is clear here. The health professionals' programme at Gainton was able to offer a significant amount of work with parents prior to the sessions in the school. These health professionals also invited the local newspaper to an evening consultation with parents. They aimed to face any media reaction in a meeting attended by senior health and education officials – in the presence of parents. This indicates again the importance of adequate funding for innovatory school projects.

School sex education programmes can make a serious effort to work with parents and negotiate content appropriate to their offspring. In Chapter 6, we discussed the fact that the majority of parents feel less than comfortable offering information and advice to teenagers. There is evidence that parents are often unaware of the level of sexual knowledge and indeed experience already acquired by their offspring. These considerations underline the importance of parents', particularly fathers', efforts to sustain communication with their children throughout their adolescence.

Toleration of difference involves the recognition that adolescents may have a value framework different from that of adults; yet in order to influence them it is important that the lines of communication are kept open (Moore and Rosenthal 1993: 203).

Gender and Power

There are significant policy implications to our data on gender. Gender codes lay down divergent blueprints for male and female behaviour in adolescence, and offer unequal access to power. A knowledge of adolescent culture casts light on some of the difficulties involved in sex education. It clarifies the blockages to effective policy development for reducing both teenage unwanted pregnancy and the spread of STDs including HIV/AIDS. In particular it makes clear the tensions between young women's gendered sexual social positioning and safer sex discourse.

Safer Sex Campaigns

A number of campaigns aimed at promoting both effective contraception and safer sex among young heterosexuals have taken as their central message the need for women to take greater control in sexual encounters. They encourage young women either to say 'No' to male sexual advances or to insist on condom use (Richardson 1996: 164). Such campaigns have problems, both of a theoretical and of a practical nature, that relate to gender issues. They unquestioningly incorporate the idea that males will press females into sexual activity: this is the convention of what is 'normal'. They thereby collude with the dominant discourse of sexuality, which assumes that men are 'naturally' less able than women to exert self-control in sexual encounters. They perpetuate notions of the insignificance of female desire in comparison with 'volcanic' male urges. All in all, they do not voice a demand that responsibility should be shared between two partners in a sexual relationship. They fail also to recognise or tackle the fact that, with the current characteristics of heterosexual sexuality, boys come under perhaps even more pressure than girls to have sex: the campaign needs to reach out to them, too.

Perhaps the major flaw in such programmes is their reliance on the expectation that girls are able to say 'No' to their male partners, or else persuade them to use condoms. This ignores or underestimates the impact of the power differential that exists between male and female in our society, and is particularly sharply focused in adolescent cultures (Holland 1992: 142). This inequality means that young women are at a serious disadvantage in any attempt they make to enforce their views of what should happen in heterosexual encounters or relationships.

It is important to be clear here that it is *men's* behaviour in relation to women that frequently puts women at risk in sexual encounters, and limits women's ability to prevent both unwanted pregnancy and avoid STDs like HIV. Such critiques of male behaviour do not belong only to feminist work: the World Health Organisation has identified heterosexual male reluctance to change behaviour as an important factor in the global transmission of HIV/AIDS.

Research on patterns of take-up of safer sex in male homosexual relationships in Britain, has indicated that there has been significant change in behaviour. This shows up in encouraging results on the rates of a number of STDs including HIV/AIDS. The suggestion is that this has been possible because male same-sex partners operate with a reciprocity that at least permits, or even facilitates, negotiation over the issue. Research suggests that patterns of power, while by no means absent here, are different in homosexual relationships. This reciprocity allows for negotiation between partners over safer sex interactions. The level of reciprocity is much higher than is characteristic of many heterosexual relationships.

We can develop policies that have real impact on teenage pregnancy rates and the STD and HIV/AIDS rates only if we begin to address the power relationships between boys and girls. There are a number of areas of work with young people in which policy needs to be developed, but one of the most significant relates to traditional models of heterosexual interaction and to available models of appropriate 'feminine sexuality' (Holland and Adkins 1996: 4).

Sexuality

In Chapter 7 we discussed 'masculinised' sexuality, which feminists argue characterises heterosexual relationships. Traditional and 'masculinised' heterosexual definitions of what *proper* sex is – and what satisfying sex is – have stressed the central place of intercourse. Intercourse is what counts as erotic behaviour in 'masculinised' views of sexuality. Women as well as men have learned and accepted these views. The feminist critique of 'masculinised' sexuality has argued that these practices are more satisfying to men than to women because they prioritise male preferences and are based on a view of women as sexual objects rather than as people with specific patterns of desire of their own.

HIV/AIDS campaigns have stressed the importance of non-penetrative sexual practices, and advocated a wide range of alternative practices – for gay men. They opened up a possibility of validating these practices as erotic and satisfying – for gay men. The dominant definition of safer sex for heterosexuals however has focused on condom use in order to reduce the risks associated with vaginal penetration. Wilton (1994: 173) has pointed out that, whether we are dealing with heterosexual or same-sex sexual relationships, '[s]afer sex demands we de-emphasise penetration'. Efforts to take the same message to heterosexuals, however, threaten to disrupt what Holland *et al.* (1990: 169) have called the 'heterosexual economy'. Such approaches challenge the dominant view of what *proper* sex should be and 'masculinised' views of what counts as erotic and fulfilling. They are likely to be resisted. Change nevertheless involves a challenge to 'masculinised' accounts of sexuality, and to male risk behaviours. One strategy is to work with young men, perhaps confrontationally, on their attitudes. This will be dealt with in the section that follows.

Holland *et al.* (1990) have suggested that the best strategy for achieving change involves creating new models of sexuality for women. Women will challenge 'masculinised' models of sexuality, because those models fail to meet their sexual needs:

> We argue that for a young woman in a heterosexual relationship to negotiate safe sex activities she has to be empowered both to develop a positive

conception of feminine sexuality and to put this positive conception into practice.

(Holland *et al.* 1990: 143)

This discovery of female sexuality carries with it the ability to resource a challenge both to male definitions of sexual practice and to male power to decide what goes on in a sexual situation. Young women who assert their own needs have to negotiate sexual relationships with men that resist commonsense views of feminine and masculine sexuality. Feminist work corresponds directly with the safer sex messages resulting from the HIV/AIDS crisis. Feminists have long voiced criticism of heterosexual sexual practices: they have specifically challenged the centrality of intercourse and legitimised ways of obtaining sexual pleasure through non-penetrative means (Koedt 1973: 173). HIV/AIDS campaigns insist on the risks associated with intercourse and stress the importance of safer sex practices. They have the ability, therefore, to promote *and* validate alternatives to intercourse. The campaigns support young women in changing behaviour by encouraging them to experiment with a range of alternative and less 'masculinised' sexual behaviours, and perhaps also to discover the 'missing discourse of desire'.

The implications of a 'positive conception of feminine sexuality' require elucidation. There is considerable evidence that girls have little understanding of their sexual urges and responses, let alone the freedom to express themselves (Lees 1986: 151). The WRAP team found that young women lacked a language in which to discuss their own pleasure and comment that this 'serves as an obstacle to these girls in many ways, but also forms a real obstacle to the development of safer sex practices' (Holland *et al.* 1990: 139). One of the aims of sex education programmes should be to provide a space for young women to discuss and explore these issues. Susan Sontag observed:

Merely to remove the onus placed upon the sexual expressiveness of women is a hollow victory, if the sexuality they become freer to enjoy remains the old one, that converts women into objects. Without a change in the very norms of sexuality, the liberation of women is a meaningless goal. Sex as such is not liberating for women. Neither is more sex.

(Sontag quoted in Keohande 1982: 190)

Sex education programmes – a radical agenda

We must question whether current work in the field of health education, and especially sex education, acknowledges or tackles these issues of male power and masculine notions of sexuality. The WRAP researchers pointed out: 'In the health promotion literature, there is little or no account of gendered power relations' (Holland *et al.* 1990: 144). An analysis of gender relations in adolescent cultures sets a more radical agenda for sex education than it has adopted in the

155

past. A recognition of the power imbalances between young men and young women has real importance for the design of sex education for young people. A theoretical analysis that includes a critique of heterosexual interactions is crucial for any health campaign aiming to change behaviour and improve the health of the nation's young people. It is important to draw attention to the theoretical and feminist work on power dynamics involved in adolescent heterosexual relationships in order to develop effective practice (Holland *et al.* 1990: 164).

In the adolescent cultures we have described, sexual visibility – in the sense of an assertion of one's sexual needs and autonomy – is allowed only to men. We have produced evidence of boys policing the sexual visibility of girls, evidence that other research backs up (see Clarke 1987: 210). More progressive models of sexuality are becoming available to young women, and magazines like *Just Seventeen*, *Sugar* and *Bliss* have an important role here. It is interesting that the Labour government has decided to work with these influential agencies in a positive way to develop new national sex education policies.

A positive model of female sexuality involves a critique of current hetero-sexual practices, which neither keep women safe nor are fulfilling to women. Trudell (1993: 188) asked the pertinent question: what counts as successful sex education? An approach that emphasises female pleasure and offers women more power would be an essential element in producing real change. Envisaging empowerment for young women could mean them not engaging in sexual activity; not engaging in sexual activity without informed consent; getting men to consent to safer sex practices; negotiating sexual practices that are pleasurable to women as well as to men. The argument is that both social justice and safer sexual practices, in terms of pregnancy and HIV/AIDS, can be achieved only by promoting alternative discourses of what counts as erotic and fulfilling for both men and women.

This analysis underlines the importance of working with young men as well as young women to secure change. For the 'masculinised' view of sexuality operates with considerable power on young men too. The WRAP team comment: 'Their male peers were usually the primary audience for their first sexual experience' (Holland *et al.* 1990: 241). In the ways we discussed in Chapter 4, young men are also under pressure to produce themselves 'in relation to a dominant conception of acceptable behaviour and action' (Holland *et al.* 1993: 34). We examine some of the implications for working with boys in the next section, below.

Educating young people in positive models of masculine and feminine sexuality, while also attempting to transform the model of male sexuality that informs young men's sexual practices is a major social undertaking. In practice it requires confronting men with the possibilities of a positive female sexuality. It requires young women to negotiate a new model of sexuality that treats female sexual pleasure as a priority, which has not yet been taken seriously by the health education establishment. The challenge to sex education now is to consider how such practices can be promoted effectively to young people. Most health and sex education material has emphasised individual choice and personal responsibility. It has not addressed the dynamics of power in hetero-sexual relationships. It is not reasonable to expect individual young women to be able to take responsibility for creating all the change. Additional supportive resources need to be in place.

There is little evidence that this feminist critique of inequalities in power and entitlement which develop from gender studies has been discernible in sex education practice. The majority of sex education programmes have been defined as actively heterosexist and to actively support a male-centred view of sex (Szirom 1988; Lees 1994). They have, in the view of many feminist commentators, worked to reinforce some of the inequalities in society (Wolpe 1987; Holly 1989). Feminist critiques of sex education call for programmes which would empower young women to take control of their own bodies, and resist abuse and exploitation. Marianne Whately (1992) has developed the notion of gender-equitable sex education. This includes emphasising male–female similarities rather than their differences; recognising female plea-sure and desire; presenting intercourse as but one of the possible forms of sexual expression; eliminating heterosexual assumptions; working against the double standard (Trudell 1993: 186).

The powerful and taken-for-granted assumptions about sexuality, rather than being natural and biologically given, are social and do not merely reflect but actually reinforce the subordinate position of girls in society. It is only with a knowledge of how sexual relations are structured by the norms and constraints of the 'gender order' that progress can be made. The focus of sex education should be to prepare boys and girls for a more egalitarian society (Lees 1993: 149). Sex education, in the traditional sense, commonly focuses on different methods of contraception and descriptions of the biological make-up and the mechanics of the sex act. A radical sex education would focus on the taken-for-granted norms and codes of contact within which social behaviour takes place. If sex education is to be empowering it needs to address and foster moral autonomy, and to do this it needs to address issues of power.

Social justice

The sex education programmes we studied in this research represent an advance on programmes that had previously been run in local schools. They gave clear evidence of a caring and concerned attitude on the part of those developing them. But we need to look at the realities of adolescent culture, and ask if the programmes were effective in tackling the underlying issues. There are questions about whether promoting a liberal approach, which offers information and support and which is essentially based on liberal values and tolerant practices, is sufficient in this situation.

Plummer has developed new ideas of 'intimate citizenship' relevant in 'life politics'. He argues that a new set of claims about the body and sexuality are in the making (Plummer 1996: 46). 'Citizenship' has been a concept of significant concern for many years. Marshall (1963), for example, saw citizenship as bestowing civil, political and social justice on particular individuals and groups in a society. Plummer suggests:

> At the century's end another 'realm of citizenship' could be added – that of intimate citizenship. It speaks to an array of concerns and it extends notions of rights and responsibilities. I call this 'Intimate Citizenship', because it is concerned with all of those matters linked to our most intimate desires, pleasures and ways of being in the world.
>
> (Plummer in Weeks and Holland 1994: 46)

Intimate citizenship, then, has claims to make about the right of individuals in contemporary society to choose their sexual behaviour, decide their sexual practices and define their sexual identities. Questions arise about the extent to which formal sex education programmes acknowledge these changes in the sexual blueprint and seek to include young people as citizens in this sense. If we return to what Iris Young said about social justice, it becomes clear that what is at issue is the freedom to make decisions and to exercise the right to choose one's own actions.

Plummer identified the scope of change in the modern world, where many traditional sexual scripts have been challenged, and claimed: 'New kinds of stories are in making around our bodies.' He also points out that 'old stories will remain side by side with the new' (Plummer 1994: 47). A major source of conflict underlies this process. Part of what is at issue in Plummer's account is the means by which traditionalists seek to buttress and defend their viewpoint and the rights that tend to be associated with it:

> Traditionalists tell stories which attempt to encompass all within one obdurate framework of authority and received truth, to lay out the one story which all should adhere to.
>
> (Plummer 1994: 48)

By contrast, progressive opinion attempts to open up the range of stories, of possibilities. Giddens (1991) has argued that we can discern a transformation of intimacy in our society, but others like Plummer are less optimistic. Plummer suggests that there is evidence of a culture war going on in the area of 'intimate citizenship'. He points out that some groups want to tell others what to do. Their moral code is a code for themselves, but they want to extend it to others as well. It is a politics of prohibition. The policy implications for formal sex education schemes are clear in Plummer's recommendations: 'It is not an easy option to keep the pluralistic, polyvocal potential of proliferating stories open, but it is probably a very necessary one' (Plummer 1994: 50).

There are political aspects to sex education work, and a case for developing a more radical agenda for sex education. The theoretical material indicates some directions for practice. It is important to create advances in sex education, and produce programmes more relevant to the interests of adolescents. Such developments may answer the 'too little too late' criticism of sex education that young people have been voicing for years. However, providing more open programmes, using health professionals, for example, and offering access to contraception are unlikely to bring about real change. The data show that their potential impact is limited. The political context and the power relations between male and female, as they are expressed in sexuality, must also be tackled:

> In sex education we need to challenge the terms on which girls participate in social life so that boys and girls can be encouraged to see their relations not in sexually stereotyped ways but in terms of human attributes.
>
> (Spencer 1984: 15)

There are real implications in what we have said for the training of sex educators and for the kinds of curriculum they need. A more radical agenda in the classroom means that sex educators need to be offered access not only to biological and physiological texts and material but to some of the theoretically informed social science work that is beginning to be produced. Sex educators also need opportunities for some of the 'considered thinking' about issues of sexuality that we have suggested is important for adolescents, too.

Working with Boys

Our research shows boys responding negatively to the sex education they were offered in school. There is a growing body of evidence to suggest that contemporary sex education does not meet the needs of young men. Biddulph pointed out that boys and young men feel left out and do not see sex and relationships' education as relevant (Biddulph 1998; see Walker and Kushner 1997). In March 1997 the Sex Education Forum published a report which held that sex education is failing to meet the needs of boys. Effort has gone into trying to get the message across to girls, and this has been made at the expense of their male counterparts (Lenderyou and Ray 1977) who respond negatively, remaining unaffected by the material and resentful of the experience. Other work done by those in close touch with young people, like Nick Fisher, expresses similar concerns. Fisher states his anxiety that in the 'current climate of sex education policies we risk ostracising teenage boys and teenagers in general by driving more of a wedge between them and adults' (Fisher 1994).

Conclusions and Policy Recommendations

A radical agenda and boys

A sex education programme with a radical agenda is likely to represent a considerable challenge to boys, and meet with considerable opposition from them. Boys are likely to be exposed to considerable criticism in such programmes. Nick Fisher has pointed out that boys complain that sex education already seems like a long list of negative messages aimed exclusively at them. In innovative programmes boys' attitudes and values may well be challenged and disapproval expressed of their culture. The old assumption that 'lads will be lads' no longer is accepted or celebrated, and social constructions that speak of the different nature of sexuality for men and for women will disappear. We have referred to a programme run by health professionals in which minor change was attempted – and we noted the quite substantial male opposition to it. The WRAP research highlights the need for substantial change in sex education work which probes and challenges a number of given assumptions in the 'heterosexual economy'. Such programmes are likely to provoke considerable opposition, and any effort in this direction needs to be planned and resourced effectively.

Finding ways to challenge some male behaviour without simply alienating boys is not easy. Raphael Reed for example questions how teachers can work with boys in ways that '[d]o not validate oppressive attitudes and ways of relating to each other' (1997: 3). Feminist work in the last decade has focused on ways of working with girls to maximise their opportunities. Raphael Reed argues (ibid.) that these models for working in an emancipatory way with girls do not easily transfer across the gender divide. Male sexuality and masculinity have never been under more scrutiny than they are now (Davidson 1990). We need to clarify our thinking about the making of male sexuality as a starting-point for deciding what it is that we have to offer young men. What kinds of information and support can we give, and how can we assist boys towards a *genuinely empowered*, responsible and enjoyable sexuality? Change is never easy, and new programmes need to understand the depth of feelings they touch, designing strategies to tackle some of these issues. As Raphael Reed points out we need programmes and strategies that can address boys' fears, anxieties and displacements (Raphael Reed 1997: 23).

New approaches to working with boys

Various groups have begun to develop programmes for non-sexist education with boys and young men. They aim to encourage boys to break out of the cycle of behaviour that oppresses women and creates problems for themselves. Theirs is a sex education that encourages the sharing of thoughts, feelings and behaviours that would not normally be discussed. It aims to liberate young men from the restrictive effects of sexism, and aims to provide a safe environment to explore feelings of inadequacy. It offers an opportunity to challenge traditional ideas of what is involved in 'becoming a man' and to revalue 'feminine' quali-

160

ties. Those involved with the development of such programmes acknowledge that it is far from easy (Davidson 1990; Segal 1990; Whyld 1990).

A number of new resources have been developed and published by agencies working in this field. *Let's Hear It From the Boys* is a new publication produced by the Sex Education Forum (Lenderyou and Ray 1997). It deals with approaches that can be effective when working with boys in different settings, including primary and secondary schools, youth and community settings and sexual health services. The chapters are written by experienced practitioners, and aim to draw on examples of successful work. There was considerable consultation in the production of the book with the boys involved in piloting the approaches.

New health promotion initiatives, like the 'It Takes Two' and the 'Men, This Is For You' campaigns were launched with the aim of informing young men about contraception and encouraging them to feel comfortable using it. The 'Men, This Is For You' leaflet offers one-line jokes, suggesting that they can be used, for example, to break the embarrassment about contraception which young men often felt with a new partner. It is backed up by a Contraceptive Education Service Helpline which offers advice and counselling. The Family Planning Association has developed a programme entitled 'Strides'. It aimed 'first to discover what boys sex education needs are, and then begin to meet them' (Wallace, *Guardian* 14 April 1999). It is interesting that the Family Planning Association has begun developing material for facilitators to work with boys-only groups.

If the new material is to appeal to young men, style is an important consideration. A reviewer in *Sex Education Matters* disliked a new video called *Johnny Condom*, produced for young men. She described parts of the video as 'aggressive and laddish', though she recognised the possibility that 'this is the point and at last we are seeing a resource whose humour and approach will be appreciated by young men' (*Sex Education Matters* 1997 14: 6). Language is another important matter in the video. It features characters asking: 'Oi do either of you two fancy a shag? Well you'd better use some of these buggers.' One of the issues here is that the humour and language in the video are likely to prohibit its use in schools. This points up again the importance of the Labour government producing new and more flexible guidelines and policies on sex education.

It is important to note that only very skilled facilitators seem to be able to 'break through the bravado to get a group including males to take the matter seriously' (Woodcock 1992: 530). There are arguments that those aiming to undertake this work need training, and a number of centres are currently offering such training. The Sex Education Forum and the Family Planning Association have developed programmes of work for sex educators who wish to develop sex education and relationships' work with boys and young men. They plan to run a programme of local dissemination seminars to publicise the programmes, and a national conference on the issue was held in April 1998. (Other sources of information on this issue are listed following the References.) The most progressive agencies working in the sex education field in the UK, then, have begun work in this area. This work needs to be adequately funded and dispersed throughout schools and other agencies working with young people.

We believe that strategies to improve the situation can be effective only if they take account of the needs of all pupils, both male and female. Arnot in 1984 wrote an article called 'How shall we educate our sons?', looking at the problems that contemporary codes of masculinity create for boys, and of course for girls. We suggest that sex education aimed specifically at boys is a particularly critical issue. We have shown how the well-intentioned innovative programmes we researched touched on core aspects of the masculine self, and were therefore resisted; and we have documented other research in this section which indicates a widespread sense of disillusionment with sex education among boys. The liberal position is that the policy challenge is to develop programmes of sex education that avoid these affronts to pupils of either sex while affording both genders opportunities to focus on those aspects of sexuality and sexual behaviour about which they are curious. The data we have presented reveal configurations of boys' informal culture in relation to masculinity and sexuality. These data suggest that it will be very difficult to create programmes that will accomplish these objectives, and which do not simply privilege male sexual entitlement.

Homosexuality

We have indicated that some young people in our study objected to the lack of information about sexual orientation. Many young people surveyed in a national study felt that their schools provided too little information on this topic (HEA 1992). We collected no data suggesting that any of the young people in the schools researched had a same-sex sexual orientation; there is, however, an increasing body of research which deals with adolescent homosexuality. It might be worth pointing out that between 8 and 15 per cent of any group of people will be gay. The starting-point in this discussion is the statistics. For the UK as a whole there has been a slight but perceptible annual rise in newly reported cases of HIV since 1993, with 2,891 cases reported in 1996 alone. Not all result from sexual contact, of course. Of these 2,891 cases, 1,670 resulted from sex between men, the next largest group being those who were infected overseas, most notably in African countries. Gay or bisexual men make up 59 per cent of the total of those infected with HIV; those infected abroad make up 14 per cent of the total.

What are the implications of these figures for school sex education? Simon Watney from the Red Hot AIDS Charitable Trust says:

> It is vital to have good generalist HIV preventative education for all children and young people within the broader context of related sex education.

However, it should be complemented by an equally forthright commitment to targeted work to reach those at greatest risk.

(Watney 1997: 8)

Well over 1,000 teenagers have contracted HIV in Britain, while young people in their 20s make up no less than 49 per cent of the total number of HIV cases since testing began in 1984. Of the 1,600 new cases of HIV among gay men reported in Britain last year, more than 500 were in their 20s. Watney suggests that those groups and individuals likely to be vulnerable to HIV after leaving school should be our priority. 'It is not some kind of "special pleading" to single out the needs of young gay men. On the contrary it is to acknowledge the realities of the epidemic' (ibid.: 9).

Above all, Watney suggests, young people at risk, and especially young men, need the provision of reliable scientific information. Offering guidance and support to all is essential. Sex education needs to ensure that all young people know how to access support in the wider community, and have information about the helplines and advice services relevant to them.

Research indicates that young people who have a homosexual or lesbian orientation may have serious difficulties in a school climate permeated by homophobia and heterosexism (Rivers 1996; Douglas *et al.* 1997). Homophobia can make schools unsafe for young gay and lesbian students. Douglas found that 82 per cent of secondary-school teachers were aware of incidents of homophobic bullying. As a result many students became truants (Rivers 1996). In more severe cases they have been driven to self-harm or even suicide (Ramafedi *et al.* 1991). The mean age of suicides and suicide attempts among young gays is 16 (Watney 1997). Research shows that while schools are aware of the presence of gay pupils and their experience of such difficulties, many teachers felt they had neither the skills nor the confidence to respond effectively (Douglas *et al.* 1997).

A number of questions arise about what schools could do to improve a serious and difficult situation. The first point relates to the legislation and to Clause 28, which makes discussion about homosexuality very difficult in British schools. On the basis of the views of young people, there is a case for the repeal of this legislation, so that effective work can be developed.

Rogers (1994) identifies a number of issues which gay young people said could have made a difference to their experiences at school. They cite open discussion of homosexuality, in a situation where homosexuality is not simply seen as a problem. They also requested open discussion of the discrimination and of the oppression they receive. Gay young people also suggested that talks by ex-students, and the use of art and literature in school which deals with same-sex relationships, could have been helpful. They also requested that teachers should stand up for gay pupils.

Blumenfeld (1992: 5) makes recommendations about a policy on homosexuality in schools:

- Are lesbian and gay and bisexual issues visible in the whole curriculum?
- Is there a statement which describes how these issues are addressed?
- How is sex and sexuality presented – is 'sex' being defined in terms only of heterosexual, penetrative and reproductive sex?
- Do the bullying policy and equal opportunities' programme include homophobia ?
- Is there a statement on how to challenge homophobia?

A checklist of this kind makes an important point. It repeats the emphasis we placed on the development of whole-school policies in relation to a radical agenda to deal with gender issues. If a school is to challenge homophobia effectively, a whole-school approach is invariably necessary. A positive ethos that acknowledges difference and actively encourages respect for all young people is required (Biddle 1998). Plummer's' demand for a 'pluralistic, polyvocal potential of proliferating stories' becomes very relevant once again.

Who Should Deliver Sex Education?

Evaluating 'Healthy Alliances'

We have throughout this study attempted to evaluate the effectiveness of the different sex education programmes from the perspective of the adolescents to whom they were delivered. Each had some advantages and some flaws in the view of their consumers. What was clear was the importance of funding. The Gainton and Tonford programmes were welcomed – with reservations – by pupils in the schools involved. Each programme's funding had allowed for a degree of careful planning, consultation and negotiation between teachers, health professionals and parents, and in either case this proved fruitful. Provision works best when sessions are well planned and integrated with a *programme* of sex education, rather than being one-offs. They need to be developed in partnership with a school and to be part of the curriculum. It is important to note, however, that the Gainton programme had funding to run for two years only. The health professional most responsible for getting the programme off the ground commented: 'My contract is only for a year and so is that of the representative from education.' At the end of that year, the programme simply stopped functioning. The Sex Education Forum has published guidelines (1994) to reflect the views of the key agencies in British sex education work. They urge that greater attention be given to the teachers' training in sex education and their ongoing support, and that 'named' funding be allocated accordingly.

The Use of Health Professionals in School Sex Education

The other theme that we want to explore is whether the health professional is the right person to take part in the sexual socialisation of young people. We have discussed the issues elsewhere (Measor, Tiffin and Miller 1999), and can offer only a brief account here. Pupils in all five schools welcomed the input into their sex education lessons of medically trained people. Nevertheless, health professionals encountered some negative reactions to their work. The programmes had dealt fully with neither the problems which arise from teaching pupil groups differentiated in terms of maturity nor with those arising from sex education provision to a mixed-gender group. On occasion, when they were asked to take over a whole class of pupils the health professionals encountered real difficulties of classroom control and discipline. Some of the reasons relate to their lack of training for classroom work with large groups. It is not reasonable to expect every health professional to have the requisite classroom skills without specific training. We suggest that it is important for the National Health Service to ensure that effective training and levels of support are provided for those health professionals who do undertake this work.

Research has indicated the importance of a multi-agency approach. Adler (1997) draws attention to the connection between socio-economic deprivation and a number of sexual health problems. Other studies, including Smith (1993), have demonstrated a reasonable statistical link between conception rates and simple measures of deprivation. There is a huge class divide in teenage pregnancy. In east London 11.5 teenage girls per 1,000 got pregnant in 1995, compared with only 32 per 1,000 in Kingston and Richmond. Adler called for the issues to be tackled across government departments. The Green Paper *Our Healthier Nation* (DoH 1998) adopts this strategy, recommending that schools are likely to have greater rates of success in these health-related areas if they form partnerships beyond the school gates. The effects of structural features are very powerful and very difficult to overcome. A health education campaign alone will have only limited effects. The issue of healthy alliances does not simply affect the behaviour of those delivering sex education but needs co-ordination at the highest level. Programmes which tackle the wider problems of deprivation and social exclusion are essential, and inevitably require cross-departmental initiatives.

Our data and other research suggest that a mixture of health professionals and well-trained teachers with good PSE skills can have some success in producing effective sex education. (There are, however, significant institutional barriers to facilitating the development of such programmes, and a role for government in effecting easier arrangements.) There is currently a significant degree of competition between health and educational professional groups the effect of which is to block successful healthy alliances. While there are some areas of Britain where these difficulties have been overcome, there are others where they remain a real obstacle to the development of healthy alliances.

Conclusion

In the conclusion to a project of this kind readers might expect a list of recommendations for policy. While this research did not have a prescriptive objective, a number of issues did emerge. For many years now there has been substantial criticism of the sex education that is offered to adolescents. We suggest that it is important to collect sound research-based information that takes account of the perspectives of users in order to develop more appropriate and effective programmes for adolescents. This research suggests that *some* of the problems identified as important in British sex education have been effectively tackled by the development of innovative programmes of the kind we studied. Nevertheless, problems remain.

Recently, doubt has been cast on the effectiveness of sex education in Britain (see Kirby 1994 for a summary of the research). In the light of these findings the Sex Education Forum calls for closer monitoring of sex education policies and the provision of sex education in schools, together with research into the effectiveness of classroom approaches. We hope the data in this study cast light on some of the issues. There are a number of problems remaining in any attempt to research and evaluate sex education. No agreement exists on what the outcomes of effective sex education might be. Effects that may be positive, like an increase in self-esteem, are very difficult to measure. They may take second place to more easily quantified measures, like a reduction in unplanned pregnancies. There is urgent need for government action, to decide on preferred outcomes for sex education work. There is also a need for increased funding, for sex education training and innovatory programmes. Most of all, though, there is need for government to take seriously the task of listening to what young people have to say about their sexual culture, and then to create policies and legislation that allow those committed groups working in this field to react flexibly and swiftly to the needs of young people.

References

Abbott, S. (1998) 'AIDS and young women', *Bulletin of the National Clearinghouse for Youth Studies* 7: 38–41.

Abrams, C., Spears, R. and Marks, D. (1990) 'AIDS invulnerability, relationships, sexual behaviour and attitudes among 16–19 year olds', in P. Aggleton, P. Davies and G. Hart (eds) *AIDS: Individual, Cultural and Policy*, Barcombe: Falmer.

Achilles Heel (1991) 'Health Matters', No. 11 (Summer).

Acton, W. (1857) *The Functions and Disorders of the Reproductive Organs in Youth, in Adult Age and in Advanced Life*, London.

Adams, G. R. (1991) 'Identity and intimacy: some observations after a decade of investigation', *Journal of Youth and Adolescence* 10: 473–86.

Adkins, L. and Merchant, V. (1996) *Sexualising the Social: Power and the Organisation of Sexuality*, London: Macmillan

Adler, M. (1997) 'Sexual health – a *Health of the Nation* failure', *British Medical Journal* 314(7096): 1743–7.

Aggleton, P., Homans, H. and Warwick, I. (1988) 'Young people, sexuality education and AIDS', *Youth and Policy* 23: 5–13.

Aggleton, P., Davies, P. and Hart, G. (eds) (1990) *AIDS: Individual, Cultural and Policy Dimensions*, Barcombe: Falmer.

——— (eds) (1991) *AIDS: Responses, Intervention and Care*, Barcombe: Falmer.

Allan, J. (1992) in R. W. Connell and G. W. Dowsett (eds) *Rethinking Sex: Social Theory and Sexuality Research*, Melbourne: Melbourne University Press.

Allen, I. (1987) *Education, Sex and Personal Relationships*, London: Policy Studies Institute.

All-Party Parliamentary Group on AIDS (1992) 'HIV/AIDS and sex education for young people', *Occasional Paper 3*, Stationery Office: London.

Altman, D. (1992) 'AIDS and the discourses of sexuality', in R. W. Connell and G. W. Dowsett (eds) *Rethinking Sex: Social Theory and Sexuality Research*, Melbourne: Melbourne University Press.

Altman, D. *et al.* (eds) (1989) *'Which Homosexuality?': Essays from the Scientific Conference on Lesbian and Gay Studies*, London: Gay Men's Press.

Arnot, M. (1984) 'How shall we educate our sons?', in R. Deem (ed.) *Co-education Reconsidered*, Milton Keynes: Open University Press.

Azjen, I. (1988) *Attitudes, Personality and Behaviour*, Milton Keynes, Open University Press.

References

—— and Fishbein, M. (1980) *Understanding Attitudes and Predicting Social Behaviour*, Englewood Cliffs, NJ: Prentice-Hall.

Bailey, C. (1993) 'Equality with difference: on androcentrism and menstruation', *Teaching Sociology* 21: 121–9.

Bainham, A. (1988) *Children, Parents and the State*, London: Sweet & Maxwell.

Baker-Miller, J. (1974) *Psychoanalysis and Women*, Harmondsworth: Penguin.

Balding, J. (1997) *Young People in 1996: The Health-Related Behaviour Questionnaire Results for Pupils*, Exeter: Schools Health Education Unit, University of Exeter.

Baldo, M. *et al*. (1994) 'Does sex education lead to earlier or increased sexual activity in young people?', Paper presented at the *World Health Organisation Global Programme on AIDS Conference, 23 June, Berlin*, Geneva: WHO.

Basch, F. (1974) *Relative Creatures: Victorian Women in Society and the Novel, 1837–67* London: Allen Lane.

Baudrillard, J. (1988) *Selected Writings*, ed. M. Poster, Stanford, CA: Stanford University Press.

Beloff, M. (1994) 'Sex education in schools: a joint opinion. Association of Teachers and Lecturers and others', BMA Foundation for AIDS, Forum Fact Sheet No. 3, *Sex Education Matters* no. London: Sex Education Forum.

Biddle, G. (1998) 'Teaching about homosexuality in secondary schools', *Sex Education Matters* 16 (Summer).

Biddulph, M. (1998) 'Teaching sex and relationships' education in secondary schools', Forum Factsheet No. 16, *Sex Education Matters* 16 (Summer).

Blackmore, J., Kenway, J., Willis, S. and Rennie, L. (1996) 'Putting up with the put down? Girls, boys, power and sexual harrassment', in L. Laskey (ed.) *Schooling and Sexualities: Teaching for a Positive Sexuality*, Geelong, Victoria: Deaking University Press.

Blake, S. and Laxton, J. (1998) *Strides: A Practical Guide to Sex and Relationships for Young Men*, London: Family Planning Association.

Bland, L. (1982) 'Guardians of the race or vampires on the nation's health? Female-sexuality and its regulation in twentieth-century Britain', in E. Whitelegg *et al*. (eds) *The Changing Experience of Women*, Oxford: Martin Robinson.

Blumenfeld, W. (1992) *Homophobia: How We All Pay the Price*, Boston: Beacon Press.

Braidotti, R. (1989) 'The politics of ontological difference', in T. Brennan (ed.) *Between Feminism and Psychoanalysis*, London: Routledge.

Boethius, C. G. (1984) 'Swedish sex education and its results', *Current Sweden* 315 (March).

Boldero, J. M. *et al*. (1992) 'Intention, context and safe sex: Australian adolescents' reponses to AIDS', *Journal of Applied Social Psychology* 22: 1375–97.

Bordo, S. (1993) *Unbearable Weight*, Berkeley: University of California Press.

Bourdieu, P. (1978) 'Sport and Social Class and Social Sciences', *Information* 17(6) 819–40.

Breakwell, G. M. and Fife-Shaw, C. R. (1992) 'Sexual activities and preferences in a UK sample of 16–20-year-olds', *Archives of Sexual Behaviour* 21: 61–5.

—— and Clayden, K. (1993) 'Risk taking, control over partner choice and intended use of condoms by virgins', *Journal of Community and Applied Psychology* 1: 173–87.

Brooks-Gunn, J. and Furstenberg, F. F. (1989) 'Adolescent sexual behaviour', *American Psychologist* 44: 249–57.

Brown, B. (1973) *Marx, Freud and the Critique of Everyday Life*, New York: Monthly Review Press.

Brownmiller, S. (1975) *Against Our Will: Men, Women and Rape*, New York: Simon & Schuster.

Buchanan, A. and Ten Brinke, J. (1996) 'The can do girls – a barometer of change', Oxford: Department of Applied Social Studies and Research.

Bunton, R. and Macdonald, G. (1992) *Health Promotion: Disciplines and Diversity*, London: Routledge.

Burchell, J. and Millman, V. (eds) (1989) *Changing Perspectives on Gender: New Initiatives in Secondary Education*, Milton Keynes: Open University Press.

Butler, J. (1990) *Gender Trouble: Feminism and the Subversion of Identity*, London: Routledge.

Campbell, B. (1987) 'Taking the plunge', *Marxism Today* December 9.

—— (1987) 'Feminist sexual politics: now you see it, now you don't', in *Feminist Review* (ed) *Sexuality: A Reader*, London: Virago.

Caplan, P. (ed) (1987) *The Cultural Construction of Sexuality*, London: Routledge.

Carabine, J. (1998) 'Constructing women: women's sexualiity and social policy', *Journal of Critical Social Policy* 34: 23–37.

Carlson, B. (1987) 'Dating violence: a research review', *Social Casework* 68: 16–23.

Carter, S. M. and Carter, D. S. G. (1993) 'Gender differentiated receptivity to sexuality education curricula by adolescents', *Health Education Research, Theory and Practice*, 233–43.

Chapman, S. and Hodgson, J. (1988) 'Showers in raincoats: attitudinal barriers to condom use in high-risk heterosexuals', *Community Health Studies* 12: 97–105.

Chessler, E. (1966) *Love Without Fear*, London: Arrow.

Chodorow, N. (1971) 'Being and doing: a cross-cultural examination of the socialisation of males and females', in V. Gornick and B. K. Noran (eds) *Women in Sexist Society*, New York: Basic Books.

—— (1978) *The Reproduction of Mothering*, Los Angeles: University of California Press.

Chrystie, I. L. L., Palmer, S. J., Kenney, P. and Banatvala, J. E. (1992) 'HIV seroprevalence among women attending antenatal clinics in London', Letter in *The Lancet* 339: 364.

Clarke, D. (1992) 'With my body I thee worship: the social construction of marital sex problems', in D. Morgan and S. Scott (eds) *Body Matters: Essays on the Sociology of the Body*, Barcombe: Falmer.

Clarke, W. (1987) 'The dyke, the feminist and the devil', in *Feminist Review* (ed.) *Sexuality: A Reader*, London: Virago.

Clarricoates, K. (1980) 'The importance of being Earnest, Emma, Tom, Jane', in R. Deem (ed.) *Schooling for Women's Work*, London: RKP.

Clift, S. and Stears, D. (1989) 'Undergraduates' beliefs and attitudes about AIDS', in P. Aggleton *et al*. (eds) *AIDS: Social Representations and Social Practices*, Barcombe: Falmer Press.

—— (1989) 'AIDS education in secondary schools', *Education and Health* 9: 1–4.

Cockburn, C. (1991) 'A politics of the Body', in *In the Way of Women: Men's Resistance to Sexual Equality in Organisations*, London: Macmillan.

Cohen, P. (1994) 'The role of the school nurse in providing sex education', *Nursing Times* 90 (23): 36–8.

References

Collinson, D. L. and Collinson, M. (1989) 'Sexuality in the workplace: the domination of men's sexuality', in J. Hearn, D. L. Sheppard *et al.* (eds) *The Sexuality of Organisation*, London: Routledge.

Confidentiality and People under 16 Guidance issued Jointly by BMA, GMSC, HEA, Brooks Advisory Service, FPA and RCGP, London.

Connell, R. W. (1983) *Which Way Is Up? Essays on Class, Sex and Culture*, Sydney: Allen & Unwin.

—— (1987) *Gender and Power*, Cambridge: Polity Press.

—— (1989) 'Cool guys, swots and wimps: the interplay of masculinity and schooling', *Oxford Review of Education* 15 (3): 291–303.

—— and Dowsett, G. W. (1992) *Rethinking Sex: Social Theory and Sexuality Research*, Melbourne: Melbourne University Press.

Corlyon, J. (1999) 'Teenage pregnancy and parenthood', *Sex Education Matters* 18 (Spring).

Cott, N. F. (1978) 'Passionlessness: an interpretation of Victorian sexual ideology, 1790–1850', *Signs* 4 (2).

Coward, R. (1994) *Female Desire: Women's Sexuality Today*, London: Paladin Books.

Daly, J. *et al.* (1992) *Researching Health Care*, London: Routledge.

Daly, M. (1978) *Gyn/Ecology: The Metaethics of Radical Feminism*, Boston: Beacon Press.

—— and Wilson, M. (1988) *Homicide*, Aldine de Gruyter.

Darling, C. A. and Hicks, M. W. (1982) 'Parental influence on adolescent sexuality: implications for parents as educators', *Journal of Youth and Adolescence* 11: 231–45.

Davidson, N. (1990) *Boys will be …? Sex Education and Young Men*, London: Bedford Square Press.

Davies, B. (1997) 'Constructing and deconstructing masculinities through critical literacy', *Gender and Education* 9 (1): 69–87.

—— Bebbington, A. and Charnley, H. (1990) *Resources, Needs and Outcomes in Community Based Care*, Avebury.

Daugherty, L. R. and Burger, J. M. (1984) 'The influence of parents, church and peers on the sexual attitudes and behaviours of college students', *Archives of Sexual Behaviour* 13: 351–9.

de Beauvoir, S. (1988) *The Second Sex*, London: Picador Classics.

Delamont, S. (1990) *Sex Roles and the School*, London: Cassell.

Delphy, C. (1993) 'Rethinking sex and gender', *Women's Studies' International Forum* 16 (1): 1–9.

DES (1987) *The Education (No. 2) Act*, London: HMSO.

—— (1987) Circular 11/87, London: HMSO.

DfE (1994) *The Education Act 1993: Sex Education in Schools*, London: HMSO.

—— (1994) Circular 5/94, London: HMSO.

DfEE (1997) *Excellence in Schools*, London: DfEE.

DoE (1988) Circular 12/88, London: DoE.

Department of Health (1992) *The Health of the Nation: A Strategy for Health in England*, London: Stationery Office.

DoH (1998) *Our Healthier Nation: A Contract for Health*, London: Stationery Office.

DiMascolo, E. (1991) 'To have knowledge and to hold power: adolescents negotiating safe sex', unpublished thesis, Melbourne: University of Melbourne.

Dixon, C. (1997) 'Pete's tool: identity and sex play in the design and technology classroom', *Gender and Education* 9 (1): 69–87.

170

Douglas, N. *et al.* (1997) *Playing it Safe: Responses of Secondary School Teachers to Lesbian, Gay and Bisexual Pupils, Bullying, HIV/AIDS Education and Section 28*, London: Institute of Education, University of London.

Durham, M. (1991) *Sex and Politics: The Family and Morality in the Thatcher Years*, London: Macmillan.

Edwards, A. (1993) 'Selling the body, keeping the soul', in S. Scott and D. Morgan (eds) *Body Matters: Essays on the Sociology of the Body*, Barcombe: Falmer.

Ehrenreich, B., Hess, E. and Jacobs, G. (1986) *Remaking Love*, Garden City, NY: Anchor Press.

Elleschild, P. (1994) 'Bad girls and excessive women: the social construction of "promiscuity"', Paper presented at the BSA Annual Conference *Sexualities in Social Context*.

Ellism, H. (1913) *Studies in the Psychology of Sex*, vols I–VI, Philadelphia, PA: F. A. Davies.

Epstein, D. (1994) *Challenging Lesbian and Gay Inequalities in Education*, Milton Keynes: Open University Press.

—— (1997) 'Cultures of schooling/cultures of sexuality', *International Journal of Inclusive Education* 1 (1): 37–53.

—— and Johnson, R. (1998) *Schooling Sexual Values*, Milton Keynes: Open University Press.

Evans, D. T. (1993) *Sexual Citizenship: The Material Construction of Sexualities*, London: Routledge.

Farey, L. (1998) Editorial, *Sex Education Matters* 15 (Spring).

—— (1998) Editorial, *Sex Education Matters* 16 (Summer).

Farrell, C. (1978) *My Mother Said …. The Way Young People Learned about Sex and Birth Control*, London: Routledge & Kegan Paul.

Feminist Review (eds) (1987) *Sexuality: A Reader*, London: Virago.

Featherstone, M., Hepworth, M. and Turner, B. S. (eds) (1991) *The Body: Social Processes and Cultural Theory*, London: Sage.

Finch, J. and Summerfield, P. (1991) 'Social reconstruction and the emergence of companiate marriage, 1945–59', in D. Clark (ed.) *Marriage, Domestic Life and Social Change: Writing for Jacqueline Burgoyne*, London: RKP.

Fine, M. (1988) 'Sexuality, schooling, and adolescent females: the missing discourse of desire', *Harvard Educational Review* 58 (1): 29–51.

Fisher, N. (1994) 'The wonder years', Paper presented at *Adolescent Sexuality and Gender: Boys and Girls are Different Conference*, Friday 6 May 1994, London: National Children's Bureau.

—— (1994) *The Best Sex Guide*, Harmondsworth: Penguin.

Fitzpatrick, P. *et al.* (1990) 'Variation in sexual behaviour in gay men', in Aggleton, P. *et al.* (eds) *AIDS : Individual, Cultural and Policy Dimensions*, Barcombe: Falmer.

Ford, N. (1991) *The Socio-Sexual Lifestyles of Young People in South West England*, South West Regional Health Authority, Institute of Population Studies.

—— and Morgan, K. (1989) 'Heterosexual lifestyles of young people in an English city', *Journal of Population and Social Studies* 1: 167–85.

Foucault, M. (1979) 'Studies in governmentality', *Ideology and Consciousness* 6: 5–22.

—— (1981) *The History of Sexuality*, vol. 1: *An Introduction*, Harmondsworth: Pelican.

—— and Sennet, R. (1981) 'Sexuality and solitude', *Humanities in Review* 1: 3–12.

Frank, A. W. (1991) 'For a Sociology of the Body: An analytical review', in Featherstone, M. *et al.* (eds) *The Body: Social Processes and Cultural Theory*, London: Sage.

References

Frankham, J. (1992) *Not Under My Roof – Families Talking about Sex and AIDS*, Horsham: Avert.

—— (1993) *Parents and Teenagers: Understanding and Improving Communication about HIV and AIDS*, Horsham: Avert.

Fruend, P. E. S. (1989) *The Civilised Body: Social Domination, Control and Health*, Philadelphia, PA: Temple University Press.

Furstenberg, F. F. *et al.* (1989) 'Teenaged pregnancy and childbearing', *American Psychologist* 44: 313–20.

Gagnon, J. H. and Simon, W. (1973) *Sexual Conduct: The Social Sources of Human Sexuality*, Chicago: Aldine.

Gaskell, J. (1992) *Gender Matters from School to Work*, Milton Keynes: Open University Press.

Gatens, M. A. (1983) 'A critique of the sex–gender distinction', in J. Allen and P. Patton (eds) *Beyond Marxism: Interventions After Marx*, Sydney: Intervention Publications.

Giddens, A. (1992) *The Transformation of Intimacy: Sexuality, Love and Eroticism in Modern Societies*, Cambridge: Polity.

Giddens, A. (1991) *Modernity and Self-Identity*, Cambridge: Polity.

Gillick, V. (1986) *The West Norfolk and Wisbech AHA and the DHSS Appeal Cases (England)* 112.

Gilmore, T. C. (1990) *Manhood in the Making*, New Haven: Yale University Press.

Goldman, R. J. and Goldman, J. D. G. (1982) *Children's Sexual Thinking*, London: Routledge & Kegan Paul.

Grafton, T., Miller, H., Smith, L., Vegoda, M. and Whitfield, R. (1983) 'Gender and curriculum choice: a case study', in M. Hammersley and A. Hargreaves (eds) *Curriculum Practice: Some Sociological Case Studies*, Barcombe: Falmer Press.

Grant, L. (1997) *Guardian* 25 March.

Griffin, C. (1985) *Typical Girls*, London: RKP.

—— and Lees, S. (1997) Editorial: 'Masculinities in education', *Gender and Education* (special issue) 9 (1): 5–8.

Haire, N. (ed.) *Encyclopaedia of Sexual Knowledge*, London: Encyclopaedia Press.

Hall, L. (1991) *Hidden Anxieties: Male Sexuality, 1900–1950*, Cambridge: Polity.

Halson, J. (1989) 'The sexual harassment of young women', in L. Holly (ed) *Girls and Sexuality: Teaching and Learning*, Milton Keynes: Open University Press.

Hargreaves, D. (1967) *Social Relations in a Secondary School*, London: Routledge & Kegan Paul.

Haste, H. W. (1981) 'The image of science', in A. Kelly (ed.) *The Missing Half*, Manchester: Manchester University Press.

Hayes, C.D. (1987) *Risking the Future: Adolescent Sexuality, Pregnancy and Childbearing*, Washington D.C, National Academic Press.

Haywood, C. (1996) 'Out of the curriculum: sex talking, talking sex', *Curriculum Studies* 4 (2): 229–50.

Health Education Authority (1992) *Today's Young Adults: 16–19-Year-Olds Look at Diet, Alcohol, Smoking, Drugs and Sexual Behaviour*, London: HEA.

—— (1997) *Health Update and Sexual Health*, London: HEA.

—— (1998) *Reducing the Rate of Teenage Conceptions. Toward a National Programme*, consultation document, London: HEA.

Health Monitor (1997) 'NOP Report for Durex', London: NOP.

172

Hearn, J. (1987) *The Gender of Oppression: Men, Masculinity and the Critique of Marxism*, Brighton: Wheatsheaf.

Heath, S. (1982) *The Sexual Fix*, London: Macmillan.

Herbert, C. M. H. (1989) *Talking of Silence: The Sexual Harassment of the Schoolgirls*, Barcombe: Falmer.

Hewitt, M. (1991) 'Bio-politics and social policy: Foucault's account of welfare', in M. Featherstone, M. Hepworth, and B. S. Turner (eds) *The Body: Social Processes and Cultural Theory*, London: Sage.

Hirst, J. (1994) *Not in Front of the Grown ups: A Study of the Social and Sexual Lives of 15- and 16-Year-Olds*, London: Pavic.

Hite, S. (1977) *The Hite Report: A Nationwide Study on Female Sexuality*, New York: Hamlyn.

HMI (1989) 'Personal and Social Education from 5 to 16', *Curriculum Matters*,

HMSO (1988) 'Section 28', *Local Government Act*, London: HMSO.

—— (1991) *Report of the Health Committee on Maternity Services: Preconception, 430*, vols I–III, London, HMSO.

Holland, J. and Adkins, L. (eds) (1996) *Sex, Sensibility and the Gendered Body*, London: Macmillan.

—— and Sharpe, S. (1993) *Wimp or Gladiator: Contradictions in Acquiring Masculine Sexuality*, London: Tufnell Press.

—— Ramazanoglu, C., Scott, S., Sharpe, S. and Thompson, R. (1990) 'Don't die of ignorance, I nearly died of embarrassment. Condoms in Context', *WRAP Paper 2*, London: Tufnell Press.

—— (1991) 'Between embarrassment and trust: young women and the diversity of condom use', in P. Aggleton *et al.* (eds) *AIDS: Responses, Interventions and Care*, Barcombe: Falmer.

—— (1992) 'Pressure, resistance, empowerment: young women and the negotiation of safer sex', in P. Aggleton *et al.* (eds) *Rights, Risk and Reason*, Barcombe: Falmer.

—— *et al.* (1998) *Male in the Head*, London: Tufnell Press.

Holloway, W. (1984a) 'Women's power in heterosexual sex', *Women's Studies' International Forum* 7: 66–8.

—— (1984b) 'Gender differences and the production of subjectivity', in J. Henriques, W. Holloway, C. Urwin, V. Couze and V. Walkerdine (eds) *Changing the Subject*, London: Methuen.

Holly, L. (1989) *Girls and Sexuality*, Milton Keynes: Open University Press.

Horney, K. (1932) 'The dread of women', *International Journal of Psychoanalysis* 13.-*Quarterly* 19: 534–44.

Houghton, W. E. (1987) *The Victorian Frame of Mind, 1830–1870*, Connecticut: Yale University Press.

Hudson, F. and Ineichen, B. (1991) *Taking it Lying Down: Sexuality and Teenage Motherhood*, London: Macmillan.

Hunter, A. (1984) 'Virtue with a vengeance: The pro-family politics of the New Right', unpublished PhD thesis, Department of Sociology, Brandeis University.

Hunter, J. D. (1991) *Culture Wars*, New York: Basic Books.

IHPS (1993) *Preventing Teenage Pregnancy: Proceedings of the IHPS Conference*, University of Southampton.

Inazu, J. K. and Fox, G.L. (1980) 'Maternal influence on the sexual behaviour of teenage daughters', *Journal of Family Issues* 1: 81–102.

References

Ingham, R. (1992) 'Sexuality and health in young people', in G. N. Penny, P. Bennett and M. Herbert (eds) *Health Psychology: A Lifespan Perspective*, London: Harwood Academic Publishers.

—— (1994) 'Sexual lifestyles of young people', in IHPS, *Preventing Teenage Pregnancy*, March 1994, University of Southampton.

—— (1997) 'The Development of an Integrated Model of Sexual Conduct amongst Young People', ESRC Project, Dept of Psychology, University of Southampton.

—— and Carrera, C. (1998) 'Liaison between parents and schools on sex education policies', in *Sex Education Matters p 11*.

—— and Edmonds, S. (1994) 'How can we meet pupil needs in sex education?', *Sex Education Matters*, No. 5.

—— Woodcock, A. and Stenner, K. (1991) 'Getting to know you ... young people's knowledge of their partners at first intercourse', *Journal of Community and Applied Social Psychology* 1: 117–32.

—— (1991) 'The limitations of rational decision making as applied to young people's sexual behaviour', in P. Aggleton and G. Hart (eds) *AIDS: Rights, Risks and Reason*, Bascombe: Falmer.

Irigaray, L. (1985) *This Sex Which Is Not One*, Ithaca, NY: Cornell University Press.

Jackson, M. (1984) 'Sexology and the social construction of male sexuality (Havelock Ellis)' in L. Coveney (ed.) *The Sexuality Papers*, London: Hutchinson.

—— (1987) '"Facts of life", or the eroticisation of women's oppression? Sexology and the social construction of heterosexuality', in P. Caplan (ed.) *Cultures and Constructions of Sexuality*, London: Routledge.

Jackson, M. (1994) *The Real Facts of Life: Feminism and the Politics of Sexuality*, London: Taylor & Francis.

Jackson, S. (1978) 'How to make babies: sexism in sex education', *Women's Studies International Quarterly* 1 (4): 341–52.

—— (1982) *Childhood Sexuality*, Oxford: Blackwell.

—— (1988) 'Constructing female sexuality', in M. Evans (ed) *The Woman Question: Readings on the Subordination of Women*, Oxford: Fontana.

—— (1996) 'Heterosexuality as a problem for feminist theory', in L. Adkins and V. Merchant (eds) *Sexualising the Social: Power and the Organisation of Sexuality*, London: Macmillan.

Jefferson, T. (1994) 'Theorising masculine subjectivity', in Stanko, E. *et al.* (eds) *Just Boys Doing Business*, London: Routledge.

Jeffrys, S. (1990) *Anti-Climax*, London: Women's Press.

Johnson, A. M. (1992) 'Home grown heterosexually acquired HIV infection', *British Medical Journal* 304: 1125–6.

Johnson, A. M. *et al.* (1994) *Sexual Attitudes and Lifestyles*, Oxford: Blackwell.

Jones, C. (1985) Sexual Tyranny in mixed-sex schools: an in-depth study of male violence', in G. Weiner (ed.) *Just a Bunch of Girls*, Milton Keynes: Open University Press.

Jones, E. F., Forrest, J. D., Goldman, N., Henshaw, S., Lincoln, R., Rossoff, J. I., Westhoff, C. F. and Wolf, D. (1985) 'Teenage pregnancy in developed countries: determinants and policy implications', *Family Planning Perspectives* 17 (2).

Jowell, T. (1998) 'Contraceptive ignorance blamed for high, unplanned pregnancy rate', Report from a speech given to the National Family Planning Association 1998, *Guardian* 9 February.

Kantner, J. F. and Zelnick, M. (1972) 'Sexual experiences of young unmarried women in the United States', *Family Planning Perspectives* 4: 9–18.

Kehily, M. J. and Nayak, A. (1997) 'Lads and Laughter: humour and the production of heterosexual hierarchies', *Gender and Education* 9 (1): 69–87.

Kelly, A. (ed.) (1981) *The Missing Half*, Manchester: Manchester University Press.

Kenway, J. and Fitzclarence, L. (1997) 'Masculinity, violence and schooling: challenging poisonous pedagogies', *Gender and Education* 9 (1): 117–33.

Keohande, N. *et al.* (eds) (1982) *Feminist Theory: A Critque of Ideology*, Harvester Press.

Kinsey, A. C. *et al.* (1948) *Sexual Behaviour in the Human Male*, Philadelphia, PA: Saunders.

—— *et al.* (1953) *Sexual Behaviour in the Human Female*, Philadelphia, PA: Saunders.

Kirby, D. (1980) 'The effects of school education programmes: a review of the literature', *Journal of School Health* 50: 559–63.

—— (1994) 'School based programmes to reduce sexual risk behaviours: a review of effectiveness', *Public Health Reports* 109 (3): 339–60.

—— (1996) Editorial, *British Medical Journal* 311: 7002.

—— *et al.* (1991) 'Reducing the risk: impact of a new curriculum on sexual risk-taking', *Family Planning Perspectives* 23: 253–6

—— *et al.* (1992) 'School-based programs to reduce sexual risk-taking behaviours', *Journal of School Health* 62 (7).

Kissling, E. (1996) 'Bleeding outloud: communication about menstruation', *Feminism and Psychology* 6 (4): 481–504.

Koedt, A. (1973) 'Myth of the vaginal orgasm', in E. Levine *et al.* (eds) *Radical Feminism: Notes from the Second Year*, New York: Quadrangle.

Koff, E. and Rierdan, J. (1995) 'Early adolescent girls' understanding of menstruation', *Women and Health* 22 (4): 1–21.

Kuhn, A. (1988) 'The body and cinema: some problems for feminism', in Sheridan, S. (ed.) *Grafts: Essays in Feminist Cultural Theory*, London: Verso.

Lawler, J. (1998) 'Body care and learning to do for others', in M. Allot and M. Robb (eds) *Understanding Health and Social Care: An Introductory Reader*, London: Sage.

Lee, J. (1994) 'Menarche and the (hetero) sexualisation of the female body', *Gender and Society* 8 (3): 343–62.

Lees, S. (1986) *Losing Out*, London: Hutchinson Educational.

—— (1993) *Sugar and Spice: Sexuality and Adolescent Girls*, Harmondsworth: Penguin.

—— (1994) 'Talking about sex in sexuality education', *Gender and Education* 6 (3): 281–92.

Lenderyou, G. and Porter, M. (1994) *Sex Education, Values and Morality*, London: HEA.

Lenderyou, G. and Ray, C. (1997) *Let's Hear it from the Boys! Supporting Sex and Relationship Education for Boys and Young Men*, London: National Children's Bureau.

Lenskyj, H. (1990) 'Beyond plumbing and prevention', *Gender and Education Journal* 2 (2): 217–31.

Lewin, M. and Tragoso, L. M. (1987) 'Has the feminist movement influenced adolescent sex role attitudes? A reassessment after half a century', *Sex Roles* 16: 125–35.

Lovering, K. (1997) 'Listening to girls' voices and silence', in M. de Ras and V. Grace (eds) *Bodily Boundaries, Sexualised Genders and Medical Discourses*, Palmerston: Dunmore Press.

McCabe, M. P. and Collins, J. K. (1979) 'Sex role and dating orientation', *Journal of Youth and Adolescence* 8: 407–25.

References

Mac an Ghaill, M. (1994) *The Making of Men: Masculinities, Sexualities and Schooling*, Milton Keynes: Open University Press.

—— and Haywood, M. (1996) (eds) *Understanding Masculinities*, Buckingham: Open University Press.

Macintosh, M. (1978) 'Who needs prostitutes? The ideology of male sex needs', in C. Smart and B. Smart (eds) *Women, Sexuality and Social Control*, London: RKP.

MacKinnon, C. (1983) 'Feminism, Marxism, method and the state', in E. Abel (ed.) *The Signs Reader*, Chicago: University of Chicago Press.

Mahony, P. (1985) *Schools for the Boys*, London: Hutchinson.

—— and Jones, C. (1989) (eds) *Learning Our Lines: Sexuality and Social Control in Education*, London: Routledge.

Mainman, L. A. and Becker, M. H. (1974) 'The health belief model: origins and correlates in psychological theory', in M. H. Becker (ed.) *The Health Belief Model and Personal Health Behaviour*, Thorofare, NJ: Charles B. Slack.

Marshall, T. H. (1963) *Sociology at the Crossroads*, London: Heinemann.

Mason, A. and Palmer, A. (1996) *Queer Bashing: A National Survey of Hate Crimes Against Lesbians and Gay Men*, Stonewall.

Mason, J. (1996) 'Gender, care and sensibility in family and kin relations', in J. Holland and L. Adkins (eds) *Sex, Sensibility and the Gendered Body*, London: Macmillan.

Massey, D. (1988) *School Sex Education. Why? What? and How?*, London: Family Planning Association Education Unit.

—— (1990) 'School sex education: knitting without a pattern', *Health Education Journal* 49: 134–42.

Masters, W. H., Johnson V. E. and Kolodny, R. C. (1987) *Sex and Human Loving*, London: Macmillan.

Matthews, J. J. (1992) 'The present moment in sexual politics', in R. W. Connell and G. W. Dowsett (eds) *Rethinking Sex: Social Theory and Sexuality Research*, Melbourne: Melbourne University Press.

Measor, L. (1983) 'Gender and the sciences: pupils' gender-based conceptions of school subjects', in M. Hammersley and A. Hargreaves (eds) *Curriculum Practice: Some Sociological Case Studies*, Barcombe: Falmer.

—— (1989) '"Are you coming to see some dirty films today?" Sex Education and Adolescent Sexuality' in Holly, L. (ed) *Girls and Sexuality: Teaching and Learning*, Milton Keynes, Open University Press.

—— Tiffin, C. and Fry, K. (1995) '"All this and not a Mars Bar in sight". The experience of a health professionals' team providing sex education in secondary schools', Paper presented at the *Annual Conference of the Association of Public Health*, Kensington, London, May 1995.

—— Tiffin, C. and Fry, K. (1995) 'Gender and adolescent cultures: the view from some boys', in L. Lawrence, E. Murdoch and S. Parker (eds) *Professional and Development Issues in Leisure, Sport and Education*, L.S.A. no. 56.

—— Tiffin, C. and Fry (Miller), K. (1996) 'Gender and sex education: a study of adolescent responses', *Gender and Education*, 8 (3): 275–89.

—— Tiffin, C. and Fry (Miller), K. (1999) 'The impact of health professionals on school sex education', *Nursing Times Research*, 4 (5).

—— and Squires, P. (forthcoming) *Juvenile Nuisance: A Study of the Issues*, Ashgate Press.

—— and Woods, P. (1984) *Changing Schools*, Milton Keynes: Open University Press.

Mellanby, A. *et al.* (1995) 'School sex education: an experimental programme with educational and medical benefit', *British Medical Journal* 311 (7002): 414–17.

Miller, B. C., Mc Coy, J. K. and Olsen, T. D. (1986) 'Dating age and stage as correlates of adolescent sexual attitudes and behaviour', *Journal of Adolescent Research* 1: 361–71.

Millett, K. (1972) *Sexual Politics*, London: Abacus.

Mitchell, J. (1972) *Women's Estate*, Harmondsworth: Penguin.

Moore, S. M. and Rosenthal, D. A. (1980) 'Sex roles: gender, generation and self-esteem', *Australian Psychologist* 15: 467–77.

—— (1991a) 'Adolescent invulnerability and perceptions of AIDS' risk', *Journal of Adolescent Research* 6: 164–80.

—— (1991b) 'Condom use and coitus: adolescents' attitudes to AIDS and safe sex behaviour', *Journal of Adolescence* 14: 211–27.

—— (1993) *Sexuality in Adolescence*, London: Routledge.

Morgan, D. (1992) *Discovering Men*, London: Routledge.

—— (1993) 'You too can have a body like mine: reflections on the male body and masculinities', in S. Scott and D. Morgan (eds) (1993) *Body Matters: Essays on the Sociology of the Body*, Barcombe: Falmer.

Mort, F. (1987) *Dangerous Sexualities: Medico-Moral Politics in England since 1830*, London: Routledge & Kegan Paul.

Mulvey, L. and Deane, V. (1988) 'Visual pleasures and narrative cinema', in C. Penley (ed.) *Feminism and Film Theory*, London: Routledge.

National Curriculum Council (1993) Spiritual and Moral Development: A discussion paper, NCC Curriculum Guidance 5 Health Education.

NHS (1997) 'Preventing and reducing the adverse effects of unintended teenage pregnancies', *Effective Health Care Bulletin* 3 (1).

Oakley, A. *et al.* (1995) 'Sexual health education interventions for young people: a methodological review', *British Medical Journal*, 310: 158–62.

Oasis Trust (1996) *Teenagers and Sex: Education, Attitudes and Pressures*, Oasis Trust.

Office for National Statistics (1996) *Birth Statistics*, series FMI 26, London: Stationery Office.

—— (1997) *Conceptions in England and Wales 1995 Monitor*, series FMI 97/2, London: Stationery Office.

OPCS (1993) *Population Trends* 74, London: HMSO.

—— (1993) *Birth Statistics: Review of the Registrar General on Births and Patterns of Family Building in England and Wales 1991*, series FMI No. 20, HMSO, London

—— and ONS (1998) *Birth Statistics*, series FMI, London: Stationery Office.

Pateman, C. (1988) *The Sexual Contract*, Cambridge: Polity.

Pearson, V. *et al.* (1995) 'Teenage pregnancy: a comparative study of teenagers choosing terminations of pregnancy or ante-natal care', *Journal of the Royal Society of Medicine* 88 (7): 384–8.

Plant, S. (ed.) (1996) *From Needs to Practice: Effective Sex Education Training and Support*, London: Sex Education Forum.

Plummer, K. (1994) in J. Weeks and J. Holland (eds) *Sexual Cultures, Communities, Values and Intimacy: Explorations in Sociology*, BSA 1996.

Pollard, A. (1985) *The Social World of the Primary School*, London: Cassell.

Pollock, G. (1988) *Vision and Difference*, London: RKP.

Prendergast, S. (1994) *This Is the Time to Grow Up: Girls' Experience of Menstruation in Schools*, London: FPA.

References

Ramafedi, A. *et al.* (1991) 'Risk factors for attempted suicide in gay and bisexual youth', *Paediatrics* 87: 869–75.

Ramazanoglu, C. (1994) 'Women and heterosexuality: a reply to Wendy Holloway', *Feminism and Psychology* 3 (3): 412–17.

Raphael Reed, L. (1997) 'Power, pedagogy and persuasion: schooling masculinities in the secondary school', Paper presented to the *BERA Conference Symposium–Special Interest Groups: Towards Social Justice*. York.

Rawls, J. (1971) *A Theory of Justice*, Cambridge, MA: Belknap Press.

Redman, P. (1994) 'Shifting ground: rethinking sexuality education', in D. Epstein (ed.) *Challenging Lesbian and Gay Inequalities in Education*, Milton Keynes: Open University Press.

—— (1996) 'Curtis loves Ranjit: heterosexual masculinities, schooling and pupils' sexual cultures', *Educational Review* 48 (2): 175–82.

Reiss, I. L. (1967) *The Social Context of Premarital Sexual Permissiveness*, New York: Holt, Rinehart & Winston.

Reiss, M. Z. (1990) 'What are the aims of school sex education?', *Cambridge Journal of Education* 23 (2): 125–36.

Rice, W. (1987) *Why Informal Methods? In Health Education in Schools*, 2nd edn, Harper & Row.

Rich, A. (1979) *On Lies, Secrets and Silence*, New York: Norton.

Richards, M. P. M. and Elliot, B. (1991) 'Sex and marriage in the 1960s and 1970s', in S. Scott and D. Morgan (eds) *Body Matters*, Barcombe: Falmer.

Richardson, D. (1996) 'Contradictions in discourse: gender and sexuality in HIV/AIDS', in J. Holland and L. Adkins (eds) *Sex, Sensibility and the Gendered Body*, London: Macmillan.

Rivers, I. (1996) 'Young, gay and bullied', *Young People Now* (January).

Roberts, H. and Sachdev, D. (1996) *Young People's Social Attitudes – Having Their Say: The Views of 12–19-Year-Olds*, London: Barnardo's Society.

Roberts, Y. (1998) 'Too young to unwrap a condom?', *Guardian* 20 December.

Rogers, M. (1994) 'Growing up lesbian', in D. Epstein (ed.) *Challenging Lesbian and Gay Inequalities in Education*, Milton Keynes: Open University Press.

Rose, J. (1987) 'Femininity and its discontents', in *Feminist Review* (ed.) *Sexuality: A Reader*, London: Virago.

Rosenstock, I. M. (1974) 'Historical origins of the health belief model', *Health Education Monographs*, no. 2: 328–35.

—— Strecher, V. J. and Becker, M. H. (1988) 'Social learning theory and the health belief model', *Health Education Quarterly* 15: 175–83.

Roth, P. (1971) *Portnoy's Complaint*, Transworld Publishers and Corgi Books.

Rowbotham, S. (1977) *A New World for Women: Stella Browne – Socialist Feminist*, London: Pluto Press.

Rowbotham, S. and Weeks, J. (1977) *Socialism and the New Life; The Personal and Sexual Politics of Edward Carpenter and Havelock Ellis*, London: Pluto Press.

Roy, D. F. (1960) 'Banana time: job satisfaction and informal interaction', *Human Organisation* 18: 156–68.

Royal College of Obstetricians and Gynaecologists (1991) *Report of the RCOG Working Party on Unplanned Pregnancy*, London: Royal College of Gynaecologists.

Sachs, J. *et al.* (1991) 'How adolescents see the media', *Bulletin of the National Clearinghouse for Youth Studies* 10: 16–20.

Salinger, J. D. (1951) *Catcher in the Rye*, London: Hamish Hamilton.

Sanger, M. (1926) *Happiness in Marriage*, New York: Brentano.

Schofield, M. (1973) *The Sexual Behaviour of Young Adults*, London: Allan Lane.

Scott, L. (1996) *Developing Partnerships with Parents in Sex Education*, London: National Children's Bureau.

—— and Thomson, R. (1992) 'School sex education: more a patchwork than a pattern', *Health Education Journal* 51 (3).

Scott, S. (1987) 'Sex and danger: feminism and AIDS', *Trouble and Strife* 11.

—— and Morgan, D. (eds) (1993) *Body Matters: Essays on the Sociology of the Body*, Barcombe: Falmer.

Sears, J. T. (ed.) (1992) *Sexuality and the Curriculum*, New York and London: Teachers' College Press.

Sedley, A. and Benn, M. (1982) *Sexual Harassment at Work*, London: NCCL Rights for Women Unit.

Segal, L. (1990) *Slow Motion: Changing Masculinities, Changing Men*, London: Virago.

Seidler, V. J. (1987) 'Reason, desire and male sexuality', in P. Caplan (ed.) *The Cultural Construction of Sexuality*, London: Routledge.

Seidman, S. (1992) *Embattled Eros*, London: Routledge.

Serbin, L. A. (1978) 'Teachers, peers and play preferences', in B. Sprung (ed.) *Perspectives on Non-Sexist Early Childhood Education*, New York: Teachers' College Press.

Sex Education Forum (1994) *Factsheet 10: Developing and Reviewing a School Sex Education Policy. A Positive Strategy*, London: Sex Education Forum and National Children's Bureau.

——(1997) 'Forum Factsheet', *Sex Education Matters* 14 (Autumn).

Shaw, J. (1976) 'Education and the individual: schooling for girls or mixed schooling – a mixed blessing?' in R. Deem (ed.) *Schooling for Women's Work*, London: Routledge & Kegan Paul.

Sikes, P. (1986) 'Teachers' careers in the comprehensive school', in S. Ball (ed.) *Comprehensive Schools: A Reader*, Barcombe: Falmer.

Smart, C. (1996) 'Desperately seeking post-heterosexual woman', in J. Holland and L. Adkins (eds) *Sex, Sensibility and the Gendered Body*, London: Macmillan.

Smith, T. (1993) 'Influences of socio-economic factors on attaining targets for reducing teenage pregnancies', *British Medical Journal* 306: 1232–5.

Smith Rosenberg, C. (1985) *The New Woman as Androgyne: Social Discourse and Gender Crisis, 1870–1931: Disorderly Conduct, Visions of Gender in Victorian America*, Oxford: Oxford University Press.

Sontag, S. (1989) *AIDS and its Metaphors*, London: Allen Lane.

Spencer, B. (1984) 'Young men and their attitudes to sexuality and birth control', *British Journal of Family Planning* 10: 13–19.

Spender, D. and Sarah, E. (eds) (1980) *Learning to Lose*, London: Women's Press.

Springham, N. (1996) *Telling Tales: An Exploratory Study of Young Men's Experiences of Schooling on Tyneside*, Newcastle and North Tyneside: Newcastle and North Tyneside Health Promotion.

Stanko, E. and Newburn, T. (eds) (1995) *Just Boys Doing Business*, London: Routledge.

Stanley, L. (1995) *Sex Surveyed 1949–1994*, London: Taylor & Francis.

—— (1996) 'Mass observation: "Little Kinsey and the British Sex Survey"', in J. Weeks and J. Holland (eds) *Sex, Sensibility and the Gendered Body*, London: Macmillan.

Stanworth, M. (1981) *Gender and Schooling*, London: Hutchinson.

References

Stears, D. and Clift, S. (1990) *A Survey of AIDS' Education in Secondary Schools*, Horsham: Avert.

Stein, E. (1992) *Forms of Desire: Sexual Orientation and the Social Construction Controversy*, London: Routledge.

Steinberg, L. *Adolescence*, New York: Knopf.

Stone, H. and Stone, A. (1952) *A Marriage Manual*, London: Gollancz.

Stopes, M. (1918) *Married Love*, London: Putnam.

Swedish National Board of Education (1986) *Sex Education in Swedish Schools*, Stockholm.

Szirom, T. (1988) *Teaching Gender? Sex Education and Sexual Stereotype*, London: Allen & Unwin.

Tappin, D., Girdwood, R., Follet, E., Kennedy, R., Brown, A. and Cockburn, F. (1991) 'Prevalence of maternal HIV infection in Scotland based on unlinked, anonymous testing of new-born babies', *The Lancet* 337: 1565–7.

Ten Brinke, J. and Buchanan, A. (1998) *The Can-Do Girls – A Barometer of Change*, Oxford: Department of Applied Social Studies and Research, Barnett House.

Theweleit, K. (1987) *Male Fantasies*, Cambridge: Polity Press.

Thirlby, D. (1998) 'Teaching about sexually transmitted infections', Forum Factsheet 15, *Sex Education Matters* 15 (Spring), National Children's Bureau.

Thomson, R. (1993) *Unholy Alliances: The Recent Politics of Sex Education*, London: Lawrence & Wishart.

—— (1994) 'Moral rhetoric and public health pragmatism: the recent politics of sex education', *Feminist Review* 18 (Autumn).

—— and Scott, S. (1990) *Sexuality in the Light of AIDS: Historical and Methodological Issues*, WRAP Paper 5, London: Tufnell Press.

—— (1991) *Learning about Sex: Young Women and the Social Construction of Sexual Identity*, London: Tufnell Press.

—— (1992) *An Enquiry into Sex Education*, London: Sex Education Forum and National Children's Bureau.

Thorogood, N. (1992) 'Sex education as social control', *Critical Public Health* 3 (2): 43–50.

Tolson, A. (1977) *The Limits of Masculinity*, London: Tavistock.

Tones, B. K. (1986) 'Health education and the ideology of health promotion: a review of alternative approaches', *Health Education Research* 1 (1): 3–12.

Toynbee, P. (1998) *Guardian* 16 March.

Trippe, H. (1994) 'School sex education: can DHAs help to bridge the divide between theory and practice?', *Health Education Journal* 53 (2): 134–40.

Troyna, B. and Vincent, C. (1996) 'The discourses of social justice in education', in *Discourse: Studies in the Cultural Politics of Education* 16 (2).

Trudell, B. N. (1993) *Doing Sex Education*, London: Routledge.

Turner, B. (1984) *The Body and Society*, Oxford: Blackwell.

Turtle, J., Jones, A. and Hickman, M. (1997) *Young People and Health: The Health Related Behaviour of School Aged Children. A Report on the 1995 survey*, London: Health Education Authority.

Valverde, M. (1985) *Sex, Power and Pressure*, London: RKP.

Vance, D. (1984) *Pleasure and Danger: Exploring Female Sexuality*, London: RKP.

—— (1989) 'Social construction theory: problems in the history of sexuality', in D. Altman *et al.* (eds) *Which Homosexuality?: Essays from the International Scientific Conference on Lesbian and Gay Studies*, London: Routledge.

Van de Velde, T. H. (1928) *The Ideal Marriage: Its Physiology and Technique*, London: Heinemann.

Walker, B. *No One to Talk With: Norfolk Young People's Conversations about Sex – A Basis for Peer Education*, Norwich: Centre for Applied Research in Education, University of East Anglia.

Walker, B. and Kushner, S. (1997) *Understanding Boys' Sexual Health Education and its Implications for Attitude Change*, Norwich: Centre for Applied Research in Education, University of East Anglia.

Walkerdine, V. (1981) 'Sex, power and pedagogy', *Screen Education*, 38: 14–24.

Wallace, C. (1985) 'Masculinity, femininity, unemployment', unpublished paper presented at Sociology of Education Conference, Westhill College, Birmingham.

—— (1987) *For Richer, For Poorer: Growing Up In and Out of Work*, London: Tavistock.

Waterhouse, R. (1991) 'The inverted gaze', in M. Featherstone, M. Hepworth and B. S. Turner (eds) *The Body: Social Processes and Cultural Theory*, London: Sage.

Watney, S. (1997) 'The epidemic is still not over! Why we (still) need HIV/AIDS education in schools', *Sex Education Matters* 14 (Autumn).

Weatherburn, P. *et al.* (1992) *The Sexual Lifestyles of Gay and Bisexual Men in England and Wales*, Project SIGMA.

Weeks, J. (1981) *Sexual Politics and Society: The Regulation of Sexuality since 1800*, London: Longman.

—— (1985) *Sexuality and its Discontents*, London: Methuen.

—— and Holland, J. (1996) *Sexual Cultures, Communities, Values and Intimacy: Explorations in Sociology*, BSA.

Weiner, G. (1985) *Just a Bunch of Girls*, Milton Keynes: Open University Press.

Wellings, K. *et al.* (1994) *Sexual Behaviour in Britain: The National Survey of Sexual Attitudes and Lifestyles*, Harmondsworth: Penguin.

Wellings, L. *et al.* (1995) 'Provision of sex education and early sexual experience: the relation examined', *British Medical Journal* 311 (7002): 414–17.

Welsh Office (1994) *Sex Education in Schools. Circular 45/94*, Welsh Office.

Went, D. (1985) *School Sex Education: Some Guidelines for Teachers*, London: Bell & Hyman.

West, C. and Zimmerman, D. (1975) 'Sex roles, interruptions and silences in conversation', in B. Thorne and W. Henley (eds) *Language and Sex Difference and Dominance*, Rowley: Newbury House, USA.

West, P., Wight, D. and Macintyre, S. (1993) 'Heterosexual behaviour of 18-year-olds in the Glasgow area', *Journal of Adolescence* 16: 367–96.

Whately, M. (1992) 'Commentary: whose sexuality is it anyway?', in J. Sears (ed.) *Sexuality and the Curriculum: The Politics and Practices of Sexuality Education*, New York: Teachers' College Press.

White, S. (1995) *Confidentiality in Schools*, London: Brook Advisory Centre and Sex Education Alliance.

Whyld, J. (1983) *Sexism in the Secondary Curriculum*, London: Harper & Row.

—— Pickersgill, D. and Jackson, D. (eds) (1990) *Anti-Sexist Work with Boys and Young Men*, Caistor, Lincolnshire: Whyld Publishing Co-operative.

References

Wight, D. (1990) 'The Impact of HIV/AIDS on Young People's Heterosexual Behaviour in Britain: A Literature Review', Working Paper No. 2, London: MRC Medical Sociology Unit.

—— (1992) 'Impediments to safer heterosexual sex: a review of research with young people', *AIDS Care* 4: 11–21.

—— (1996) 'Beyond the predatory male: the diversity of young Glaswegian men's discourses to describe heterosexual relations', in L. Adkins and V. Merchant (eds) *Sexualising the Social: Power and the Organisation of Sexuality*, London: Macmillan.

—— *et al.* (1996) 'From theory to practice: developing a theoretically based teacher delivered sex education programme', in *Proceedings of the Symposium 'Sexual Awakening: Making Sex Education Work'*, 3 April 1996, London: Medical Research Council.

Willis, E. (1992 [1989]) 'The social relations of medical technology: condoms in the AIDS' era', in R. W. Connell and G. W. Dowsett (eds) *Rethinking Sex: Social Theory and Sexuality Research*, Melbourne: Melbourne University Press.

Willis, P. (1977) *Learning to Labour*, Farnborough: Saxon House.

—— (1984) *New Society* 29 March.

Wilson, D. (1978) 'Sexual codes and conduct', in B. Smart and C. Smart (eds) *Women, Sexuality and Social Control*, London: RKP.

Wilton, J. and Aggleton, P. (1990) 'Condoms, coercion and control: AIDS in heterosexual practice', in P. Aggleton, P. Davies and G. Hart (eds) *AIDS: Responses, Intervention and Care*, Barcombe: Falmer.

Winn, S. and Roker, D. (1995) 'Knowledge about puberty and sexual development in 11–16-year-olds: implications for health and sex education in schools', *Educational Studies* 21 (2).

Wolpe, A. M. (1987) 'Sex in schools: back to the future', *Feminist Review* 27: 37–47.

Wood, J. (1984) 'Groping towards sexism: boys' sex talk', in A. McRobbie and M. Nava (eds) *Gender and Generation*, Basingstoke: Macmillan.

Woodcock, A., Stenner, K. and Ingham, R. (1992) '"All these contraceptives, videos and that …": young people talking about school sex education', *Health Education Research, Theory and Practice* 7 (4): 517–31.

Wright, H. (1930) *The Sex Factor in Marriage*, London: Williams & Northgate.

Young, I. M. (1990) *Justice and the Politics of Difference*, New Jersey: Princeton University Press.

Zelnick, M. and Kantner, J. (1977) 'Sexual and contraceptive experience of young unmarried women in the United States 1976, 1971', *Family Planning Perspectives* 9: 55–71.

Resources

Organisations

Acceptance: a helpline offering support for parents of gay young people. Tel. 01795 661463

Avert: 11–13 Denne Parade, Horsham, West Sussex, RG12 1JD. Tel. 01403 210202

Body Positive

Brook Advisory Centre: 165 Grays Inn Road, London WC1X8UD. Tel. 0171 713 9000

Contraceptive Education Service: Tel 0171 837 4044

Families and Friends of Lesbians and Gays (FFLAG): Tel. 0191 537 4691

Family Planning Association: 2–12 Pentonville Road, London N7 9FP. Tel. 0171 923 5230

Health Education Authority: Trevelyan House, 30 Great Peter Street, London SW1P 2HW. Tel. 0171 413 1995

Lesbian and Gay Switchboard: Tel. 0171 837 7324

Lesbian Information Service: Tel. 0171 681 7235

National Childbirth Trust: Alexandra House, Oldham Terrace, Acton, London. Tel 0181 992 8637

National Forum on AIDS and Children: National Children's Bureau, 8 Wakely Street, London EC1V 7QE. Tel 0171 843 6000

Sex Education Forum: National Children's Bureau, 8 Wakely Street, London EC1V 7QE. Tel. 0171 843 6000

Publications

Epstein, D. (1994) *Challenging Lesbian and Gay Inequalities in Education*, Milton Keynes: Open University Press.

Forrest, S. *et al.* (1997) *Talking about Homosexuality*, Horsham: Avert.

Frankham, J. (1995) *Young Gay Men Talking*, Horsham: Avert.

Mole, S. (1994) *Colours of the Rainbow*, London: Camden and Islington Health Promotion Service.

Prendergast, S. (1994) *Helping Girls Cope with Menstruation in School: A Guide for Governors, Teachers and Parents*, London: FPA.

Ray, C. and Wents, D. (eds) (1995) *Good Practice in Sex Education: A Sourcebook for Schools*, London: National Children's Bureau.

Resources

HEA (1994) *Sex Education, Values and Morality* offers a useful guide on how to develop a moral framework. There is also a National Curriculum Council Discussion Paper on spiritual and moral development (NCC 1993).

Thomson, R. (1993) *Religions, Ethnicity and Sex Education: Exploring the Issues.*

Index

Index

110; incidence of 4, 5; information
107n3, 123; responsibility 53; sex
education 22, 23, 46–8; *see also*
HIV/AIDS
Shaw, J. 62, 64, 91, 109, 111
Sigma survey 3
Sikes, P. 143
Simon, W. 56, 81, 118
single-sex classes 55, 65–8, 111, 137–8,
145 n1
small group teaching 138–9
Smith, T. 165
social class: morality 17–18; teenage
pregnancy 165
social conditioning model, sexuality 68 n1
social constructionism 56–7, 58, 59, 160
social engineering 144
social justice 151, 157–8
social learning theories 55, 56
social purity 17
social sciences 2, 7
socialisation: multiple positionings 59, 81;
psychoanalytic approach 58, 61; school
64; sexual 55, 64–5, 150–1
sociology of body 91–2
sons, parental sex information 101–5, 141
Sontag, S. 155
speculum 74
Spencer, B. 159
Spender, D. 64, 73, 110, 137
spots 88, 91
Squires, P. 100, 131, 132
Stanworth, M. 111, 137
status 71, 73, 74, 77; *see also* reputation
STDs: *see* sexually transmitted diseases
Stears, D. 3
Stenner, K. 39, 55
Stopes, Marie 18, 106–7 n1
stratification 63
'Strides' programme 161
subject choice, gender 63–4
suicide, homophobia 163
surveillance, teachers 77
Swedish National Board of Education 52
symbolic interactionism 55, 59–60, 81
Szirom, T. 157

Tappin, D. 5
teachers: embarrassment 44; gender
142–4; legal position 25, 35–6, 127;
supporting girls 86, 134–7; surveillance
77
teaching policies, potential changes 137–9

teasing 105; to cover ignorance 99; focus
group 86; girls' reactions 85; power
108; sexual activity 109–10; teacher
intervention 134–7, 137–8
teenage fathers 136
teenage pregnancy: class 165;
government policy 148, 152–3, 154;
statistics 4, 5
Ten Brinke, J. 123
Theweleit, K. 95, 105, 120
Thomson, R.: age at first sexual
experience 121 n1; AIDS/HIV
campaign 30; legislation 21, 24;
personal/public 15; school ethos 139;
sex education 16, 19, 29, 147; Sex
Education Forum 6, 26, 33, 136;
sexuality 2, 29, 144
Thorogood, N. 7
Tiffin, C. 70, 164–5
Tolson, A. 82
Tones, B. K. 146
touching, harassment 95–6
Toynbee, Polly 149–50
Trippe, H. 6
Trudell, B. N. 1, 8, 9, 12, 16, 156, 157
trust, confidentiality 35–6
Turner, B. S. 91

US 3, 31, 125

Valverde, M. 87
voluntary organisations 18, 19

Walker, B. 159
Walkerdine, V. 137
Wallace, C. 112, 161
Waterhouse, R. 87, 94–5, 95
Watney, Simon 162, 163
Weatherburn, P. 3
Weeks, J. 2, 9, 55, 56, 57, 60, 158
Weiner, G. 28
Wellings, K. 3, 121 n1
Welsh Office Circular 45/94 16, 22, 27
West, C. 74
Weyman, Anne 149
Whately, Marianne 157
Whyld, J. 139, 160
Wight, D. 3
Willis, P. 75, 83 n2, 112, 113
Wilson, M. 82, 112
Wilton, J. 154
Wolpe, A. M. 33, 76, 157
Wood, J. 93

192